My Music

MUSIC / CULTURE

A series from Wesleyan University Press

Edited by George Lipsitz, Susan McClary, and Robert Walser

Published titles

My Music by Susan D. Crafts, Daniel Cavicchi, Charles Keil,
and the Music in Daily Life Project

*Running with the Devil: Power, Gender, and Madness in
Heavy Metal Music* by Robert Walser

Subcultural Sounds: Micromusics of the West by Mark Slobin

My Music

SUSAN D. CRAFTS,

DANIEL CAVICCHI,

CHARLES KEIL

and the Music in Daily Life Project

✣

WESLEYAN UNIVERSITY PRESS

Published by University Press of New England

Hanover & London

WESLEYAN UNIVERSITY PRESS
Published by University Press of New England, Hanover, NH 03755
© 1993 by Wesleyan University
All rights reserved
Printed in the United States of America 5 4 3 2 1
CIP data appear at the end of the book

Contents

Young Adults

Adults

Older Adults

Elders

GEORGE LIPSITZ

Foreword

A few years ago, a reporter for a national magazine asked the jazz pianist Abdullah Ibrahim to explain how he first became interested in music. Recognizing the question as a standard opening for interviews with performers, Ibrahim nonetheless refused to answer directly. Instead, he challenged the question's premises in order to illumine an important difference between music making in the United States and in his native South Africa. "People always ask this question, you see, and I understand why [laughs], because here it seems as if it's a concerted effort which you have to go through when you're a child, that you have to *start* singing or start playing. In Africa, you're born into it. It's all part of the day-to-day living."[1]

Ibrahim insisted upon representing music as a social rather than an individual activity. Where he grew up, music played a vital role in medicine, in religion, and in politics—not as an ornamentation or commentary on them, but as a vital and organic part of the practices themselves. Rephrasing the interviewer's question, Ibrahim replied, "it's not when *I* started to play; music was there . . . you open up your eyes, it's in the home, in the community."[2]

Ibrahim's insight illumines an important aspect of music anywhere— its inescapable identity as a social practice. When you open up your eyes, it's there. Although Ibrahim delineates important differences between musical practices in South Africa and in North America, we are helped by his formulation to notice an often ignored reality about music making in the United States and in all advanced industrialized countries. Here, too (in part because of the powerful African presence in all European and American popular music), musical practices do not "start" when we pick up an instrument or when we pay attention to what is happening in any given song. We enter a world of music already in progress around us. No less than in Africa, we encounter music everywhere—at the schools and the symphony halls, in the churches and the taverns, on the radio and the television. Our musical practices do not blend life and art as thoroughly as they do in some parts of Africa, but they nonetheless function as nodes in a larger network, as complicated and diverse ways for people to reaffirm old identities and to forge new ones.

Interesting in their own right as public expressions of things that are generally kept private, the interviews in *My Music* provide some clues to more general questions about exactly how and why music plays such an important role in the modern world. They offer evidence and insights capable of adding significantly to the existing scholarly and popular literature about music by musicologists, journalists, and social scientists.

Expert musicologists, journalists, and social scientists have written many important and interesting works about music, but only rarely have they confronted the complicated and contradictory ways that people use music to make meaning for themselves. In their accounts, musicologists tend to give greatest attention to the content of musical texts: the melodies, harmonies, and progressions that give determinate shape to the sounds that we hear as music. Journalists, on the other hand, almost never write about music itself; their concerns center on artists and audiences, on the personal histories of musicians and on the passions of their adoring fans. Social scientists, for their part, tend to downplay the importance of artists and audiences, focusing instead on the commercial and social apparatuses that promote, distribute, and regulate musical production and reception, especially institutions within the music industry, conservatories, critics, and government regulators and censors.

Musicologists, journalists, and social scientists all illumine parts of the truth about music, but they have not as yet produced an adequate way of understanding (and theorizing) how interactions among the artists, audiences, and apparatuses collectively create the world of musical production, distribution, and reception.

We are now at a moment when it is possible to think about music in important new ways. Before 1970, popular music criticism tended to revolve around anxiety about the effects of commercialism and mass marketing on music that originated in "folk" settings, like blues, jazz, and country. This period produced many brilliant works that remain essential to understanding music today. Americo Paredes's brilliant analysis of the popularity of the "Ballad of Gregorio Cortez" among Chicanos in south Texas demonstrated how a song could serve important social functions, not because of its innate artistic qualities, but because of the ways in which it was deployed and understood by people in a concrete social and historical situation.[3] Similarly, LeRoi Jones's *Blues People* demonstrated how the history of black music encapsulated the broader historical experiences of African Americans, as well as revealing the many ways in which music has served as a site both of domination and of resistance in the black struggle for dignity and justice.[4] Along with Charles Keil's *Urban Blues*, an ethnography of the contemporary blues community in Chicago, Johnny Otis's *Listen to the Lambs*, a passionate reflection on black music and the Watts riots, and the jazz criticism of Sidney Finkelstein and Ralph Gleason, these works formed the cornerstone for accurate, subtle, and meaningful investigations of popular music and its role as a social force.[5] Yet, with the possible exception of David Riesman's knowing exploration into the practices of popular music fans in a 1950 article in the *American Quarterly*, the best popular music criticism of this era tended to assume that commercial culture and mass media could only dilute and destroy the strengths of traditional forms of music.

Starting in the 1970s, critics around the globe began to explore the possibility that commercial culture might extend the reach and scope of traditional "folk" music, while at the same time generating new cultural and political opportunities. The success of the Beatles and the rise of a global youth culture directly linked to alternative and mainstream music created a new agenda for cultural criticism. Dick Hebdige's analysis of the relationships among reggae, punk rock, and traditional working-class culture in England, Steve Chapple and Reebee Garofalo's examination of the rise of rock'n'roll in the United States, and Greil Marcus's presentation of popular music as a medium for the reproduction of traditional themes and images within American culture—all opened new possibilities for understanding popular music as an important locus for the creation, maintenance, and subversion of individual and social identity.[6]

The new approach to commercial culture among music critics and scholars found firm theoretical grounding in the emergence of new and exciting theories about culture. The psychoanalytic theories of Jacques Lacan and the structuralist Marxism of Louis Althusser provided a new language for speaking about the relationships among popular culture texts, social power relations, and individual identity. British and French feminists further expanded this inquiry, as did political theorists influenced by the Italian Marxist Antonio Gramsci.[7] In a particularly influential 1979 essay, Fredric Jameson rejected the modernist division of art and culture into separate spheres, contending that the pervasiveness of popular culture mandated criticism capable of seeing how the very commercial processes that destroyed communities and turned traditional cultural expressions into commodities also called into being new communities through promises of social harmony and justice.[8] The appropriation of these theories by the literary critic Raymond Williams, sociologist Stuart Hall, and film scholar Laura Mulvey invigorated writing about popular culture around the globe. By the mid-1980s, writings by Simon Frith, Lawrence Grossberg, Angela McRobbie, and others presented new explanations and interpretations for the processes and practices of creating, receiving, and distributing popular music.[9]

As we enter the 1990s, a new synthesis is possible. Writings on popular music before 1970 lacked an appreciation of the emancipatory potential of commercial culture, but they also tended to situate investigations of music within the concrete social and historical experiences of actual individuals and communities. Popular music writing since 1970 has brought a necessary theoretical sophistication to the subject and has brilliantly assessed the positive and negative effects of commercialism on culture and politics, but it has tended to lose touch with the ethnographic, historical, and social connectedness of the earlier critiques. Recent writing by Susan McClary, Lisa Lewis, Tricia Rose, Eric Lott, Chris Waterman, and others, however, points the way toward a new paradigm for popular music studies, one capable of synthesizing and extending the strengths of the earlier two periods, while also demonstrating an engagement with the present and its unique and specific dangers and opportunities.[10]

My Music summons up a special kind of expertise—i.e., the knowledge that people have about how they use and enjoy music in their own lives. From interviews conducted in Buffalo, New York, during the 1980s with forty-one individuals of diverse tastes and backgrounds, we learn about the pervasiveness and power of music as a social force. The people who speak to us in this book range in age from four to eighty-three, and they represent a variety of racial, ethnic, and national experiences. The authors make no claim for their selection of interviewees as a statistically representative sample; rather, the interviews are evidence of one conversational network that emerged from ties and associations among students in the Music in Daily Life course at the State University in Buffalo. Yet those interviewed reflect widely varied experiences, tastes, and interests. Some are musicians, but most are not. All actively employ some kind of music in their lives, whether they make it themselves or have it made for them by others. As one would expect from any practice so laden with emotional investment and so central to the invention of one's own identity, the use of music inevitably becomes conflated for these individuals with other important issues: how they make meaningful connections with others, how they monitor and remake themselves, how they remember the past, and how they dream of something better for the future.

Clearly, music as a social experience is broader and more complex than the musical activities encompassed by social institutions concerned with music. Music educators, recording studios, publishers, promoters, and musicians' associations are only a small part of a social practice that is deeply rooted in the everyday life experiences of a broad mass of people. Perhaps the most important message that emerges from these interviews concerns just how complicated people's encounters with music can be. As creators and receivers, performers and spectators, active and passive listeners, people's musical tastes and interests reveal far more complexity and far more self-directed searching, testing, and experimenting than either music schools or commercial market categories can account for. The divisions within music education that divide "classical" from "popular" music, that create separate departments of "musicology" and "ethnomusicology," and that substitute a classical canon of "good taste" for an open-ended exploration into the ways that different cultures and communities transform noise into music—all this poorly represents the musical practices described in these interviews.

For their part, radio programmers, concert promoters, and recording executives find it convenient and profitable to split up audiences into discrete market segments. They target specific genres to specific audiences identifiable by age, race, gender, and class. But these interviews show just how badly such market categories distort the musical interests and experiences of individual members of the audience. We encounter here, instead, people who find their way to an astonishing range of musical choices, despite the inhibiting constrictions of the music industry.

As Rob Walser points out, "Few listeners can be grouped into the usual sociological subcultures or commercial market segments with assigned musical tastes; real tastes are multiple, just as real people are more complex and contradictory than most sociological abstractions."[11] People listen across the spectrum of genre categories, and very few individuals identify themselves as interested in only one kind of music. Through nervous (and sometimes defensive) admissions, some of those interviewed show that they realize that their eclectic combinations of musical tastes transgress societal expectations, but they transgress anyway.

In these pages we will meet Elaine, who displays equal knowledge and discernment when discussing Strauss waltzes and Jelly Roll Morton's jazz, and May, who, we discover, plays Mozart on the violin but has the themes from the "Flintstones" and "My Three Sons" television shows running through her head during the interview. Beth, we learn, likes Rickie Lee Jones but got interested in classical music while playing pool in the basement with her father. And Ralph listens carefully to cartoon sound tracks in order to hear music by Wagner, Lizst, and Fats Waller.

We also see how people listen with varying degrees of attentiveness. Billy likes it when "they bang the drums twice after they say the words" in his favorite music video. Beth says she listens to music mostly to hear the words, but she knows only half the words to her favorite song. Molly listens for arrangements with maracas in them, and often loses track of the melody while listening to hear what the background instruments are playing. Victor tries to listen to the sounds produced by each instrument in any given song and says it takes him ten or twenty times before he can listen to them all together. Wanda doesn't hear the instruments playing because she's too busy imagining what kind of dance would fit with the music most effectively.

These interviews demonstrate how different locations take on a special meaning for the creation and reception of music. May, a violinist learning to play classical music at the Juilliard School of Music, tells of her enjoyment at taking her violin to play for commuters outside a New York City subway station. Anita has many recordings of her favorite band, the Grateful Dead, but she never listens to them except to prod her memory about her experiences at their live concerts. Beth reports that she owned a Steve Forbert album but never listened to it until she heard him play before an enthusiastic crowd at a concert, because, for her, fans "*are* the experience." Stella explains that she listens to the country and western music that she likes mostly while driving in the car, because that is the only time that she is able to get away from her husband and son and the tyranny of their musical tastes. James speaks fondly of a local night club because of the diverse crowd it attracts that makes you "surprised who comes to listen to who."

Although choices about preferred musical sites and sentiments vary widely, they are nonetheless constrained by many factors, ranging from the parochialism and prejudice of individuals to the monopolistic practices of the commercial entertainment industry. People's tastes are not as narrow as the confines imposed upon them by marketing specialists, but neither are they infinitely open. The taste preferences that emerge in these interviews reflect the contestations and confusions of an extremely complex social world with all of its contradictory limitations and opportunities. For example, despite a diversity of musical preferences and a plurality of musical practices, we also hear bitter complaints about the constraints imposed on music by commercialism and by cultural conservatism. Ralph treasures the memory of finding radio stations with unusual programming lists, because he feels deep resentment against the narrow range of music normally available to him through most mass media outlets.

Interviewees also contradict and limit themselves, criticizing narrowmindedness, but then routinely condemning music they haven't heard—especially country and western, heavy metal, and punk. They often feel scornful of what they perceive as the lower status and presumably lesser listening abilities of fans of music that they despise. In some cases, they seem genuinely offended and puzzled by other people's tastes, as when Charles, a musician, observes that when people come to him and ask if he can play Led Zeppelin's "Stairway to Heaven," his response is to say "Well, yes, I can play it, but why in God's name would I ever want to, and why would you like it?"

But the music that appears in these interviews is more than a matter of taste. Four-year-old Heather likes music videos because the people in them "dress up." Johnny, who is five, knows that you need quiet songs to help you get to sleep. Seven-year-old Billy remembers the time that a snow cave collapsed on him and he came home cold and wet and crying, but after watching the tape of "Chartbusters" that his mother made for him he felt fine. Molly, eleven years old, explains that she likes different music at different times, that she listens alone to pieces that she wants to think about, but shares "fun" songs with her friends. Jennie exercises to "kids" music with her dad but tries *so* very hard to learn dance. For these children, music provides models for fantasy and dreaming, relaxation when they are tense, compensation when things go wrong, and an opportunity for both solitude and social connection. In those respects, the youngsters are not very different from the adults in this book, who use music in similar ways.

Even when questions of taste come up, many of the speakers recognize that people go through stages with music, that whatever people listen to may also be preparing them for something new. Beth doesn't like Led Zeppelin, but tolerates them because she remembers that they were "the thing to listen to" when she was thirteen. Alan listens to the Psychedelic Furs and U2, but remembers that he started out listening to pop groups like Styx, the Bay City Rollers, and Kansas. Carl began his involvement with music when he took accordion lessons from a local television personality, but found his way to rock'n'roll and jazz later on.

Musicologists and sociologists have often advanced exceptionally broad generalizations about popular music, but the interviews in *My Music* reveal the importance of time, place, and circumstance in shaping the social meaning of musical practices. Discussions about disco, MTV, and Michael Jackson locate these interviews within one particular time period (the 1980s) whose particular dynamics might be very different from earlier or later periods. The repeated references to Rick James and to Polish-American polka music reflect part of the specific local culture and demographics of the city of Buffalo where the interviews took place. Certainly other cities would have different icons and signifiers of local memory. But the general principle of locality remains important nonetheless; clearly, one factor in making music meaningful is the way in which it is shared with a larger community.

The role of the university as the institution generating these interviews also shapes their content; an interviewing project emanating from a day care center or a labor union hiring hall might show very different results. Yet the very qualities of time, place, and circumstance that would render this study invalid if it purported to be a statistically representative sample, give it great explanatory power as a case study. To borrow a metaphor from the anthropologist Renato Rosaldo, these interviews are not a microcosm of the nation's or the world's experiences with music; they are an afternoon at a busy intersection that reveals many individual vehicles creating the surface appearance of continuous heavy traffic. Many of the specific details of time, place, and circumstance will diverge from the most powerful associations elicited by music for people in other times, places, and circumstances, but the importance of shared histories, local memories, and common associations in the musical worlds represented here suggests the presence of dynamics that pertain elsewhere as well.

My Music, and the series of which it is a part, represent attempts to contribute to a new phase of inquiry into popular music in the 1990s. They are empirical (grounded in investigation and evidence) without being empiricist (believing that the facts speak for themselves). They explore the positive and negative dimensions of commercialism and electronic mass mediation, but try to see how individual agency and action provide crucial local inflections to broader systemic practices. The potential of this moment cannot be realized by avoiding theoretical issues or by merely devising a better theory about why people act as they do. It must come instead by drawing on what people already know, think, and believe.

The editors and interviewers in *My Music* have taken an important first step. The conversation in these pages, and the broader cultural conversation that it is designed to provoke, are important components in an emancipatory cultural project, one based not so much on the hope of transcending or escaping the injustices and oppressions of this world as on working through them to envision new social relations emanating from the hopes and desires of people as they are, and of the world as it is.

For me, this book helps answer what I have come to call the "In-A-Gadda-Da-Vida" problem. In twelve years of teaching about American popular culture, I have never been able to understand "In-A-Gadda-Da-Vida," a song recorded by an obscure San Diego–based band named Iron Butterfly in 1968. The single record and the album on which it appeared both reached the top echelons of the music industry's bestseller charts, but the song's importance as a cultural symbol far exceeded its commercial success. In the winter of 1968–69, "In-A-Gadda-Da-Vida" blared out of car radios and college dormitory room stereos. Its appearance on turntables provoked parties and its mysterious (and some would say incomprehensible) lyrics generated impassioned arguments. As so often happens with commodities circulated as devices for commercialized leisure, "In-A-Gadda-Da-Vida" emerged as an emblem of its time, a song whose affective power and social presence seemed to define for much of its audience what it meant to be alive at that moment.

Yet, for all of its influence at the time, in retrospect "In-A-Gadda-Da-Vida" seems unbelievably trivial, insubstantial, and meaningless. When we listen to it today, we are struck mainly by Iron Butterfly's notable lack of musicianship and by the song's unimaginative and unaffecting melody and rhythm. At a time when virtually every other 1960s hit has been recycled in some form (as a movie theme, a commercial, or a remake for the pop charts), "In-A-Gadda-Da-Vida" appears virtually unlistenable. When I play it for my classes, students seem surprised that it could ever have been popular at all, and they can only surmise, as one did, that "maybe people were feeling major depressed in those days." How could so many have been moved so deeply by so little?

There are of course many possible answers to the "In-A-Gadda-Da-Vida" problem. The large amount of pharmaceutical products circulating among 1960s audiences might have enabled each listener to hear a very different version of the song. Perhaps the hunger for novelty among jaded popular culture consumers and the sophistication of the marketing apparatuses aimed at them might have combined to make "In-A-Gadda-Da-Vida" seem more significant than it was. But when we read the interviews in *My Music* and see how they demonstrate the way music gets instantiated in everyday life, other possibilities about the popularity of "In-A-Gadda-Da-Vida" emerge.

For instance, Edwardo explains that he listened to 1950s "oldies" when he lived among Mexicans in California, but when he moved to Buffalo he had to "switch to catch up" and listen to 1980s rap and heavy metal. However, when he's with his brother he listens to 1970s music. The music he likes depends on the social situation that he's in: each friendship has a music attached to it and the music's significance to him depends upon how and with whom he experiences it. Alan defends his preference for "alternative music" by arguing that "it helps you be depressed . . .'cause . . . everybody has to be depressed." Paula says that she listens to music because she can't stand quiet, she has to have noise. She likes music that's "fast and so raw," that "appeals initially to the barbarian part of you." But she also feels that her musical transgressions are part of a larger rebellion against her middle-class father and his values. "I just wanna scare the shit out of him," she confides.

Fan identification also forms part of the experience of music in these interviews. Rhonda feels that Pink Floyd's Roger Waters has important answers to the world's problems, while Betty can't wait to return home from vacations so that she can resume listening to Neil Diamond's singing. Like Anita in respect to the Grateful Dead, Rhonda and Betty forge special bonds with friends based on their shared enthusiasm for their favorite musicians. Similarly, Violet learned to like Bruce Springsteen because her children did, and she developed a taste for country music after being introduced to it by her husband.

We can see, then, that musical tastes sometimes reflect important social statements and experiences that may seem only incidentally related to the music itself. Perhaps the fans of "In-A-Gadda-Da-Vida" forged a certain kind of solidarity with each other through that song. For others, its appeal might have come from the very negative reactions it could provoke. Maybe it legitimated feelings of alienation, anger, or depression for individuals in important ways, or provided a ritualized way of calling a community or subculture together through the emotional and somatic releases of listening and dancing. But in any case, the significance of "In-A-Gadda-Da-Vida" lies both in its affective content as a piece of music and in its historical role as a social actor in a given time and place. Understanding the song's significance depends upon an appreciation of the plurality of musical practices evoked by any one work and upon a respect for the complicated and complex relationship between cultural texts and social experience.

My Music makes an important contribution to our understanding of music. It brings to the surface some of the contradictions and serendipities of cultural creation and consumption, and it reveals the multiple layers of meaning embedded in any social practice. It provokes us to rethink our own relationships to music and it enables us to learn about the role of music in the lives of others. Most important, it warns us against facile generalizations and judgmental conclusions about other people's musical likes and dislikes. As James observes in his interview, "Regardless of what it is, somebody likes it. You don't have to be in love with it or anything like that, but just be aware of it. And everything you hear comes from some kind of ethnic background, and from somewhere. So why do you want to be narrow?"

Notes

1. Karen Bennett, "An Audience with Abdullah Ibrahim," *Musician* (March 1990): 40.
2. Karen Bennett, "An Audience with Abdullah Ibrahim," 40.
3. Americo Paredes, *With His Pistol in His Hand* (Austin: University of Texas Press, 1958).
4. LeRoi Jones (Amiri Baraka), *Blues People* (New York: William Morrow, 1963).
5. Charles Keil, *Urban Blues* (Chicago: University of Chicago Press, 1966); Johnny Otis, *Listen to the Lambs* (New York: W. W. Norton, 1967).
6. Dick Hebdige, *Subculture: Revolt Into Style* (London: Methuen, 1976); Steve Chapple and Reebee Garafalo, *Rock'n'Roll is Here to Pay* (Chicago: Nelson-Hall, 1978); Greil Marcus, *Mystery Train* (New York: E.P. Dutton, 1975).
7. For a description of these changes see my "Listening to Learn and Learning to Listen: Cultural Theory, Popular Culture, and American Studies," *American Quarterly* (December 1990).
8. Frederic Jameson, "Reification and Utopia in Mass Culture," *Social Text* 1 (1979).
9. Simon Frith, *Sound Effects* (New York: Pantheon, 1981); Lawrence Grossberg, "Another Boring Day in Paradise: Rock and Roll and the Empowerment of Everyday Life," *Popular Music* 5 (1985); Angela McRobbie, "Dance as Social Fantasy," in A. McRobbie and M. Nava (eds.), *Gender and Generation* (Basingstoke: Macmillan, 1984).
10. Susan McClary, *Feminine Endings* (Minneapolis: University of Minnesota Press, 1991); Lisa Lewis, *Gender Politics and MTV* (Philadelphia: Temple University Press, 1990); Tricia Rose, "Never Trust a Big Butt and a Smile," *Camera Obscura* 23 (1991); Eric Lott, "Double V and BeBop," *Callalloo* 20 (1990); Chris Waterman, *Juju* (Seattle: University of Washington Press, 1990).
11. Robert Walser, "Reader's Report on Susan Crafts, et al., *My Music*," for Wesleyan University Press, September 1990. I cite Walser here because I am quoting him directly, but want to acknowledge his general influence on all of my thinking about this project through our many conversations about this manuscript.

Acknowledgments

In her talk on the importance of acknowledgments at a collaborative learning conference a few years ago, Elaine Maimon made it clear that all knowledge is "acknowledge": receiving, recognizing, owning, admitting, confessing, affirming that every single thing we know comes from outside us, expressing our appreciation and gratitude for other people and their unique ways of knowing the world. All of the Music in Daily Life Project could be presented as a series of thank you notes to each of the graduate student editors, the 40 or so interviewers and the approximately 150 people interviewed. No author can acknowledge the multiplicity of sources adequately. But what is especially unfair in the presentation of these interviews is that the interviewers have been edited more than the interviewees, deliberately turned into "Q"s so as to highlight the subject. And, of course, the editors who diminished these interviewers are even more invisible, though their efforts to make the interviews shorter and more enjoyable to read represent the crucial step between a file drawer full of data and a book available to a broad public eager to acknowledge what is inside.

Ellen Koskoff interviewed people in depth about music in their lives over a decade before we started this project and she also developed a useful model for diagramming a person's musical tastes in relation to the rest of their values. Her imaginative and careful work inspired the Music in Daily Life Project and is still the starting point for any further research and analysis in this area.

The other starting point for our work was SUNY Buffalo student Carol Hadley's independent study project in 1984. Her first interviews were surprising and idiosyncratic. A hundred and fifty interviews later we still haven't found ourselves filing away an interview saying, "Yeah, this is a lot like . . . ." Each person is unique. A parallel starting point was the research done by Jennifer Giles and John Shepherd at Carleton University in Ottawa; four English-speaking teenage girls in Montreal were very carefully interviewed by Giles and all of this material was graciously shared with us as we began our editing. Many thanks.

Looking back we are proud that this book represents a model of collaborative work at the university. The Music in Daily Life Project consisted of two undergraduate courses to do the interviews and three semesters of graduate seminars to discuss, edit, and organize the interviews into something close to their present form. There are a great many other issues that can be explored in courses where students learn how to interview, analyze, edit and construct a text for an audience. Projects like this don't happen often because it takes time, a series of semester classes, and a supportive environment. Thanks to the American Studies Department at SUNY Buffalo—Larry Chisolm, Bob Dentan, Hester Eisenstein, Mike Frisch, Bev Harrison, Rick Hill, Endesha Ida May Holland, Liz Kennedy, June License, Oren Lyons, Alfredo Matilla, Ruth Meyerowitz, John Mohawk, Francisco Pabon, Barry White—for providing the freedom to explore and much encouragement along the way.

Joe Wetmore was only with us for the last semester, but he quickly clarified the virtues of grouping the interviews into six generations and he led the democratic forces against the "reflexives" who wanted to put more of us profs and grad students into the collection. "Isn't the main point to hear from more people rather than from the critic and expert types again?" Well, yes.

Barry Morris edited and commented insightfully for two semesters, taking special delight in thinking up new names for people, and in finding the representative quotation that summed up a basic theme. A lot of the very first impressions you get from these interviews are thanks to Barry.

Nicolas Tulus, Andy Proehl, Andy Byron, Alexandria Gelenscer, Kevin Mogg, Tony Sylvestre, Yvette McKoy, Crystal Albert, Rita Johnson, and Lee Wysong contributed substantially to the editing work at one time or another. Mike Huber, John Frink, and John Cicchetti did fine interviews as undergraduates and then joined the editing team for a semester.

A great many sparkling interviews did not make it through the many editing stages but the following students gave us a variety of material to choose from and together they created the core of this book. Many thanks to Charlie Weigl, Lynn Gowgiel, Yvette Evans, Wilma Lange, Lisa Weinberg, Gina Pasquale, Henry Hilska, Tony Grajeda, Evan Bauer, Alyson Bader, Tammy Lynn Brown, Kathy Ralabate, Mary Kay Rigney (who also interviewed children in France), Norman Schwagler, Kelli Scott, Kristen Shannon, Stephen Vujcec, Mark Zarrillo, Robin Stone, Jennifer Mohan, Rhonda Kram, Mark T. Kough, Jeffrey Kless, Hollie Kerling, Doreen DeFranco, Robert Maghran, Sidney Horton, Jacqueline Campbell, and Norma Bianchi.

Finally, George Lipsitz has been an exemplary final editor, making the cuts we couldn't bring ourselves to make, doing the final trimming and shaping, consulting with us conscientiously, giving our work some context in his fine foreword without preempting reader responses to people speaking for themselves about their music. Thanks to George; his co-editors in this series, Rob Walser and Susan McClary; and to Terry Cochran and the team at University Press of New England for all the work that makes a book possible.

December 1992   S.D.C.

                                                       D.C.

                                                       C.K.

My Music

CHARLES KEIL

Introduction

This book began in 1984 when Carol Hadley decided to do an "independent study project" interviewing a few people about music in their lives. Her first report was surprising. What her interviewee had to say about the role of music in her life seemed to be a unique configuration: Bette Midler was at the center of this personal-world-of-music as a kind of alter ego, the musical person she would like to be if she could, providing songs to weep and catharse over and supplying categories like "thirties music" and "Broadway show music" with which to organize a record collection; the Allman Brothers seemed to be another set of star-friends to call on whenever she wanted to put her life in a partying direction; a third corner—the "live" dimension—was occupied by Joni Mitchell concerts "where you see all the good bumper stickers for worthy causes." This Midler/Allman/Mitchell pattern represented a set of complementary musical orientations to the world that we had never imagined existed. Yet, once revealed, this specific musical world seemed clear, logical, and even necessary. Unfortunately this first report was more of a narration wrapped around a few quotations than an interview, so we haven't included it here.

The next interview that Carol brought in was completely different from the first. This time it was a woman who had moved from "classical" to "soft rock" and Neil Diamond, finding many ways to keep Neil's music intertwined with her life. She is called "Betty" in this collection, and perhaps she is a bit more typical than the Midler/Allman/Mitchell woman, or at least somewhat representative of Neil Diamond fans. But a hundred and fifty interviews later we still haven't found anyone like her. In fact, aside from a few Grateful Dead fans (who also have their marked differences), none of the hundred and fifty interviews can easily be clustered into subcultures.

And that is the main point of this collection of interviews. Each person is unique. Like your fingerprints, your signature, and your voice, your choices of music and the ways you relate to music are plural and interconnected in a pattern that is all yours, an "idioculture" or idiosyncratic culture in sound. This may seem obvious or will seem so by the time you have read half of these interviews, but we believe most people think of the musical tastes of others in highly stereotyped ways that are based on layered prejudices or prejudgments along the lines of "rural white people listen only to country and western music," "urban black people love only soul music," "older upper-middle-class women like easy listening," and so forth—what might be called a Billboard Charts view of other people's musical worlds. We hope this book convinces you that our musical lives are much more complicated than that.

When we first organized a class of undergraduates to go out and do interviews, the leading questions were about mediated music and record collections, but after the first set of interviews we arrived at the open question, "What is music about for you?" so as not to prejudge the situation, and also to give the respondents more room to define music of all kinds in their lives. What is the relative weight of live and mediated music in each person's life? In this collection most of the children and teens are doing something musical for themselves, but less than half of the older people are engaged in making music, and a number of the "musicians" seem very ambivalent about it. For example, you could read "Beth" and "Alan" in the "Young Adults" section and perhaps not realize that they are musicians who play for friends or in bands. Electronic recordings and mass mediation have given us opportunities to put much more music into each of our lives, but reading all these interviews may leave you wondering if this is entirely a good thing. Are we enriching our private lives at the expense of a broader sociability?

The reader may also be able to form an impression about music's role in contemporary American lives and in American society along three other major dimensions: age, gender, and "white America."

By including two foreign visitors, "Victor" and "Chad," in the middle of the book, and one African American voice in five of the six age-grades (as well as "May," an Asian American, and "Edwardo," an Hispanic American, in the "Teenagers" section) we are not necessarily enabled to generalize about foreigners, African Americans, or minorities, but we do find an interesting contrast to the voices from the white American majority.

By dividing the interviews into six sections from "Children" to "Elders" (while emphasizing the adult personal-worlds-of-music) we hope to give a fuller picture of music in our society and a sense of music's place in the life sequence. Each reader can thus place his or her own musical world in a broad comparative context.

Twenty-two females and nineteen males of the species Homo Americanus are represented here, and when you listen for differences in their voices and what they are saying about music you will certainly find them.

We would like to let each reader evaluate the gender and age differences, and the many other issues and questions raised by the interviews, without generalizations from the editors. From person to person and, within interviews, from answer to answer you may find yourself asking, "Is one verb better than another to describe this?" Is this person *finding* music to explore and express an identity or being *invaded by* musics to the point of identity diffusion, *using* music to solve personal problems, *consuming* music to fill a void and relieve alienation and boredom, *participating* in musical mysteries to feel fully human, *addicted* to music and evading reality, *orienting* via music to reality? And, of course, these verbs and predicates can be shifted around too: *consuming* to feel fully human, *using* to express identity, and so forth. Do these unique voices make you want to shout "hooray for American individualism!"? Or are there underlying negative themes running though the interviews that spoil the celebration? Each person with a walkman and headphones may indeed be gaining a "most intense, most unexpected sense of self," as Simon Frith puts it in *Facing the Music* (1988:4), but looked at as a social phenomenon aren't all these headphoned people alienated, enjoying mediated "my music" at the expense of a live and more spontaneous "our music"? Are people in general and women in particular being turned into passive consumers of music as they get older? Enjoy each tree as you wander through the forest, but pause occassionally to think about the ecological balance.

Finally, we hope this book will find its place on the still small shelf of books where people not ordinarily heard from get to have their say at last. Music critics, experts, commentators, authorities, all hope (or make believe) that they know who they are writing for and why. Well, here is what some people out there have to say for themselves.

CHILDREN

"I dance to 'Dude Looks Like a Lady.'"

Heather is four years old and was interviewed by her mother.

Q: What's your name?

A: Heather.

Q: How old are you?

A: (holding up four fingers) Four.

Q: Do you like to sing?

A: Um hum. The Elephant Show. Care Bears song.

Q: Do you like to dance?

A: I dance to "Dude Looks Like a Lady." [by Aerosmith]

Q: What kind of singers do you like?

A: I like some people who play horns and guitars. I like to see the Elephant Show singers. I like the guy in Labyrinth [David Bowie] who sings. Tina Turner and Bon Jovi.

Q: Why do you listen to the radio?

A: Because it's my favorite music. Um, and the records too. I like it when they dress up.

Q: Do you want to be a singer when you grow up?

A: Yes, 'cause I look beautiful when I dress up.

Q: What's your favorite thing to play music with?

A: Piano. I love pianos because they have white keys on them to play music, and black things too, and little doors to open and close. I like the guitar, because I like it. I like the drums 'cause they have sticks and they make lots of noise when you hit on them.

"You have to have a lullaby before you sleep. I told you . . . that's what lullabies means."

Johnnie is five years old. He was interviewed by his aunt.

Q: Johnnie, I want you to help me play a game. Okay?

A: Sure. What kind of game are we going to play?

Q: It is a game of pretending. I want you to pretend that you have never seen me before . . .

A: (interrupting) You mean, make believe that you aren't my aunt, but some bad person I'm not supposed to talk to?

Q: (laughing) I want you to pretend that you don't know me but don't pretend that I am a bad person. I just want you to make believe that you have never met me before and tell me who you are, where you live, what you like to do. Stuff like that, okay? Stuff that I already know but I want you to pretend that I don't know it. Do you understand?

A: Sure I do. We do this in school. Well . . . did you know that it's called roleplaying?

Q: (laughing) Yes, that's what I want to do. Roleplay. So why don't you start telling me about you.

A: Well, you see, my name is Johnnie Reluto. I live at 32 Hill Road, in Scranton. That's very far away from here, unless you fly. Then it's not so very bad. (pause)

Q: Good. Keep going.

A: Well, I am in kindergarten. I go to St. Luke's School. My teacher is named Linda.

Q: Can you tell me what kinds of things you do in school? Do you ever sing?

A: Oh, sure. I think . . . I think that we sing every day.

Q: What kind of things do you sing?

A: Well, we sing all sorts of stuff. We sing songs about animals and . . . we sing songs about Christmas . . . and we sing songs about Chanukah. 'Cause, you know, not everyone has a Christmas. Just the people that go to church. Some people go to a place that's like a church . . . 'cause Jesus lives there . . . only it's called a temple. (Johnnie shouts this last word.)

Q: Well, what kind of songs do you like to sing best?

A: The loud ones.

Q: The loud ones. How come?

A: Because then we are allowed to run around . . . and we can jump up and down if we want to . . . just not near the record player, because then the record skips . . . it skips . . . and it says the same thing that it just said. Only over and over again. Timmy and I think it's funny, but Linda says it's not supposed to do that.

Q: So, if the music is loud, then you can run around?

A: Yes. We can run as fast as we want and we can jump up and down as much as we want and . . . and . . . well, we play this game about hearing the music.

Q: Johnnie, I don't understand. What do you mean?

A: Well, you see, Linda puts on some music and whoever hears it the most wins a prize. It's not usually a present or anything, but we win a snack or candy. I win all the time, except the other day my friend Timmy Morgan won.

Q: How do you hear the music?

A: Well, we are supposed to do whatever the music does. Don't you know . . . don't you know . . . when the music gets loud, we are supposed to jump up in the air and be loud. (Johnnie starts jumping up in the air with his arms above his head as if he is reaching for the ceiling.) Just like this. And if the music gets fast, then we are supposed to run fast. Like this. (Johnnie starts running quickly in a very small circle, around and around.)

Whoa, I'm dizzy, Aunt Diane. You are spinning all around. (laughing very hard)

Q: Okay, Johnnie, calm down, okay? So, how else do you hear the music?

A: Well, when the music gets quiet, then I get very quiet. Very quiet. Like this. (Johnnie bends over, almost folding himself to the floor, and ends up crouching very low with his head and shoulders hidden by his hands.)

Then, when the music gets loud, we are supposed to get louder very slowly. (Johnnie tries to unfold very slowly and starts out okay, but he loses patience about halfway there and stands upright.)

Q: So, what happens if the music is kind of in-between? You know what I mean? If it's not really loud but not really quiet either?

A: Well, it usually is. You see . . . you see . . . music can be either fast or slow. I like it when it is fast better because then I can run around.

Q: But you like slow music sometimes. Do you know when you like it?

A: (thinking) No, I don't. When do I like to be quiet?

Q: How about before you go to bed, when Mommy sings to you. Don't you like it then? (Johnnie has a ritual with his mother: first he brushes his teeth, then he says his prayers, then he gets to pick which song his mother will sing to him. He usually sings along.)

A: Oh, yes. Then I like quiet songs. But you know what? Don't you know . . . those special kinds of quiet songs . . . those are called lullabies. Because after I hear them I go to sleep. That's what lullabies means.

Q: What is your favorite lullaby?

A: Oh, well, I like all kinds of them. I like . . . (Johnnie says some unclear German name which refers to a song that his mother sings to him in German, and he knows all the words.) That is also a lullaby. I also like the one called "Mommy's Little Boy." (Johnnie starts to sing it. It is a song about a mother that always loves her son and never goes away. Part of the words are: "Even when you are a grown man and big someday . . . Mommy never goes away.") That's my favorite.

Q: Can you go to sleep if Mommy doesn't sing to you?

A: Well, when she is home she always sings to us. If there is a very special occasion, and she isn't home, then she can't sing to me. Sometimes she goes out.

Q: Then what do you do?

A: Well, if Grandma DeMarco is babysitting for us . . . if Grandma DeMarco is there . . . then she sings to us. But I don't think she sings lullabies. I think . . . I think she just sings regular songs, because only Mommy sings lullabies. (pause) If Aunt Judy is babysitting for us with Uncle Mike, then she doesn't sing a song to us. Then I sing to Paul and Ricky [his younger brothers] instead, before we go to sleep. But Aunt Judy still hears us say our prayers.

Q: Johnnie, wait. So, if Mommy isn't there and Aunt Judy is, then you sing a song to Paul and Ricky?

A: Yes.

Q: How come?

A: Well, because before you go to bed, you have to say your prayers and have a lullaby.

Q: What if you didn't?

A: Well . . . then you couldn't sleep. You have to have a lullaby before you sleep. I told you . . . that's what lullabies means.

Q: What kind of song do you sing to your brothers? Do you let them pick it out?

A: (pause) Well, sometimes. Sometimes Paul picks one out . . . but he doesn't like the right ones. He always wants to sing Christmas songs. So, most times I pick one for him. Then I kiss him goodnight, like Mommy does, and tell him he better not get out of bed in the middle of the night or I will spank him. He gets out of bed when he's not supposed to, but I don't see it because I am asleep.

Q: Do you like to sing at school as much as you like to sing at home?

A: Yes, I do. I like to sing.

Q: Do you feel funny singing in front of other people? Do you like to sing better when you are alone?

A: Well, no. No, I don't. I like to sing in school. But I like to sing at home. I think . . . I think that I like to sing better at school because then I can sing loud. Really loud. (He starts jumping up and down.) Well, Aunt Diane, can I go downstairs and play now?

Can I go now? (Johnnie runs very quickly downstairs.)

"I just play with my songs . . . it's like I . . . I sing them out and then I roll them up into a ball."

Carley was interviewed by a male graduate student who has been a friend of the family for a number of years. At the time of this interview, Carley was about to turn six years old and was in kindergarten.

Q: What kind of music do you like?

A: Well . . . mostly . . . when Doris plays the song of Johnson on a videotape.

Q: Who's Doris?

A: My music teacher. In school.

Q: What kind of music do you learn in school?

A: Well, lots of different things.

Q: Do they teach you singing?

A: Well, some singing.

Q: What other kind of things do they teach you?

A: They teach us . . . things that we do and Doris plays along to. Like there's an elephant thing where we put one hand in front and hold the other person's hand and put one hand in back and hold the person's hand in back of us. And the person in front of us . . . the one person, the person that just was called, when they come around to the time, they pick someone. If it's a girl they pick a boy and if it's a boy they pick a girl. And then we get like this . . . . (demonstrating) It's called "Elephants in Song."

Q: "Elephants in Song." So it's kind of a game?

A: Yeah, a game with music to it.

Q: Wow. So that's . . . that's the special music part of the day. So Doris comes to your room to see you?

A: No, we go there.

Q: So that's the only music that you have in school, right?

A: Right.

Q: Okay. What kind of music do you listen to at home?

A: . . . Well, CDs, and also, in school . . . sometimes we also learn music in our classroom. You know what's so funny? In the class . . . sometimes Doris plays things up when we go to music. And then our teacher, Diane or Alice . . . that is, they're both our teachers, whoever's there. They sometimes . . . they . . . you know, do the same thing. Like, we learn a song, but it's the song we learned in music.

Q: And they don't know that?

A: Yeah! (both chuckle)

Q: So you do the same stuff sometimes in class.

A: Yeah. And then all of our class raises their hands and . . . Diane kinda calls on us all at once and we say altogether, "WE DID THIS IN MUSIC!" (giggles)

Q: And what do the teachers do?

A: The teachers say, "Well, okay, what didn't you do?" (both chuckle)

Q: So, what songs do you listen to here on CD?

A: Well, we sometimes . . . listen to . . .

Q: You don't remember?

A: I don't remember.

Q: Is it stuff you like a lot?

A: Well, yeah!

Q: Yeah?

A: My favorite song is called "American Pie."

Q: "American Pie." Okay. I've heard of that one. Do you listen to it a lot or . . . ?

A: It's not on a lot.

Q: So . . . what? You mean your parents don't play it a lot or you . . .

A: I don't even know if I have it.

Q: So you hear it on the radio mostly.

A: Right . . . that's the first place I heard it.

Q: Do you ever play music here or do you just listen to what your parents play?

A: Well, sometimes I play little tunes on my little piano and on the real piano.

Q: Oh, really? Are you taking music lessons?

A: No, but I know how to play one song.

Q: One song? Okay. So, what song is it? Do you know the name?

A: Yeah. It's called "Hot Cross Buns."

Q: "Hot Cross Buns." Do you like it? (Carley nods vigorously)

Q: I've noticed when I've been here before that you sing a lot. When you're just kind of walking around.

A: Sometimes I hum.

Q: Sometimes you hum and sometimes you sing little things. Do you do that all the time?

A: Well, sometimes in school . . . at recess when I don't have anyone to play with. I just play with my songs. (laughs nervously)

Q: Yeah?

A: Yeah, it's like I . . . I sing them out and then I roll them up into a ball.

Q: How do you mean, you roll them up into a ball?

A: (giggles nervously) It's just one of my little jokes.

Q: It's just a little joke? (Carley nods, giggles) How about the video tapes? Is there anything on those that you like to listen to?

A: Well, sometimes. Last night I watched one with songs on it. It's called *Comedy and Magic*. *Comedy and Magic* has Disney songs on it. It has "Supercalifragilisticexpialidocious." (both giggle)

Q: How about other things on TV. Do you notice music on TV?

A: Well, sort of. When I went to tape with my mom . . . the tape happened to be . . . there was this song, there was this movie on and it had singing in it.

Q: Supercalifragilistic?

A: No. Not kids' music. Grown-up music. A grown-up would mostly like it. I was just hanging around and listening to it.

Q: What's grown-up music. As opposed to kids' music?

A: Well, Disney music is mostly like a kind of kids' music. Some Disney music grown-ups like, but my parents mostly don't like Disney.

Q: But you do? (Carley giggles, nods yes) But you don't like their music?

A: (continues giggling and shakes her head vigorously, no) Well, you know, there is some, well "American Pie" is sort of grown-up music. And I *like it*. (bursts out giggling)

Q: Is there anything else you can think of to talk about right now?

A: Yeah . . . . We sometimes watch musical videos. At school. In the music room.

Q: What kind of stuff is that?

A: *Peter and the Wolf* . . . and *Eine Kleine Night Music. Eine kleine nacht music* means really "a little bit of night music."

Q: So is that music you'd like to try to get a tape of so that you can listen to it here?

A: Well, no, because it was boring. (both laugh) The video was about the person who made it, that is, who wrote the music of "Night," and it was kind of boring.

Q: But the music was nice?

A: Yes.

Q: Well, I don't know, you've done pretty well. Can you think of anything else?

A: Do you want to know some of the things we sing around Christmastime?

Q: Do you like that? Do you like to sing around Christmastime?

A: Yeah, 'cause I like the songs we sing. There's one about snowmen. (pause)

Q: Do you usually think about music?

A: We sing "Frosty the Snowman" in class, and . . .

Q: During the winter, right?

A: Right, and (singing) "Rudolph the Red-Nosed Reindeer."

Q: When do you do that, that's in music class?

A: Well, sometimes we sing it in music, sometimes we sing it in our classroom.

Music's my favorite thing in school. The reason I don't like gym the most is because sometimes we go in with older kids and we get called names, and in art some people say that they don't like me and other kids' pictures and that's upsetting, too. No one does any of those things in music, so that's why my favorite thing is music.

Q: So, in music, why don't they make fun of you? Is it because everybody's singing?

A: It's because everybody's singing. So they don't have time to make fun.

Q: But they don't make fun of you afterwards?

A: No, because in the classroom no one makes fun of anyone.

Q: Do you think everybody likes music?

A: Well, most of the kids' favorite things are gym or art.

Q: But everybody sings in music class?

A: Yeah.

Q: I'm kind of interested in how grown-up music is different than kids' music. What makes it different?

A: Well, one thing is strange about Raffi's music. My parents like it and I like it. So I don't know whose music it is. (laughs)

Q: So, your parents like grown-up music and you like kids' music, that's what the difference is.

A: But there is an in-between music. Raffi's music. Things like "Supercalifragilisticexpialidocious" are kind of for kids. My parents don't like them. (giggles)

Q: Well, I think we've done pretty good. Thank you for talking.

A: (melodically) You're welcome.

"I was stuck in the snow cave, and I felt like listening to music."

Billy is seven years old. He was interviewed by his
older sister, a college student, in her bedroom.

Q: Are you ready? Who are you?

A: (shouts) Billy!

Q: (laughing) How old are you?

A: Seven. (laughs because he is still shouting)

Q: Um, what do you like about music?

A: Ah . . . I like it because it's on every single day and you don't have
to worry about having no music at home.

Q: Do you like music?

A: (enthusiastically) Yes!

Q: What kind of music do you like?

A: Rock'n'roll. (both laugh)

Q: What kind of groups do you like?

A: Singers? I like Belinda Carlisle . . . George Michael, Richard Marx,
Debbie Gibson, Whitesnake (laughs), Bill Medley, and Jennifer Warnes.

Q: What do you like about Belinda Carlisle?

A: (laughs) She's pretty!

Q: She's pretty. (Billy is still laughing.) What's your favorite song?

A: "Heaven is a Place on Earth."

Q: (laughs) What do you like about it?

A: Mmm, the people that are in the video that they have. They raise
their hands and go "Heaven!" (both laugh)

Q: Do you like to dance?

A: Yes, with it!

Q: Do you dance with other songs? What are some of your other
favorite songs?

A: Um . . . um . . . let me think . . . um . . . "Faith," "Father Figure," "I've Had the Time of my Life," um . . . "Is This Love?" "Here I Go Again," . . . "Don't Shed a Tear for Me," "She's Like the Wind." I like to dance to music because I have all the right moves 'cause I watch them on "Chartbusters." And every night. Sometimes they're on every night. Sometimes they aren't.

Q: Where do you like to listen to music?

A: Um . . . (laughs) on my brother's stereo.

Q: On your brother's stereo! Do you like to listen to music in the car?

A: Yes! Absolutely! My favorite station is 93 Q.

Q: Do you ever want to be in a band?

A: Yes.

Q: What kind of a band?

A: Can I say it?

Q: What?

A: Can I say it? (laughs)

Q: Yeah.

A: Okay . . . Belinda Carlisle Fan Club. I'd like to join one.

Q: Her band or her fan club?

A: Her band. I like it when they bang the drums twice after they say the words.

Q: (laughs) You really like Belinda Carlisle don't you?

A: Yep! I certainly do! (laughs)

Q: So you still like to go down and watch the marching band, right? What do you like about it?

A: That . . . (stutters) that they, they do very neat things . . . every kind of instrument . . . and play good music.

Q: They play good music?

A: Um hum. (both laugh)

Q: Do you like to sing to it?

A: Yeah.

Q: You like doing the flag stuff? And conducting?

A: Um hum.

Q: What do you like about it?

A: (laughs) Well, um . . . you get to shout. Do slow things and get to shout them out. We have music in our school and we act out things with our costumes and act them out in the back 'cause they have this stage and we do . . . and we play lots of music and I'm in the band that they do. I just sit there and we have a book which tells us what keys to do. Because one of the kids in our classes is twelve . . . not in third grade . . . is twelve and comes down at the same time and plays the piano. 'Cause he's a good piano player. Real good piano player, and he plays real good music.

Q: In your music class at school? What other things do you do in music class?

A: We . . . we sing lots of songs.

Q: What's one of your favorite ones?

A: "Halloween is coming." (sings it) "Hal-lo-ween is com-ing, Ha Ha Ha . . . ." I forgot the words.

Q: What other kind of things do you do in music class? What do you like?

A: Um . . . we get to listen to the stereo.

Q: Do you like listening to the radio?

A: Yes, and she [the teacher] has records that she plays and we get to dance like popcorn where you have to jump up and down. Whoever jumps the highest gets to go in the back and, um . . . sing the song that they like best.

Q: Do you have any records?

A: Oh yes!

Q: How many do you have?

A: (laughs) Hold on, I'm counting them. (laughs) Can I say them? Belinda Carlisle, "She's like the Wind," George Michael, George Harrison, Debbie Gibson, um . . . Pretty Poison, and . . . "Heaven is a Place on Earth."

Q: So you have seven of them.

A: No, I have, I got one more . . . um . . . trying to think of it . . . "Tunnel of Love." So I got eight.

Q: Eight! That's a lot. How often do you listen to them?

A: Every single day. (both laugh)

Q: Do you like watching videos a lot?

A: Yep.

Q: What do you like?

A: The "Chartbusters" where they count down and they . . . whoever reaches the number one song of the week, they are on the "Chartbusters" chart that week. They put them on there and write their names and then the show is over.

Q: (laughs) You love to watch them?

A: Yes, but I never get to stay up at eleven.

Q: (laughs) So what do you do?

A: We tape them on our VCR.

Q: And then you watch them later?

A: We watch them later in the morning.

Q: Every morning?

A: Yes. (laughs)

Q: How often do you watch videos during the day?

A: Ah . . . once or twice. Yep, and Belinda Carlisle is on it too!

Q: What about movies with music in them? Do you like them?

A: Oh yes! *Dirty Dancing* and the *Berenstein Bears*. They have a whole bunch of music in them. And they sing songs.

Q: Do you like music in all of the cartoons and stuff? What are some of your favorite TV shows that have music that you like?

A: "Scooby Doo" . . . "Space Station Reach Star" . . . that's on at eight in the morning. And . . . my other favorite show is the "Super Heroes." They're not on TV. They took them off, but they sometimes are on because they put them on for other shows. Oh . . . and I also like the movie the *Wizard of Oz*.

Q: What do you like about it?

A: I like all of the actresses that are in there, and the little dog, Toto, is cute.

Q: Did you like the songs that they sang?

A: Yep. (sings "We're off to see the Wizard")

Q: (laughs) What do you think about music?

A: It's fun. It makes you happy. If you're really tired of listening to the TV and you turn on the radio and more music and it's fun. And you get to dance, and actresses sing songs. My most favoritest song that they play every single day is "This Must be Just Like Living in Paradise" and it's on in the morning but in the afternoon they play Belinda Carlisle.

Q: (laughs) You said you're in her fan club?

A: I'm in her fan club. I joined it. I got five things on my list that I wanted from her. I wanted a poster, a record, two tapes, and a little small record of another song that she sings. Her new song, whatever it is, and it should be coming in a week and a half or something.

Q: What if there wasn't any music? What would you think? Would you miss it?

A: Yes.

Q: Why would you miss it?

A: Because. All my favorite songs are on the radio, and I don't get to hear them 'cause if you don't get to hear them you . . . it's kind of boring. Around the house like if you didn't have any toys or anything it's so boring. If you were caught in a snow cave you'd be even more . . . .

Q: (laughing because Billy was) Um, do you get mad when people don't let you listen to music? Like if they want to . . .

A: Yes! My brother comes out and turns the stereo off and he never turns it back on and I have to get the chair to climb on the cupboard to try and turn it back on.

Q: (laughs) What about when you are in the car? Do you like to listen to one station or a lot of them? What happens if a song comes on that you don't like? What do you do?

A: I tell them to turn down the volume.

Q: What if one comes on that you do like?

A: Tell them to turn it up real loud! If it was "Heaven is a place on Earth" I'd really tell them to!

Q: So you like to listen to music on TV, right?

A: Yeah, every single day I hear music and all my favorite characters are on TV sometimes. Like they have the new "Out with Alf" and they play music and he . . . one of the kids has got a kitten on the chair and, um, he comes up and Alf's on the couch, and the little boy pushes Alf, and the cat runs.

And also one of my favorite shows is "Pee Wee's Playhouse." I love it. When Pee Wee comes over, the music starts out . . . my brother likes it . . . "Get out of bed, there'll be no more napping," and all the people come out and they go bananas, and then everybody else and the rest of the playhouse comes in, and they ask Pee Wee what the secret word of the day is, and the music goes . . . . (sings) It's really funny. We really like it. My brother says it's a queer show 'cause it's got all of that funny kind of music. His playhouse is nice, and I like it when all of the actresses come over and sing songs. (sings a song from the show)

Q: So, do a lot of your friends like music as much as you?

A: Yes, one of my friends likes Belinda Carlisle and we always sing the songs together in lunch. Did you ever hear "Heaven is a Place on Earth"? And then we start singing it.

Q: So, do you like music more so than other kids?

A: No, one of our kids listens to the radio every day. He doesn't stop. Even when he is going on vacation he turns on the radio.

Q: Is there any music that you don't like?

A: Yeah, I don't like that old-fashion music.

Q: Like what?

A: Like "Stay Just a Little Bit Longer?" I like the song but it's an old song. Today my mother went up to B.J.'s and we went next door to Fay's. And they didn't have any music [in B.J.'s] and that was what was boring about it. Then they played all kinds of music in Fay's and they had all kinds of records. Thousands. They had all kinds of tapes and they had Belinda Carlisle. She was at the very end and they had Tiffany. Oh! That's it! Tiffany, "Could Have Been." That's nine!

Q: Oh, nine records.

A: Nine, 'cause I was trying to think of it. I probably have one more, but I don't know about it.

Q: So for you music is fun.

A: It's fun, happy. It makes people very happy. Is the tape almost out?

Q: No, not yet. Um . . . so if you didn't have music you'd be really bored?

A: Really bored with no toys and being stuck in a snow cave and not getting out. But I was stuck in the snow cave, and I felt like listening to music. At the end of the day I was all stiff 'cause I was laying on my back in the snow cave and my hand was stuck and I tried to get my hand up and I jammed the snow and got my hand up. And there was a big hole in the top and I stuck my hand out of it and I started calling my nextdoor neighbor, Martha. She was out and she heard me calling and she came over and started digging to try to get me out. My brother looked out and said, "The cave collapsed, is Billy in there? 'Cause he's not out here in the front." He thought that I might be in the cave 'cause he told me not to go in there, but then I was getting my ski poles and I heard the snowplow go by and piled more snow up and the cave collapsed and I started calling and started to cry. I couldn't stop and then when I got in I just felt like listening to music so I played all of my records.

After, I felt a little better, and then that night I watched . . . my mother taped me some "Chartbusters" and I watched them and I was fine. Then, one time in the morning, I was all stiff up, I didn't think I'd go to church. My back was all stiff. I told my mom if I could listen to some music and I turned it up. When I turned it on they were playing Belinda Carlisle and I was going "Uh, oh." And I turned the radio up too loud. And they were all sleeping and they came down and said, "Why you got the music so loud?" " 'Cause my song is playing!"

"They teach us that so we know what to do with our kids when we grow up."

Jennie was eight years old when she was interviewed by a
woman who is a family friend and graduate student.

Q: Did your mom tell you what I wanted to talk to you about?

A: No.

Q: Well what I'd like to know is what kind of music you like—got any special kind?

A: Rock and roll.

Q: You like rock and roll? Do you have a favorite star?

A: Yes, Madonna.

Q: What do you like about her?

A: She sings well. And there's a group named Bon Jovi. My brother can sing that, my dad can sing it too.

Q: When you listen to rock and roll do you ever listen to your dad's records? Do you have any favorites there?

A: Yeah. It's a blue tape and it has rock and roll songs on it. All sorts of songs on it and I like it.

Q: Now, you dance too? What kind of dancing do you do?

A: Jazz and ballet.

Q: Do you like one better than the other? Because they have kind of different musics that go with them, don't they?

A: Yeah. Jazz is good because you get to move around a lot and ballet is sort of slower. . . .

Q: Do you have to do more rules with ballet than with jazz?

A: Yeah, you have to speak in another kind of language.

Q: French?

A: Yeah. That's sort of hard. . . .

Q: Can you remember any of the words?

A: Yeah. Umm . . . your arms are "bra" and umm . . . and your nose is . . . I think so. Does it begin with an "n"?

Q: Would it be something like "nez"?

A: Yeah.

Q: Tell me how ballet works.

A: We have to stand up on our toes, 'cause you wear toe shoes when you do ballet. Yeah, so you don't really stand up on your toes you go like that (demonstrating how foot is held) . . . stand on your feet. And a different ballet, you have to stand right up on your toes. That's hard.

Q: And you don't do that when you do jazz dance?

A: No.

Q: Well, tell me a little bit about jazz dancing.

A: We do skips and we have to point our toes. We do gallops, and . . . we do warm-ups . . . we do flatbacks.

Q: What's a flatback?

A: A flatback's when you go down and you have to have your . . . your back really straight . . . then you go down like that, and you have to move your arms and then you go down and then up, down then up.

Q: Do you get to make up the steps that you do when you do dance?

A: Rachel makes them up. She practiced a long time to be dancer.

Q: She's your teacher, right?

A: Yeah.

Q: Does she dance with you?

A: She dances with us, but when it's almost time for the recital she wants us to do it all by ourselves, the whole thing. It's so hard.

Q: You have a recital coming up pretty soon, don't you? Have you started to practice?

A: Yeah. We did a couple new steps. We went backward and the other group puts their leg up there and the other one goes and touches the other and then you do that with the other one . . .

Q: Have you picked out the music that you're going to dance to?

A: In ballet, I can't remember the name but it's sort of really slow and it's a nice song.

Q: And what about jazz? Do you know what the music will be?

A: Yeah, "One, Two, Three, Four." Same one again.

Q: Same one? But you're going to do different steps this time? Do you dance together and help each other with steps?

A: In ballet we do.

Q: But not in jazz? Do you make up ballet dances, too?

A: No, Rachel makes them up. And they're always different. There's tons of dances. I don't know how she can do it. She has tons. She has the "Fat Boys" too.

Q: Is that what they call rap music?

A: Yeah.

Q: You don't dance to that, do you?

A: No. (laughs) Jackie and Alissa do.

Q: What kind of dance are they doing to that?

A: They have to wiggle their butts and go down and side, side, down, up.

Q: How do you practice?

A: She tells us what to do and we have to do it. See, if whoever can't do it, she'll go over there and help them. Most of them can. Probably two or three can't.

Q: So, you get an assignment each week and you practice that and then go in and see how everybody's working when you work all together.

A: We take about four weeks to get it. And then we do a new thing.

Q: So do you dance in school? Do you have gym or anything in school.

A: Yeah, you have to do square dances.

Q: Oh, yeah? Do you dance with boys?

A: Yeah, we have to.

Q: How are they at dancing?

A: Sort of good. There's two different kinds of square dancing.

Q: Oh, tell me. Tell me about that.

A: One of them's you have to get in a circle. I know some of them. You bow to your partner and you bow to your corner. Then they both do it a different way. The ladies curtsy and the boys bow. And, then we have to go like that and skip around the circle until we get back to the spots. We have to keep skipping until we get back to our spots.

Q: To where you started from?

A: Yeah, and then we have to hold hands and go to the right in a circle and then the left in a circle. And you have to go like that. Cross your arms. And then the other one puts their hands just like that. The boys go like this and then the girls go like this. They put their hand on their hips and then they go around the circle, to the partner and then the corner. And then that's all.

Q: Well, now you said there were two kinds. What's the other kind?

A: There's just two lines going down, then we just do it with our partners and we hold hands and then somebody goes under. We did that in Mrs. Cristopher's class the other time.

Q: You make like a bridge and the person goes under it?

A: Yeah.

Q: Do you have somebody special that you dance with?

A: You just go around. We don't just pick partners. Mr. Jackson does them.

Q: Do they have band at school? Is there an instrument that you could play at school?

A: Yeah. In music, she has bells, drums, tambourines, sandpaper.

Q: What's your favorite?

A: Umm . . . sand scrapers.

Q: You like them?

A: Yeah.

Q: You know, in Africa they make music like that too. They rub things together to make sounds. Do you mostly play instruments in music or do you sing in music too?

A: We sing the song named (singing) "Let's Make Music, Yes Indeed."

Q: I don't know that. Do you know the words. Can you sing it?

A: (singing) Let's make music, yes indeed, yes indeed, yes indeed. Let's make music, yes indeed, yes indeed, everybody . . . yes indeed, my darling. That song. And we march in band. We play in there with drums and instruments. It's really fun.

Q: Do you get to play all kinds of sounds? Can you make as much noise as you want?

A: Yeah, if she tells us to. 'Cause the door is closed. They're making a new building there and it makes lots of noise. That's why she let's us do it.

Q: So you can make as much noise as you want, when you're in music.

A: Yeah.

Q: Have you ever been tape recorded before.

A: Sometimes I tape myself on our tape recorder.

Q: You've got your own little record of yourself then, huh?

A: Yeah.

Q: That's kind of neat. Do you have tapes of your own with music on them?

A: Yeah. Kids' music.

Q: What's kids' music?

A: There's this thing about church and they got church songs and Christmas songs. Chip and Dale. The Disneyworld tape, the Disneyworld exercise tape. The Care Bears tape.

Q: You've got quite a few. Do you have any Madonna or Bon Jovi?

A: Nope. My dad has them.

Q: Does he share them?

A: Yeah.

Q: You probably have to ask, don't you?

A: It seems like I have to ask all the time.

Q: That's the trouble with being a kid, isn't it? You know what? It doesn't change much when you get older.

A: Yeah—but they teach us that so we know what to do with our kids when we grow up.

Q: (laughs) That's right. So. Dad sometimes shares his tapes with you? The kids music that you've got—does your dad ever listen to that?

A: Yeah. But I have to talk him into it sometimes. Except, he does the exercise with us—on the tape.

"I like to look for things that people don't really recognize."

Molly is eleven years old and is in the fifth grade. She was interviewed by the mother of the man who has been giving her piano lessons for many years.

Q: Who are you? How would you describe yourself if you were to tell someone about yourself?

A: I'm Molly and I play piano and flute. I've been playing piano for a long time, since I was in first grade. And I started flute last year. I really enjoy both instruments but flute is sometimes easier because . . . well, you don't have to concentrate on both hands . . . well, you do but . . . and the thing that is not so great about it is that you lose your breath on the flute, while on the piano you don't.

But I think piano is more musical sometimes because you can make it louder or softer than a flute and you can have chords . . . a flute doesn't have chords. And you can play all kinds of notes on the piano but on the flute it's how long you've been playing, or how good you are, that you can go lower, but on the piano you can go as low or as high as the piano goes and it's a wider range of notes.

Lots of my friends play piano too. Most of them play piano and another instrument. One plays the oboe, a couple play the clarinet, one plays the French horn, and I tried to play the French horn. It didn't really sound too good (laughs) but I played the oboe a couple of notes and I've looked at a lot of other instruments. My dad plays the trumpet and so I've played the trumpet a little bit.

Q: Does your mother play an instrument?

A: No, she used to play piano when she was younger but she doesn't anymore. She can still, like . . . she reads music much better than I can.

Q: Well, your friends all play instruments . . .

A: Not all, just a lot. (laughs)

Q: Do you get together and play your instruments together?

A: Yes, my friend that plays the oboe and my friend that plays the clarinet . . . we usually get together a lot. We're all in band together in our school and we play band songs and things but, when we get together with my friend that plays the French horn, it's kind of hard because if we don't want to play our band songs, we're not like in the same note. Since most of my friends play the piano, sometimes we play duets and stuff.

Q: When you get together and have fun with your different instruments . . . does that make you feel different about your music?

A: Well, yes . . . because a flute can take on a whole different sound when you're playing with an oboe, and if you're not, there's a whole different sound there too because when you play instruments together, you have a different sound than when you are playing them separately.

Q: What is it about this sound that you like?

A: Well, I think . . . for example, when my band conductor gives everybody a song and says, take it home, practice it, and next week we will try to play it with the band. And so I take it home and practice it and I'm thinking, "This sounds horrible," and "I must be playing something wrong," but when I get there and I play it exactly as I was playing it at home, it sounds ten times better because of all the other instruments. I think it really sounds neat when you're with all the other different instruments.

Q: How about listening to music? Do you prefer to listen alone or with your friends?

A: Sometimes when there's a piece I want to think about, I like to listen to it alone but if it's just some fun song or something, I like to listen to it with my friends and then we talk about it and everyone has a different opinion on it, sometimes.

Q: What do you mean, "When it's a piece you want to think about?"

A: Well, if it has some interesting quality that you need to concentrate on like when you're reading a book and it has some really tough words and you have to read it slowly and think about each word. . . . I think it's the same with music. When it's a hard piece you have to listen carefully. But, if it's easy, you can just sit back and listen not too close, and it still calculates in your brain.

Q: When you are listening to a piece closely and thinking about it, do you ever have any special feelings about it?

A: Well, sometimes music makes pictures in my mind . . . makes you think of things and when you're listening to a piece that's really kind of soft you feel real carefree . . . but when you're listening to a real suspenseful piece, loud and scary, you feel strange and it makes you think of different things.

Like if it's a pretty, sunny day out and you are listening to scary music, the day doesn't look too great . . . whereas if you're listening to nice music, it makes it better. Just like in a movie when they're showing a scary part, you're not going to play some beautiful song. They play some scary music and you feel scary.

Q: What do you like about music? Why are you taking these two instruments and playing together with your friends?

A: I think that music sounds neat and people like to hear it, and I would feel pretty empty if I didn't play any instruments. I like playing with my friends, and when I'm practicing flute I like to flip through my flute book and find a piece and just try and play it. I like to start a new piece and see what I can do that I didn't think I could. So, I just like how it sounds, and I can do different things with it.

Q: Okay. Your father is a musician, so you've probably always had a lot of music in your house. What kind of music do you like?

A: I don't like heavy metal. I like ragtime. I like classical but I like to play pieces that I recognize so that I know what they are supposed to sound like. I like rock music, something that has a nice beat because it sounds really nice if it has a good support, a bass to it . . . because if it's only strings it gets boring after a while. When I'm at a concert, I usually don't like to listen to a piano the whole time. I like listening to a band or a variety of music so that you can have different things to listen to and you can pick out different parts of it. But when you're listening to a piano or something like that, you just have one thing to listen to and that gets kind of boring after a while.

Q: When you listen to music, what do you zero in on? The words, or the whole sound, or the beat, or the group? What do you like most?

A: Well, most people recognize the vocals or the main instrument, but I like to look for things that people don't really recognize. Like some songs have maracas in them and you don't really notice that unless you really listen. I was listening to a song the other day and mostly it was just the downbeat and you might just hear the main instrument but I found five other things playing and I was trying to listen for those. It was really neat.

Q: It's like doing a puzzle.

A: Yes, but you can't be doing something else while you are doing that—listening for other things in the music. You have to really think about it.

Q: What do you think about today's music?

A: Well, I don't like songs that are too loud and it's just a blur of all these instruments pushed together. I don't like anything that doesn't have much of a beat to it. I like kind of a slow rock, not fast and loud, that has a good beat to it . . . a good rhythm.

Q: Any favorite rock groups?

A: Not really. I like all kinds, but sometimes I don't like groups that sing about useless things.

Q: Do you listen to the words?

A: Yes, if I really find them interesting. If they are stupid, I don't listen to them.

Q: What do you think of the music videos that you see?

A: I like to look at how well they put pictures to the music because some people that make those videos don't do that too well. If it's a really good video, I look for the good video part of it. How well the pictures or whatever they're doing describes the music.

Q: Does watching the videos influence the way you feel about the music, or interrupt the music?

A: Not really. But if you're watching the video and later on you hear the song, then you picture the video . . . but that really cuts off on how well you imagine things when you are listening to the music because you just think of what you saw on TV and not what your mind sees.

Q: Do you collect records or tapes?

A: I collect some tapes but I'm not really into it that much. I just get tapes of groups or music that I like. My dad collects records, but not like a hobby . . . he just has thousands of them. I think it's hard to find a record that you want when he has piles and piles of them.

Q: What are some of the tapes that you have?

A: Some of them are rock music. Some of them are presents and I don't really like all of them. My dad has a CD player and he got a ragtime for it. I really like ragtime piano music. I don't really know why. I just like how it sounds. I listen to that.

Q: How do you feel when you listen to it?

A: It's really cheerful music, so it makes me feel cheerful.

Q: (laughter) We need that sometimes. Do you like to dance?

A: Yes. I take ballet lessons, and I used to take jazz and tap. I like ballet. It's pretty neat. You can stretch while you're dancing. And sometimes I dance to music, and I try to dance to it that would show how the music is . . . like if it's cheerful music, I'm not going to go moping around. (laughter)

Q: So, do you choreograph your own stuff according to how you feel about your music?

A: Yes. Sometimes I do that and sometimes I just listen to music and I can picture a ballerina or I can picture a tap dancer. It's all different.

Q: Do you ever dance to change the way you feel?

A: Sometimes I do. But never to make myself feel sad. (laughter) When I'm sad I do something I really like. I like to read a book by a good author that captures the reader's attention. Good music does it too . . . they both capture the reader's attention.

Q: Where do you like to listen to your music?

A: Sometimes I like to listen to it in a big auditorium or gym, or even outside where it seems to flow all over the place. Sometimes I like to listen to it in a small place because it goes straight to your ears. There is no place else to flow and sometimes you just hear it better. But I also like listening to it sitting on a couch, or doing something else like playing a game on the floor.

Q: Do you play different kinds of music if you are playing a game than if you were sitting on the couch and wanted to listen?

A: If I like the music and played and thought about it a lot, I can usually then think about doing something else while I'm listening to it.

Q: How about singing? Do you like to sing?

A: Yes. I like to sing in chorus. I don't like to sing alone . . . just singing. I like to sing in chorus because I like to listen to the music and sing it with other people. There's a song in chorus called "Flying Free" and I really like that song because . . . the notes are nice and the altos and the sopranos are singing different from you and it sounds good together. I like listening to piano duets, or other instruments because they sound good together.

Q: You mentioned a favorite song, "Flying Free." Can you tell me more about how you feel when you hear that song?

A: I'm not sure, but if I thought about it I could probably tell you. (pause) Well, I feel like a bird because it's about a bird and I feel like I'm flying free when I listen to it or singing it because it's pretty and it makes me feel good.

Q: Can you remember a time that you felt something especially powerful?

A: Well . . . we sang a song in school about America and I felt really proud that I lived in America because we talked about all the rights we have that other people didn't and I felt really special.

Q: Is there anything else you can think of telling me about how you feel about music?

A: Yes. My friend Georgette started to play the flute and then she quit. She said she quit because she didn't have much time or she didn't like it. In the beginning, when I started to play the piano, I hated it and then, when I started to play more interesting pieces, I started to like it and now I really like it. The same thing happened with flute. I started out where I didn't like it and I stuck to it and now I love it. So, I think you should stick to what you are trying to play for a time; that you will get better at it. Some people told me . . . my father's sisters or people who were older . . . that you should stick with the instrument that you pick because you get lots of advantages because of that instrument. In general, if you are playing an instrument, you get to do a lot of things.

TEENAGERS

"What would the human ear do, just listen to nothingness?"

Lisa, twelve years old, was interviewed by her older sister.

Q: Tell me about yourself.

A: Well . . . my name is Lisa. My mom's a social worker. My dad's an insurance man. He's a pretty cool dude. I'm also your sister; I've got four brothers and you. I love horses, uh . . . I'm pretty smart and . . . hey, I'm just an all-around person.

Q: Great. Okay. And what is music about for you?

A: Music . . . music to me is . . . it really doesn't have that much meaning in my life. I just turn on the radio and listen to whatever comes on. Maybe a song will come on that I just happen to like. It just doesn't matter to me.

Q: Like what songs?

A: Well, this one song by the Bangles, "Shady Day of Winter" ["Hazy Shade of Winter"]. That was really from Simon and Garfunkel. They made it upbeat, and I like it, and that's about the only song I really like on the radio.

Q: When do you listen to music?

A: Whenever I'm doing homework, before I go to sleep, and when I'm cleaning the kitchen. Or whenever someone else is listening to the stereo. That's the only time really because it has no meaning to me.

Q: No meaning at all?

A: No!

Q: It doesn't make you feel good?

A: Well, I guess I like upbeat songs except some are pretty stupid, like what's his name . . . George Michaels' songs are stupid. They have no real meaning. Some of them are pretty sick, too. Like "I want Your Sex." Oh, now *that's* a great song. (sarcasm)

Q: What are your favorite songs right now besides "Hazy Shade of Winter"?

A: Tiffany's all right, except some of her songs are pretty stupid, too. I like Irish music. That's about it. Hey, I just listen to whatever comes on the radio.

Q: What about performing? Do you sing?

A: Dumb little songs like . . . (laughs) no, I don't sing, I just . . . no, I just hear songs on the radio and then it pops into my head, and then I just bounce around a lot thinking of the song even though it's dumb. (sister laughs) I live an exciting music life, what can I say? (sister laughs) Glad you find this amusing. (sister still laughing) It's pretty depressing to me.

Q: Why?

A: Because I have no music life. I can live without music.

Q: Really?

A: No.

Q: What makes you think you can't?

A: It's because you always need some song, a little music that just makes you happy. If you're in a bad mood, and you hear a jumpy song, even if it's dumb, it makes you happy. Reggae's all right, it's pretty neat. (laughs) They're not dumb, though I don't understand half the words they're saying, but it's jumpy.

Q: So you listen more to the beat than the words?

A: Yeah, because if you listen closely . . . pretty dumb words.

Q: Do you like to sing or dance in public?

A: In public? (laughs) Yes, while doing my papers with Karen, I start singing "Glory Glory Hallelujah" (sister laughs) or "It's a Small World After All." That's the only time I sing in public. I may get some funny looks, but why not?

Q: Do you tend to listen to music by yourself or when other people are around?

A: Well, the only time I usually listen to music is when someone else plays it, so there's got to be someone else around, unless I'm listening to my radio while doing my homework. I like to listen to the tape move. (both laugh)

Q: You said you get songs in your head. Are they usually yours or someone else's?

A: They're the songs I hear on the radio. Sometimes I get the Beach Boys song in my head because I saw it in the movie. Or one of those songs on the radio, like Tiffany or "Hazy Shade of Winter" comes into my head a lot. I know it means a lot to some people like Greg, our brother, for instance. He's a drummer, and he loves all sorts of music. He likes jazz. He appreciates classical, and he's got his own songs. And Paul just likes a lot of songs. And John, he likes pretty much what Greg and Paul like.

Michael, he's like me. He doesn't really have a music life. No, he doesn't even listen to the radio. He just usually listens to what Greg has on tape. My friend Karen really likes music although it's not really music. It's Bon Jovi and Whitesnake. And Jennifer, she's starting to get into it. She sings a lot of songs like I do. She gets a song in her head and then she thinks about it a lot, and she listens to the radio. My friend Brynn, she does not really care about music either, but I think she will really begin to enjoy music sooner or later.

Q: Do you think you will?

A: Maybe, depends, whatever songs come out or old songs I like.

Q: Old songs?

A: I like old Billy Joel. Beatles are okay; they were pretty funny people. I did enjoy their haircuts. Now, I just listen to the radio really, and whatever comes on, you know? Nothing really exciting. A boring music life like I said eighteen times already.

(pause) I enjoy going to plays. I enjoy those types of music, when it has real meaning. If someone is depressed and they're trying to cheer him up like "Singing In the Rain." Some guy was really depressed, and his friends tried to cheer him up by singing and dancing to a song. That's the kind of music I like.

Q: What do you think of all the styles that come out of music?

A: Music pretty much controls the world. It does. If some great music star does something, everyone else is going to want to do something. When Bon Jovi had long hair, everyone wanted long hair like the Beatles. Michael Jackson started a big fad with break-dancing, and that totally hit the nation, and everyone was break-dancing. It didn't seem like anybody didn't like it. It pretty much controls the world. I think so because everyone listens to music, and whatever they do, they are the idols. It's not like some great leader is the idol. If you ask someone who their idol is, it's either a music star or one of those wrestlers . . . Hulk Hogan for instance. "I want to grow up to be Hulk Hogan or G.I. Joe."

Q: Who do you want to grow up to be like?

A: (sings) "I just wanna be me!" . . . 'cause I think I'm a pretty neat person. Not trying to sound conceited, but I am.

Q: So you think the media controls a lot of people?

A: Yes.

Q: Do you think it does you?

A: No, it doesn't have any effect on me. I don't understand how some people just singing a song can have such a great influence on people. I don't see why I should dress like them just because I like their songs. I just do what I want to do.

A lot of people try to make a good song by doing it for a good cause. I think people should make a song for cruelty to animals. I really love animals so I think they should make a song for cruelty to animals to get people more aware of what they do to animals.

Q: You don't think it's more important to save people than it is to save animals?

A: They were here first. We don't even think about all the little things behind us all. Say you become a great leader. Maybe you became that great leader because you had such great influence from your animal. Some people like to talk to their animals and figure out their problems from their animals. Look at Paul Revere. He had his horse. He's famous for riding his horse. Some people like that. Rin Tin Tin, what would everyone do without Rin Tin Tin? And Lassie, one of the most famous animals in America, although he's probably dead.

I think people should do things about animals. Sure they should help people, but we do that all the time. Let's do something different for a change; help the animals. Sometimes I think they are smarter than us. For one thing, they don't cause problems, they are not causing pollution, big fat wars, and they are not too worried about diseases.

Q: How do you use music in your life?

A: I listen to it. I just use it for amusement. To cheer me up when I'm depressed, I listen to an exciting song. Sometimes I use it if I'm studying for a test. A song comes on, and when it comes to the test, I remember the song, I remember the question, and I remember the answer. But usually I remember the answer because I'm so smart. Uh . . . I like to whistle. Give me a song and I can whistle it although you may not understand the song, but I'll just whistle. Whistle little words, and make up my own little songs.

That's what I like about our keyboard. You can make up your own beat, your own song, and it doesn't have to be good, and it's just yours. I really enjoy that . . . combining instruments and things even though they sound really bad because I'm tone deaf.

(pause) But music is always good to have. I mean what would the human ear do, listen to nothingness? They need something to listen to, so it may as well be music. But I always wondered who started music. Who started it? Maybe the cavemen started it. Maybe they went around banging sticks. Maybe that's what did it. 'Cause its been around a long time. Flutes and harps. I just wonder who started it all. Who was that main person? 'Cause it's one of the biggest trends, and will always be a big trend, but it's more than a trend to most people, but it's hard to explain. (pause) The Monkees are neat. (sister laughs) I mean the band. (sister laughs more) They made songs about making fun of people. They showed how stupid people are sometimes and they made them into funny situations. (several interruptions from family)

. . . also it affects religions. The Baptists pretty much put everything to music. Songs . . . songs are made for praises because singing is praying twice . . . and Catholics, they love to sing, like, praises. It's pretty interesting how music has such a big effect on people when you think about it. You can't just turn around and see nobody listening to music. Music will never stop. Even Amish people. They don't listen to radios and stuff, but they still sing their songs. They still have their music. Radios are always on in cars. Music is just everywhere. People are singing, they have walkmans, there's music at the beginning of shows.

Q: What do you think of walkmans?

A: They are good, but they are bad. They hurt people's hearing, but they are also good because say some elderly people don't like our type of music. They let them listen to what they want to listen to. It's pretty interesting. I never really thought about it. It's part of the American way, and everyone else's way. Look at our national anthem. All countries have music for their anthem to show their pride for their country, and it's pretty amazing. Look at when Mozart was alive. Everything was operas and that meant music.

Everywhere there's music. People are always listening to music, operas, there's music everywhere. Can't stop it either. Keep playing the music. Since long ago, there's been music. Even in our modern science world, there's always going to be music, and people are always going to be affected by it. Some songs may get stupider, but some may even get better, and that's all I've really been trying to say this whole time even though it took so long.

"They play weird songs you have to be so old to know."

Matthew was interviewed by his older brother. He is twelve
years old and likes to play computer games and basketball.

Q: Okay, what does music mean to you?

A: Well . . . I usually listen to the radio while I'm playing my computer in my room or when I'm playing basketball. I don't sit down and just listen to it. It's sort of a side thing, you know?

Q: What do you listen to?

A: Well, I usually listen to the radio stations because my other brother always has my tune box. I listen to all kinds of music. I can listen to it all. Some things are not my favorite, but I really don't have any I hate and detest.

Q: Why do you put it on when you're using your computer?

A: Well, because I want to hear something, you know . . . not only just kind of sitting there . . . you know, listen to music, sing along . . . .

Q: What stations do you listen to?

A: I usually put on radio stations that play popular stuff that's going on now. But the problem is . . . I think they do like a recording or something because you just hear the same five songs. I hate that, because a lot of times when I play on the computer I just play it all day, and I listen to the radio all day.

Q: What do you listen to?

A: Ah, I listen to rap. I like that a lot.

Q: How did you start listening to rap?

A: My brother listens to rap. And in music class we had a talent show and Tom, me, and Joe did a rap. We were D.J. Dizzy Tom and the Fat Prince, and I was the Fat Prince. I had to rap. My favorite line was (raps),

"Some people think I'm a genius and have a big brain, but . . . ." (laughs) You know, problem was we couldn't put any violence or anything in it.

Q: Cause it was for school? (Matthew nods) Is there a lot of violence in rap?

A: Yeah, because in most of them you listen to, you hear like (raps) "Twenty dead men on a dead men's chest/Shot them all and I'll shoot the rest." Or, um, killing people with a big shotgun. There's a lot of violence.

Q: Does that bother you?

A: Yeah. I don't like listening to violence.

Q: But you like listening to rap.

A: Yeah, rap's good. Some of it's not violence. You know, some groups do and some groups don't.

Q: What rap groups do you listen to?

A: Rap? Well, usually the major ones like Run D.M.C., Fat Boys . . . I like them . . . Tone Loc . . . I like him. You know, he does "Wild Thing." You know, mostly because I watch "Yo MTV Raps." Great show.

Q: You like that show?

A: Yeah, it's funny. See it on Saturdays and Sundays. Because that's when the good ones are on. You can always see the stupid one, the really stupid raps that people from down the street made. You know, they have no rhythm or anything.

Q: No rhythm . . . . So what do you like about rap? What's good about it?

A: I don't know. I just like to listen to it.

Q: The rhythm, the words . . .

A: I don't know. I just like it. The rest of the family pretty much hates it. Problem is when I'm listening to the radio I always think Ma's calling. Always can hear her. So I can't listen to it loud. Most people in my school are like, "Yo, Guns and Roses! They're really cool!"

Q: They're all into heavy metal at school?

A: Yeah. A lot of them are into heavy metal . . . Metallica and things like that.

Q: So, do you like heavy metal?

A: Not really, no. You know, I'll listen to it to be cool and everything, but I won't go out and buy the new Guns and Roses tape. Or Metallica. We had a lip-synching contest at school, and someone did a Metallica thing. I didn't understand a word of it . . . because the only one I've ever heard is "One." I didn't understand a word of it. The kid just sat there and went doo-do-doo-do-doo with a guitar and everything, and it's ten minutes long! They sang Metallica that was ten minutes long! . . . and this guy was still there (mimics guitar part) . . . . It was really long.

Q: How about other stuff in school? You have music there?

A: Yeah, we have a music class, but the teacher's a jerk. She's doing this whole thing . . . "From Bach to Rock." (sarcastically) Yeah! And she likes classical music too much. Don't say it's boring or too slow or too fast. You know, some people like it, so you have to listen to it. But my last music teacher, she did music exercises, she played rock and everything, but Mrs. Ames, all she does is crap like "Potbello Orchestra!"

Q: Potbello Orchestra?

A: Yeah, "Potbello Showdown." And we're all supposed to bring in one-liter bottles and everyone keeps forgetting. And she had us pan-tomime "Billy the Kid." It was like a three-minute production and she brought the whole sixth grade in to see it. And we had this showdown and everyone went . . . (shoots with fingers). They couldn't have a real gun. You just had to use your fingers and you had to do it in beat with the music. And everyone kept dying.

And we were doing this thing on "Card-playing Under the Stars," and they had two girl singers smoking pieces of paper and everything. And then we heard "Boom!" and we all ran out shooting our guns . . . aaaaah . . . and killed people. I killed five people because I was messed up. And I had to dive behind a rock because I couldn't die.

Q: Uh huh. How about trumpet?

A: Trumpet? Yeah, I like that. Because I like when we play good music. Like when we play "Melodies That Were Broadway," I don't like that because it's "Grand Old Flag" and things, but we also play "Tequila" and "La Bamba," so that's pretty good.

Q: What?

A: "Tequila," "La Bamba," and "Shakedown."

Q: So what do you do in band?

A: Well . . . on Tuesday mornings and Friday afternoons, for one period, we come in and sit down and play our music and the director says, "No, no, you're doing it wrong, flutes play it . . . . Okay flutes. No. No, clarinets . . . !" Like this year he yells at the clarinets much more than he did last year.

The worst thing is when he makes you play individual, because I never practice. I'm one of the first trumpets in third trumpet. You sit there and he'll say like "First trumpets play," and I'll play it like five times, you know, and he'll go, "You can't get the high note," and I'll get the high note, and then he'll move on to the second trumpets who play all air.

Q: So you don't practice. How come?

A: Well, I don't know. Trumpets are really heavy to take home sometimes. (laughs) Because I ride my bike a lot or I just kind of forget or I don't have enough time. But I try to practice.

Q: So do you like it? Are you going to continue?

A: Oh, yeah, I'll probably continue. But I don't want to play in a college marching band.

Q: (pause) Do you buy albums and tapes? What's the medium through which you listen to music? Do you listen to live music? Or . . .

A: I've never been to a concert or anything or a live band. I usually listen to the radio. I don't buy tapes that much. You know, if someone gives me a gift certificate to the record store, I'll go out. Or at Christmastime I got tapes because I was there. But I don't usually take time out to go to the music store.

Q: Let's get back to school. What do other people think about you rapping and stuff?

A: Well, I don't usually rap a lot. Sometimes I do. A lot of people hate rap, you know? Like Maggie, she wanted to make her friend's boyfriend really mad, so she kept asking me about rap things. And I just kept telling all the little rap things I'd heard in songs.

Q: What was she going to do with them?

A: She was going to make a big rap song. She was just going to say them all, keep rapping to him in his face.

Q: He doesn't like rap or something?

A: Yeah, he hates rap. There's a school-store rap, you know. Mrs. Porter . . . or Porker, whatever you want to say . . . runs the school store. "Yes! You can buy buttons! Pencils! Oh!" So there's an activity called "School Store," and they don't do anything. So they made like a rap for the new school t-shirts. But, you know, I don't think rap's as big as it used to be.

Q: How come?

A: I don't know. I think maybe it just kind of dies out. It's sort of like a fad. A lot of music . . . it's sort of with the times.

Q: So what's big now?

A: Oh, I don't know. I think heavy metal is kind of big. Everyone likes that.

Q: What about MTV, do you like that?

A: MTV? I don't know. I'm not really into music videos unless it's an exciting video. You know, like D.J. Jazzy Jeff. I like that video. Then there's The Fine Young Cannibals . . . . You know "She Drives Me Crazy"? The guy's got such a high voice. And I like "Remote Control."

Q: The game show?

A: Yeah. But I can't just sit down and watch "The Headbanger's Ball." But I did see the "Top 100 Videos," I watched about fifty of them.

Q: Do you have tunes in your head and stuff?

A: Oh, yeah! I always get tunes in my head. Especially when I'm on my paper route . . . because I talk to myself when I'm alone on my paper route. Or not really talk to myself, but think . . . and I really get into my thinking. So I start talking out loud or make hand signals, you know, or I start singing. Like I've been singing and people look at me. Once I was walking along and people go, "You want the collecting money?" And I go, "No . . . oh, what?" Because I was thinking.

Q: What do you sing?

A: I just sing anything. You know, if a song is in my head like "Stand" or something. (He sings the refrain.) You know, I'll sing or get a little thing in my head. Like once I had that GMC Truck thing . . . "It's not just a truck anymore" . . . in my head. And you know, I get a song in my head because I sing it, and I just can't stop singing it, and then you get another song in your head . . .

Q: Is there anything else?

A: (stammers) Well, I don't really like sing-alongs. You know, because everyone always messes it up. That's why I hate music in school . . . singing songs. Because I always mess up. I can't sing solo. Once we had this thing at school: "I Bought Some Grapefruit From Tampa." And it was like (sings like Sinatra) "I bought some grapefruit from Tampa." And I went . . . (sings it poorly and laughs).

Q: Did the teacher tell you to be quiet or something?

A: No. She makes you do solos. And I can't stand doing solos! I (mumbles) . . . I don't like it. I think the teacher's a jerk for forcing you to.

If I don't want to do music, I don't have to take it next year. It's not even an elective anymore. Because there's band and chorus. I can't be in chorus because . . . well, last year, there were 150 boys in chorus because it was during homeroom period. Then they moved it to an activity period and there were nine people left in the class. Because nobody wanted to take it as an activity, you know. (pause)

But I sing a lot. I just sing, you know. Sometimes, especially when you're practicing the trumpet, take the trumpet music and start playing it on the piano, and you just play the piano for a while, and then you just leave and you're done. You know, because when I play the piano I just fool around. It's fun.

Q: You've stopped piano lessons?

A: Yeah, I stopped lessons. I didn't like it. See, they always told me, "You don't have to go to the audition if you don't want to." But they never told me, "Matthew, don't go to the audition, because you're gonna go in and you're gonna hate it, because you're just gonna keep on playing the same music over and over again, every single day. You're never going to get anything new, you're never going to get to the synthesizer, you're just going to keep playing 'Scarborough Fair' every other week. They're going to tell you 'Hold your hands up!'" They never told you that. I said, "I'll do it," and I hated it because she only made me practice for the audition. So I quit. And I wanted to go to synthesizer, but she said, "No, you have to get better at piano." And I said, "You never get better." But I was told that once you can do it you can always get better. You just have to practice more. But I know my basics, I know what an arpeggio is, I know how to read music. . . .

Q: So you like fooling around on the piano there?

A: I always play with chords and stuff, you know? And play big long things. It's not just "doo-do-do-doo." You know, it usually has a rhythm or something. I always try to make it sound good. I remember we did this report on Leningrad in front of the class and Jim, who was in our group, goes, "That report wasn't great." And Dan goes, "How about the music?" Jim goes, "Aw, all our music stinks." And Dan goes (singing), "Lenin-grad, oh, Lenin-grad, please come back to our ci-ty." It was like the "Trinidad" song. You know? So we all followed Dan going "Lenin-grad, oh, Lenin-grad. . . ." And we all sung it and everything. We had a big song and got extra credit points for that.

Q: Sounds good!

A: But, Mr. Andrews, our teacher, he told us about how he used to live in Texas and all the girlfriends he went out with. He's girl crazy. He talks about, "I went out with this girl . . . whoo!" . . . all he talks about. He talks about country-western music, how it's in Texas, how you can't get away from country music because you always hear it, you know? And he said, "It's not bad, you know?" He doesn't say it once, but all the time. He talks about Willie and Waylon . . . that's Willie Nelson and Waylon Jennings, you know, and he said when country-western's on, it's like, "Yeah, I went down to the depot/to get some coffee/and my dog died/because he drank it too fast, yes. . . ."

Q: This is what your teacher said? Have you ever listened to country-western music?

A: Yeah.

Q: Do you like it?

A: Well, it's not that bad. You know, some country music you hate.

But I like Kenny Rogers. If it's not like real down country. Sort of a country-rock. I can't sit there and watch "Fandango."

Q: What's "Fandango?"

A: (rolling his eyes) The Nashville Network! Channel 39. They have game shows: "You Can Be a Star" . . . they interview all the country-western singers and if you can match their answers you win a free TV. Then they have "Fandango" where you have to answer music questions. And the best thing is "Face The Music," because I think they're showing repeats from the 1970s or at least have people who think they still live in the seventies. Because the people who are on the show are totally spaced geeks.

They play weird songs you have to be so old to know. They have the weirdest people on it. Total idiots. They don't have a normal person like you see on, um, "Classic Concentration" or "Jeopardy."

Q: (laughing) They have normal people?

A: They have cool music like when they ask a question.

Q: All right, if that's all you had to say . . .

A: Ah! My Dungeons and Dragons game! Let me see if it's here still. . . . It has this thing . . . it's called "Song of Goldmoon." It's from that *Dragonlance* book. Goldmoon has this song she sings, and it says, "Whoever is Goldmoon, have them read this line; if they are musically inclined, have them sing it." So we're playing, and I said, "Here, Dan, you're Goldmoon, you have to sing this." (laughs) That was fun.

"Rap is things you say fast . . . and rock and roll is things you say medium-sized with the beat."

Connie was interviewed by a male graduate student. She is about
thirteen years old, attends junior high school, and is black.

Q: Why don't we start with you telling me a little about yourself . . .
about the music you like.

A: Okay. I'm a new kid here. I come here to enjoy myself, to get away
and think through things I have to do. I like music like Ready for the
World, Michael Jackson, New Edition, and mostly rap.

Q: Tell me a little bit about rap. Why you like listening to it.

A: I like to get the lines so I can put together my own fashion show of
a rap. You know. Sort of a thing we like to do on weekends, like Saturdays or Fridays. Then you get together and you make a group. Then
you come on stage and you say your part. We've been just auditioning
for turns.

Q: Oh. So you're just imitating rap groups? Can you give me an
example?

A: (to a rap beat) "My name's Connie / and I'm here to say / I'll rock
your mind all night / on this spot."

Q: Okay. What else do you do with rap? Do you listen to it by yourself or . . .

A: With friends.

Q: What makes you decide when you're going to listen to rap versus
when you're going to listen to rock and roll?

A: Mostly it's like when me and my friends get together, that's when
we listen to rap. But when I'm by myself, that's when I want to listen to
rock and roll.

Q: Do you prefer rap or rock and roll?

A: Both. (laughs) I can't decide. They are both so . . . unique, down-to-earth, in the eighties, I mean, like really.

Q: But you find that rap music is a more social thing? Do you ever listen to rock and roll with your friends?

A: Yeah. Sometimes. It's like when I'm feeling down and out. Then I go with my friends and listen to rock and roll . . . and rap.

Q: Do you listen to rock and roll with the same friends you listen to rap with?

A: No. It's just like either friend . . . I have so many of them. You know, it's hard to tell which ones I'm going to listen to rap or rock and roll with. It's like a two-part story. Most of the friends I hang out with prefer rap to rock and roll.

Q: They all listen to the same kind of rap?

A: No. Not really. Some of them listen to different ones. like ladies' rap . . . like JJ Fads. And Miss Prince, Miss Jolowesa, or whatever her name is.

Q: What's the difference between ladies' rap and the other kinds of rap?

A: Well, ladies' rap is different. See, ladies go around here and they punk off the boys. They just put them down completely, like out of it. And the men's rap, they just punk off the girls, they put them down like just out of it.

Q: Can you give me an example of ladies' rap?

A: Like (sung to a rap beat), "Let me tell you baby doll / I'm here to stay. / I'll rock your mind all night long. / You can't do nothing / 'Cause you're not worth it. / So why don't you go / Turn around / and stuff it."

Q: So you prefer ladies' rap?

A: Definitely. I'm a lady. (laughs) And . . . sometimes I prefer men's rap, because I like to listen to the things they call their women!

Q: Tell me about it.

A: Well, they be . . . they call them stuck up, not worth it. All they want to do is take the men's money. (laughs) And then they lay around like they ain't got nothing to do.

Q: Would you consider that accurate?

A: Yes. (laughs) Me, myself . . . I wouldn't do that.

Q: What kind of music does your family listen to?

A: Oldtime music. Like Elvis Presley. Old King Cole [Nat King Cole]. The Jackson Five. Destiny.

Q: Do you enjoy that kind of music? Do you listen to it with them?

A: Sometimes. I enjoy their music. I do.

Q: You sometimes put it on yourself?

A: Yeah. I have to steal my mom's tape to do it, but I still do it.

Q: Do you listen to it with your friends sometimes?

A: Noooo! I don't think they'll like it much.

Q: Does your family ever listen to rap music with you?

A: Yeah. They like rap too. They're into it.

Q: Is listening with your family different than listening to it with your club group, your friends, that you listen to it with?

A: Yes, very different. With my family, I just explain some of the things that be going on with this tape. But with my friends, I explain EVERY detail.

Q: What kind of things wouldn't you explain to your family?

A: Like how hard it is, these days, to catch boyfriends. And how hard it is to put them down, like they be doing.

Q: Is listening to music different when listening with your brother than it is when listening with your sister?

A: YES! It's like a brick wall. (laughs) I'm serious. Because when rap music is on around my brother, he goes nuts. I mean, he knows every verse of it. He has to sing it to you.

Q: And how do your sisters react?

A: Well, they just sit there and bob their heads and enjoy it.

Q: What's it like, listening to rap music with your parents?

A: Well, they don't like it so much so they ignore it or else turn up the TV loud.

Q: Is there anything else you want to tell me about music and how it affects your life?

A: Music has, well . . . I have my advantages to music. I'm addicted to music. I'm a music freak myself. I mean, when music's on, I have to listen to it.

"Sometimes I think about life, and all the problems I have. Sometimes I just dwell on the lyrics and just listen to the music."

Edwardo is fifteen years old and is enrolled in an auto
mechanics program at a vocational high school.

Q: What kind of music do you like to listen to?

A: Basically, I listen to anything. I prefer rap and regular . . . R and
B and rock.

Q: What groups do you listen to when you get a choice?

A: When I'm by myself, I listen to rap like Eric B, MC Hammer, and
KRS 1. People like that. When I'm with my friends, I listen to Ozzie,
and Pink Floyd, Iron Maiden, Metallica. You know, groups like that.

Q: Why do you listen to different stuff when you're by yourself?
Different than when you're with your friends?

A: Usually when I'm over at their house they have control of the
radio, and they don't like to listen to rap that much.

Q: What kind of things do you do when you are listening to music
by yourself?

A: I lip-synch it in the mirror. I pretend I'm doing a movie. Kind of
embarrassing, but I do that. And I listen to it while I'm in the shower.
And . . . that's about all.

Q: Would you like to be a professional musician?

A: Kind of. Yeah.

Q: If you pictured yourself as a musician, how would you picture
yourself? What kind of music would you play?

A: I'd probably rap. If I didn't, I'd like to play the saxophone.

Q: When you're walking along, do you ever have a song going
through your head? Do you have specific songs that you listen to and, if
not, do you ever make up songs?

A: Yes. I rap a lot to myself. I make up rhymes and have one of my friends give it a beat. Sometimes we put it on tape. Sometimes we don't.

Q: Could you give me an example of some of the stuff you have put together on your own?

A: I made up one that goes something like, "Now I have many mikes / stepped on many floors. / Shattered all the windows / knocked down all the doors." That's just a little part of it. This is hard for me. I'm nervous.

Q: So what kind of things do you try to put together in your songs? What kinds of things do you try to talk about in your songs?

A: I make up different stories. Like people running around. Sometimes I talk about drugs and drinking. Most of the time I just brag about myself.

Q: Do you have any brothers and sisters who listen to the same sort of stuff?

A: Yes. My older brother . . . he's the one who got me into rap. We're originally from the Bronx, in New York, and he doesn't listen to anything else. My cousin, he listens to heavy metal but he's kind of switched to late-seventies, early-seventies rock. He listens to Pink Floyd and all them, so I listen with him sometimes. I listen with my friends. That's about all.

Q: How long have you been listening to rap?

A: For about seven or eight years.

Q: What kind of stuff were you listening to before that?

A: Actually, I don't remember. Oh yeah. We used to live in California and I was listening to oldies . . . like the Four Tops and all them. In California . . . the Mexicans down there, they only listen to the oldies and stuff like that.

Q: Why would you say you changed to rap?

A: When I came down here, everything changed. People were listening to different kinds of music and I was, you know, behind times. So I just had to switch to catch up.

Q: So you would say that your friends really influence you and the kind of music you listen to by yourself?

A: Yeah. I would say that.

Q: When you're listening to music by yourself, what kinds of things go through your mind? Are you concentrating on the words or what?

A: Sometimes I think about life, and all the problems I have. Sometimes I just dwell on the lyrics and just listen to the music.

Q: Do you ever use music as a way to change your mood? If you're really depressed, is there a record you put on?

A: No. Usually when I listen to music and it changes me is when I'm bored and I don't have anything to do or I just get that certain urge to listen to music.

"I still have my violin from when I was five. I used to sleep with it at night."

May is a sixteen-year-old Asian American high school student
who also attends Juilliard. She was interviewed by a male college
student, a brother of one of her friends at her high school.

Q: How would you identify yourself?

A: Well, first, I would say I'm a girl, and then I guess I would describe myself as the kind of person who's not too social, and I guess because of that, I lean towards music.

Q: What is music about for you?

A: Well, music to me is the only medium where I can sort of . . . like with the violin, okay, when I play the violin, it's the only thing I can put all my emotions into, and I don't have to express myself. I just do it. It's the only thing where I give so many emotions that no one can understand what I'm doing. I relinquish so much. It's a whole different . . . it's like a different language. Does that make sense?

Q: Yeah. When you said it's the only time you express your emotions, when you listen to music, is it a similar thing?

A: Yeah. I like to listen to music alone and with people. It varies. If I have a choice I like to listen to Italian opera, Mozart, *The Marriage of Figaro*. This is with people who are into classical music. But I also like to listen to new wave music. I like new wave music a lot. Most of the time when I listen to Italian opera, it's usually in the car and I'm driving and then my friends and I don't talk to each other. I'm just driving in New York.

Q: And it's the same when you're alone?

A: Yeah, but it's not always Italian opera. Mostly it is. That's what was on sale. I have lots of tapes like Berlioz and Jane Siberry . . . but usually it's classical. Actually I have a tape of a collection of stuff like all sorts of pieces. It's weird. Stuff like classical music, and jazz, and it's got a few Talking Heads songs all mixed together.

Q: What about at home? Do you listen to music at home?

A: Yeah. I listen to gospel music.

Q: Just gospel?

A: Sometimes . . . well, I guess I shouldn't have said that I listen to gospel music all the time. It varies.

Q: Does gospel music have the same effect as classical music?

A: In a way. It gets me excited. Not only that, I think it gets my mind off of classical music, whereas new wave, it's more like background music.

Q: How often do you play and how often do you listen to music?

A: I usually practice between seven and eight hours a day. I really don't listen to music a lot. And when I'm not practicing I usually watch TV. I like the show, "Head of the Class." That's on Wednesdays.

Q: If you practice seven or eight hours a day and you go to school about six hours a day, what else do you do?

A: Sleep.

Q: How often do you go to New York?

A: I go to New York every Friday night, and I come back Sunday night. Friday nights, I come into Laguardia Airport and go to my friend's house and go to sleep, and then on Saturdays I have classes. I have orchestra from 8 : 30 to 11 : 30 . . . (unintelligible) until one, a lesson from 1 : 30 until . . . (unintelligible), 4 : 00 to 5 : 00 I have chamber music, and then at 5 : 00 I have theory. Saturday nights I go out to a concert.

Q: How long have you been practicing seven or eight hours?

A: It wasn't until my sophomore year that I became this involved. I went to a music festival and I was really inspired by the musicians. This was the summer after freshman year, and then I came back to high school and I thought, "Well, I don't know." I just wanted to practice more and then some day . . . I just wanted to practice more to get into Juilliard [School of Music]. And then I got in and I started going to New York.

Q: When you practice seven or eight hours, how often do you take breaks?

A: Okay. I usually wake up at 5 : 30 or 6 : 00 and I play before school. It helps get my fingers warmed up. And then I have orchestra for forty-five minutes. Then I go to school and come home and watch "General Hospital." I watch that and I watch "Attitudes." About 4 : 30 I go upstairs and I practice until 7 : 30 and then I eat dinner. Then I go back and practice until 12 : 30 or 1 : 00. Sometimes I study, but usually not.

Q: So how old are you?

A: Sixteen. Actually before my freshman year I knew it. I wanted to play violin, and I also wanted to be an artist, or go into acting.

Q: When did you start violin?

A: I started when I was five, but I have to tell you the story of how I started. See my smile here? I have this dimple? It's not a real dimple. It's a fake dimple. When I was five, my mom came home with a Pepperidge Farm chocolate cake, and I was so excited, I went running into the corner of a table. I used to do wild things like jumping out of my crib when I was one year old. My mom said, "Well, she's gotta calm down. By the age of ten she'll be all over." She said, "Well, you better start the violin" . . . to calm me down.

Q: Did it work?

A: Yeah, I think it did, but I think that's one of the reasons why all my teachers used to call me the human volcano on the violin. I get really into it I guess. I get really emotional about it. I took the Suzuki method, and what that is is you have a series of tapes that you constantly listen to so you don't learn how to read notes. You memorize the pieces so that you have it in your head. You just play it on your violin, and that's how I got into it.

Q: Before then, do you have any memories of music? Did you listen to music?

A: Yeah, actually I remember my father said that . . . he's a doctor . . . and he always said, "I'm going to take conducting lessons. I'm gonna be a conductor." I said, "No, don't do that. Stick to being a doctor." 'Cause he'd always conduct in the car. He really liked classical music and when he heard . . . he'd always listen to orchestra music and he'd constantly ask me, "May, wouldn't you like to play the flute or piccolo?" And I'd say, "No, I want to play the violin," and he'd say, "Oh, okay." And so one day my parents said . . . after this happened . . . "Well, May, we're gonna have to start you on the violin and we couldn't afford a piano." They thought about piano first because they thought in their minds it was a basic instrument of all instruments.

Q: But you wanted to play violin before? Why?

A: Well, I just remember this girl, my parents' friends' daughter, played the violin, and we were always competing against each other.

Q: You mentioned your father likes classical music. Does your mother like classical music?

A: Yes, she does. She does very much. Everyone always asks me if . . . "Is your mother a musician? Is your father a musician?" Because a lot of people at Juilliard, all their mothers are violinists or pianists. I said,

"No." My mom used to play piano, but she had to quit because they moved or something.

Q: Did your parents play a lot of music around the house?

A: Yes, they did. They were into it.

Q: I know they got you started. Were they the first ones to push you or were you self-motivated?

A: I was really self-motivated. I still have my violin from when I was five. And I used to sleep with it at night.

Q: Did you have a teddy bear or doll or just the violin?

A: I had a pet kangaroo, a stuffed kangaroo. I slept with both.

Q: How have your listening habits changed as you grew older?

A: In middle school, I really liked the Rolling Stones and the Who. I really liked them, but then all of a sudden. . . . I'm actually glad I learned that music because I think that now . . . like one day I got up in the "commons," the cafeteria, and started playing, this was right before my competition at Carnegie Hall, and I didn't want to feel pressured when I got on stage and saw thousands of people. I had to get my anxiety out in front of the school, and afterward someone said, "Well, can you play Grateful Dead rock from America," and I said, "Yeah," and I started playing it.

Q: Was there a time you started getting into new wave?

A: Yeah, I started getting into new wave in eighth grade. I remember one of my friends' sister went to the University of Toronto and she knew all these groups like Japan and David Sylvian and things like that.

Q: You mentioned playing in school. How do your peers react to your playing?

A: I was really shocked because I thought they would think it's really stupid because in middle school and elementary school it was looked at as kind of antisocial, it was weird, nerdy. I guess that's why sometimes I think people won't like it too much. Actually I played in front of Astor Place train station in New York just to see what it's like and I made sixty-nine bucks in one hour. It was fun.

Q: Is there a difference between that and on a stage when people are there to see you?

A: Yes, definitely. It's also a different character. With classical music you have to be more concerned with what the composer was like. If you're playing Mozart, for instance. At the time they wore big costumes and all his pieces are dances and so when you play them you have to almost put yourself in the time's frame of mind. That's why I like acting . . . when I play the violin, it's almost like I have to act. I have to change my playing for that character.

Q: When you play in Astor Place, you don't take on a character, you're just yourself, or is it a different character?

A: I guess when I just play like that . . . sometimes when I play pieces that are by a composer, I sort of put on some character, but street performances are just laid-back. It was fun. It was kind of a joke. It was a dare from my friend and I didn't want to, but I did it.

Q: Would you do it again?

A: Yeah, I'd do it again actually. I took myself out to dinner. I bought a sandwich for about a dollar. Well, actually what happened with the money is my mom called in that hour because I was staying with a friend and we weren't home. When I got back, I called her that night and she said, "Well, where were you?" and I told her and she said, "Don't ever do that again. We're supporting you to go to New York, not to play in the streets, to go to Juilliard." And she took all the money and gave it to Cerebral Palsy.

Q: Are there any times when you experience music in a particularly powerful way?

A: There are some kinds of music that get me all excited or all sad. It usually depends on what it is. If it's something which reminds me of something . . . I guess any kind of music that would be true.

Q: Gospel music, you mentioned, gets you excited.

A: Yeah, I listen to that before I play competitions; whenever I play I like to glorify the Lord with my music. I like to think of it as a religious sort of thing.

Q: Do you hear music in your head when it's not actually there?

A: Always.

Q: Is it your own?

A: Usually someone else's.

Q: Is it voluntary or does it suddenly come up?

A: It always comes up.

Q: Is there music in your head right now?

A: Yeah.

Q: What's in your head?

A: Actually it's the "Flintstones" because this morning we were playing this piece by Leonard Bernstein and it's sort of like the "Flintstones" so I had the TV hits in my head all day.

Q: Do you have any other TV hits in your mind?

A: Yeah, I had "My Three Sons."

Q: Do you sing?

A: Before I look at a piece I have to sing it. It's kind of required.

Q: Are there any other times?

A: I think I do, but I don't notice it.

Q: You're not sure if it's out loud or not?

A: Yeah, actually I do when I listen to gospel music.

Q: Do you dance?

A: Yeah. I dance at parties. Sometimes when I'm feeling depressed, I turn on the radio and I stand in front of my mirror and I shake around. I just do that to make myself look foolish and I start laughing.

Q: Do you think the media manipulates people's tastes?

A: Definitely. Like MTV and also . . . well, right now I find it hard to . . . some violinists who are up there . . . right now I'm looking for a manager, which is kind of hard. If you want to solo, you have to find a manager before you are twenty. They like to have little people on stage all the time. It's like their product. So that's what I'm trying to do and a lot of people who are so-called concertizing, they're not so good. Some of them maybe won a big competition and then they get a big name, and they get advertising in the papers so the public believes they're good when they're really not—the people who really don't know too much about the music.

Q: Do you think the media influences your own taste in music?

A: Not really. Usually when I go to hear someone play, I know what to expect from that particular composer. I have a taste for it.

Q: Do you remember any time when some music you never liked before suddenly touched you or made sense?

A: Yeah, I used to hate Mozart because it was so hard to play. It's not meant to be played so fast. I guess this century is the only century where musicians don't play the music of the composers who are living in this era, maybe with the exception of Bernstein. We play from the past because we also have tape machines and we can listen to what Mozart and Paganini sound like, whereas in Brahms's time they couldn't listen to what Bach and Mozart sounded like so . . . I was really turned off by Mozart. He was so easy, but so hard to bring across. Where Paganini is all over the place, Mozart is so simple. The more simple it is the more hard it is to play. Especially at Julliard, everyone wants to show off their technique on the Paganini concertos which, to me, it's not music, it's kind of like a circus act. Now I really like Mozart a lot, to answer your question. I didn't like Mozart before, but now I do.

Q: When did it change?

A: It was hard for me because when I was at the conservatory my teacher said, "You're too much of a human volcano. Paganini, it sounds great with you. Now we have to work on your Mozart. We're going to start with the Mozart concerto number seven." I just hated it, but now

I practiced it and I like it. I listen to Italian operas to get the feel of Mozart.

Q: What do you use music for?

A: I use it first to express myself. And also I confide in it, because it's generally very hard and lonely going into music because—especially at this school—because a lot of people are ignorant of what I do. . . .

Q: Like a companion?

A: Yeah.

Q: Any other ways?

A: When I play it, it always makes me feel better. After I have my last class, I just want to go home and listen to music and play.

ANITA

"*I listen to other music and then I go see the Dead.*"

Anita is a high school senior who was interviewed by a
friend who has known her for a few years. Anita lives with her
father and brother. The interview took place at her home.

Q: Tell me a little bit about what music in general means to you. What are your likes, your dislikes? When do you listen to it? Do you have any special music that you like . . . ?

A: I like a lot of music. Quality music. I don't even mind listening to rap. I mean, it's pretty poetic, it's a whole new way of saying . . . of communicating, just like jazz was. I don't . . . well, let me see . . . I guess I like rock and roll basically because . . . I like the music by people who seem to have a grip on life, and they're not just selling themselves out or being superficial . . .

Q: Is that what you mean by "quality"?

A: Yeah, yeah. So I like The Dead, Joni Mitchell, and I also like U2 and REM . . . .

Q: . . . I'd like to talk to you a little more about the Dead. Would you call them your favorite band?

A: Yeah, because they're like the only band I listen to really. I mean Joni's not a band, she's a singer.

Q: Do you consider them to be a part of your music or are they separate? In other words, do you listen to music and then listen to the Dead?

A: Well actually, I listen to other music and then I go *see* the Dead, I really don't listen to them that much at all.

Q: You don't have many recordings?

A: Oh, I have many, but I haven't listened to them lately. I can kind of get sick of them. A lot of them aren't very good. But I still can put on a very good version of whatever and remember . . .

Q: So you like the concert idea a lot better than the recording?

A: Yeah.

Q: How many concerts have you been to?

A: (without hesitation) Seventeen.

Q: Seventeen? And you say that you don't do much listening at home?

A: Well, I do before I go to a concert or when I come back. Or if someone gives me a new tape. There are a few songs that I don't know, that I haven't got on tape, but once I do I'll listen to them a lot. Because they have that mystery about them. (chuckles)

Q: What about your friends? Do they listen to the Dead?

A: (pauses, unsure) Well, it's strange because I have my friends at home . . . and I have my friends on tour who I'm really close to even though I've spent probably only two weeks collectively with them, but I still have strong bonds with them. I guess that half of my friends at home don't listen to the Dead and half do.

I really like it when they do because it becomes such an integral part of my life. It is such a big part of my life that it's hard . . . when half of my friends want to do something that relates to the Dead, and the other half wants to do something because they don't like to do things that relate to the Dead, it gets kind of tense. Like tonight, the Wild Knights [a Grateful Dead cover band] are playing, and Janie and Pam and I were standing right over there and one said, "You want to go see them?" and I said, "Sure." And the other said, "You want to go to dinner?" and I said "Sure." Pam doesn't like the Dead and Janie does, so Pam didn't want to go to the Wild Knights and Janie didn't want to go to dinner. (laughs) They were kind of conflicting at the same time, so right now I don't know what's going to happen.

Q: (chuckles) Would you like to share a favorite story about a concert? Or a story about your favorite concert?

A: Let's see . . . Oh! Janie and I, last fall . . . I made up a story that I told my dad . . . that I was going to run cross-country in the morning and I'd be gone. . . . I snuck out of the house at about six in the morning with a long dress on and my guitar and I went to the park and Janie was waiting there in her car and we drove down to Maryland. It was Saturday morning when we left and we got there at around five in the afternoon. That concert was the first time we discovered . . . the life that we live now in regards to the Dead. We always stayed in the arena and watched the show, and I couldn't take my eyes off them all the time. But for the second set we went out in the hallways, and there are just so many people out dancing in the halls. That was when we kind of found these things out, what we were missing. Then we spent the night in the parking lot, we slept in the car, actually I didn't sleep because I was shrooming after the show, so I stayed up all night.

Q: . . . Do you consider yourself to be a "Deadhead" or not? Or do you dislike that kind of labeling?

A: I dislike the labeling, but if somebody were to describe me to their friends, that would be appropriate. You know, I wrote an article last year for the newspaper about the strange connotations to the word "Deadhead." I get angry when people . . . it's kind of snobby of me . . . when people who don't really deserve the title call themselves Dead-heads. Because the real Deadheads are the "tourheads" who go to every show. And their lives revolve around it. But . . . it depends on who calls me a Deadhead really.

Q: When I went to their last show in Rochester—that was the only show I've seen—I was kind of surprised because I had heard all of this "community-unity" talk being preached to me about the Grateful Dead. When I got there, it didn't seem like that to me at all. It seemed to be just another concert. Sure there were all the hippies and all there, but it did feel like just another concert for some reason. What is your comment on that?

A: Okay, the reason it sounds like just another concert is because of all of the people there because they know the name and they want the drugs and the beer. So they really detract from it.

And the tourheads do totally preach that community thing but they're very restrictive about who they preach it to because they know that there are a lot of people out there who are idiots. And also, they're very careful about police because they do massive marketing. . . . So you have to kind of (hesitation) get into the inner circle, and then you can feel the community. It takes a while. I finally got into it when I met Dick because he was in . . . and he brought me into it, and his friends were some of the highest people there. Not on drugs, I mean high spiritually. They have these bongo players there . . . did you see them? They just play and play and they get such . . . emotion going. People just dance around them and, during intermission . . . nobody can stop, you know, when the feeling starts . . .

Q: So besides just seeing the band, an attraction of the Dead concerts for a Deadhead would be to be with friends and be with all the people hanging around. Do you think that's as important as seeing the Dead?

A: Yeah. I mean I've *seen* the Dead. I've seen them drive by in cars. Peter actually saw Phil in an elevator and he talked to him. The Dead . . . they're slowing down. I believe that they should stop playing. They're so old and tired, and it's hard on them. But I also don't want them to stop because it's my outlet to them and to my friends. But you can tell, we can all tell . . . like Jerry's voice is not what it used to be and he'll not hit all the notes or he'll cut them short. So it's very sad. But still, sometimes they'll be great and they'll really have something going.

Q: What do you do after the concert is over?

A: I just stay . . . usually you're really tired after dancing, or, if you're on drugs, you're not . . . (laughs) so you just stay up all night or you worry about how you get to another show.

Q: So is everyone at a Dead concert alike or does everyone have their own kind of philosophy, their own outlooks?

A: It's very diverse. There's the people that are against drugs, that are still there. There's people that eat meat without even thinking . . . there's people that go to Burger King without a care in the world . . . people who will throw their beer bottles on the ground, but then there's the people that get upset if you throw a nonfiltered cigarette on the ground. There's people that preach human rights for everyone—they see no justice and they won't take anyone else's advice, they just try and get what they want—but then there's the people that are *so* open. Like Janie is the most carefree person. She is—she never has a worry in the world when she's high. And because of that, I take on a lot of the worry. (laughs) Like if we're together, I'll get stuck with finding a ride and, if I don't do it, it's not going to get done.

Q: Okay, you said before that you dislike the labeling of "Deadhead" . . . but if I could use that expression for a moment, does being a "Deadhead" allow you to . . . see things or do things that other people can't? What's the advantage?

A: (after a pause) It's definitely the seeing and the doing. I've been all over the northeast, seeing the Dead. I have connections all over the country. So even if now I'm not able to . . . well, I could just go out to California with friends, and they would show me around . . .

Q: All right. You took the practical side of the doing and seeing. How about "seeing"? Now that you know about what's going on with the whole scene, the "Grateful Dead Experience," if you want to call it that, now that you're on to that, do you think that you're able to catch something that maybe the average person wouldn't?

A: Yeah, yeah. It made *me* aware of evils in life, because the society we have tries so hard to keep them out . . . . From all the experiences I've had, I've got a better definition of what I want to do with my life and where I want to be. Preferably somewhere where other people have the same philosophy as I do, to an extent. I mean, you have diversity at the Dead shows, but it's not a complete high, like . . . insanity. Usually. I mean, people, my friends, aren't trying to be diverse, they just turned out that way, and they're individuals. There's no real effort, it just comes out. Which is better than . . . people trying to make an effort to be different.

YOUNG ADULTS

BETH

"It's the first remedy for trying to get out of my boredom . . . whether it makes me tap my toes or sing along, it takes me away from whatever I want to be taken away from. . . ."

This is a self-reporting statement from the 1984 Music in Daily Life class that, at this stage, was still focused on mediated music. Students were asked to keep logs of music in their lives during a twenty-four-hour period as a starting point for writing about music in their lives. Beth is a white student living in the dorms.

From sunup to sundown music is always somewhere in the background. It can be annoying when trying to study, sometimes you can't even hear yourself think. Writing down every time I heard a song wasn't hard to do, except when I subconsciously blocked it out, which was hard not to do. Especially at the one point in which three different musics were playing, and I was trying to listen to them all to write down what I was hearing. Nobody wanted to listen to anyone else's music so they turned up the volume to the point I thought I was gonna die. Yes, it was a typical day. Whenever I'm not studying, I'll always have the music on. When it's not on and the TV's not on something feels empty. It's the first remedy for trying to get out of my boredom. It gets my mind off of the problems of the day kind of like an escape. Whether it makes me tap my toes or sing along, it takes me away from whatever I want to be taken away from. Depending on what there is to be taken away from also influences my choice in what I put on the stereo. When I'm happy, I generally put on happy music, something upbeat: Rickie Lee or somebody to "join me in my good mood." When I'm down, like when I have a lot of work or something, I tend to put on something less invigorating (Joni Mitchell—old stuff) or something of the sort to join me in my mood. It's like having someone with you at all times good and bad who you don't have to talk to about *why* you feel a certain way. It seems the musicians always know what's on your mind like if you miss a close friend. They always pop a song or two on the album you put on about how you feel like they know you or something. Like your best friend, somehow spelling out the depression or good happy mood makes me feel like I have control over my mood, because I didn't fully understand why I felt like I did or do but now that Joni spelled it out for me I know exactly why I'm so depressed. For example, on her *Blue* album she sings a song called "My Old Man" in which when he (her old man) leaves her for some unknown reason, she sings of her loneliness—for instance "The bed's too big, the frying pan's too wide." When I haven't seen my boyfriend for a while I get to feeling my frying pan's too wide also. We can now share that without having to tell somebody else of my misery to feel better. You know the old expression "If you talk about it you'll feel better." I don't only—oh God forbid—I don't only listen to music to get out of depression. For example Rickie Lee Jones does a song on her *Pirates* album where the beat is really funky. I can't very well explain it but it makes your feet just start bopping all over the room, it's really fast moving. It's about her and all her buddies (mostly, if not all, guys) going out on the town. The best line is: "Dude—you got a map to the next joint?" I can really relate to that as if I was right there going to all the joints with her. Actually I probably only know about half the words to the song (which has been my favorite for the past three and a half years). The way she sings makes it impossible to figure the words out, but she and her friends seem to be having the greatest time and you can't help but have a great time with them. I never really loved music that was well liked by many other people. If anyone is going to play out my music, it's going to be me. I can't believe how many people are so into the Grateful Dead to the point where that's all they listen to. You never have to ask them what they want to hear—it's always the same. I have trouble with that—their lives must be so monotonous. My music goes with me. I'm not the moodiest person in the world but I could never listen to Rickie Lee Jones only and all the time. It's like having only one friend to "play with." I love my best friend but I don't think I could ever just have her as my only friend. I'd get so bored! I love to go to concerts to see live music. There is nothing like it. I don't know if I feel this way because I'm a musician, or because it's a time when I can "be" with my "friends" who've kept me happy for so many hours—or some of each. This past summer [July 1984] I saw Steve Forbert at "My Father's Place," Roslyn, L.I. What a hot show! I had bought his *Jackrabbit Slim* album years ago, never really got into it because the only time I could listen to it was at a friend's who had a turntable, and I really just didn't love him at that point. Around '78 I went to his concert with my pal Simon who loves Forbert and asked me to go with him. Boy was I surprised when I saw how few people were there. The place wasn't even half filled with people. We got first row seats which were great. When Steve came out, the crowd went wild. Everyone in the place loved Steve to death! There were people dancing on the tables, including me and Simon, and I think everyone in that place had a great time—including Steve. We all got to meet him afterwards downstairs from where it happened, and it turns out he was really impressed with the bunch that showed up. It just goes to show ya that it's quality not quantity that counts. The people in the audience definitely make the concert. Come to think of it, they *are* the experience. An audience that doesn't dance makes the show so much less. Whenever I go to a show, up front is the best and I will do my damnedest to get up there with all the folks who want to get the best experience. When I saw the Fixx it was a wide variety of people all condensed at the not-so-large stage and field. *Way up* front, everyone danced and loved it, while the people in the back barely tapped a foot and didn't move at all. I wandered back and forth from front to back as my friends were standing in the back. Those are just two of the most recent concerts I've been to. The one before that was one of another sort. I saw a classical orchestra and I still don't even know their names. I don't really even care to. It didn't impress me that much. Sure the unison was incredible, but next time I'll stay home. The strangest thing about my collection is that nobody else I know has half of the same albums, except my sister who lives in California. It's kind of eerie in the fact we rarely turn each other on to things, we just find many of the same musicians at around the same time. We'll be on the phone and she'll say, "I've been into this new person Joan Armatrading," and I will be also, it's strange. She did, however, turn me onto the Roches. Three sisters who are from New Jersey and now live in N.Y.C. who formed a trio. They have very beautiful voices; one a very low, one a very high, and one kind of in between. Their best (most talented) song they do (and also the most and only serious one) is "Hallelujah." They don't use any instrumental accompaniment just their three voices. It's beautiful. They really are very silly most of the time. They sing songs like, "Oh Mr. Sellack, can I have my job back, I've run out of money again . . ." and "Even though my baggage and I are taking up a two-person seat, I'm not trying to be funny but the guy who sits down next to me is even bigger than that; we are overflowing out of the seat!" Not too many people I know are into the Roches, you have to hear them with an open mind. I would say most of the music I listen to (that has words), I listen to because of the words. Tom Waits is great at picking the right words for the right times. His burlappy kind of voice makes you unsure of his race—is he black or white? He's white really. He's perfect for listening to after coming home from a club at around 4:00 in the morning. One of his songs, "Night Hawks at the Diner," is Tom Waits at his best. It's about the people you see in a diner at around 4:30 A.M. and why they're there.

There really isn't any music that I can't stand. I do have my priorities obviously, but there is rarely a time in which somebody will put something on and I absolutely can't handle the music. Led Zeppelin doesn't thrill me to death, but I can tolerate them on the grounds that when I was thirteen years old, I too listened to them, because that was the thing to listen to! So if someone puts it on, it brings back a lot of memories—the same goes for the Doors and Jethro Tull. This Michael Jackson business is overwhelming. I remember childhood days, having every one of their albums (the Jackson Five). Every Saturday morning we'd be watching their cartoons on TV. At around nine or ten years old we realized they weren't the cool thing to be listening to, so we stopped! When Michael Jackson came out with the *Off the Wall* album I didn't even know it! When he came out with *Thriller* (before much of the publicity began) I found myself loving the songs "Beat It" and "PYT" as well as most of the others. I had no intention of buying the album though. Last summer at the New Jersey shore I won an album on one of the wheels; I didn't know what to get, so I picked *Thriller* and not once played it (well maybe once but that's it). I think I stopped liking this album because of all its publicity. I don't know of a person in America who wouldn't agree that the *Thriller* album is *played out*. I never before have really gotten into such a superstar. For some reason that turns me off (when everyone likes the same thing). Maybe I feel this way because I use music partly as part of my identity. When everyone does something all alike, it's not part of their identity anymore. It's like owning a pair of blue jeans except worse because there is only one of him (and it's not like people have specific albums, that others haven't heard of—everyone has the same one or two). At least there are varieties in blue jeans. I love Michael Jackson's dancing and "look" but I think the media has gone too far this time folks. It doesn't make me feel good to see Michael Jackson on my can of Pepsi or on my television interrupting my movie. If it was Rickie Lee Jones—maybe. I doubt it though. Even if my own mother was omnipresent like Michael Jackson is, it wouldn't make me feel good, just bored.

Disco is something that I will try to explain my feelings for. That beat. It never brings me down. If I'm already up, it brings me more up.

Makes me feel good about myself. Many of the words in disco tunes are very sexy. "I'm So Excited" by the Pointer Sisters is a typical example. Hearing songs like this, makes me excited about doing whatever it is I'm going to do—dancing mainly.

In general most of the words to many disco songs don't make too much sense. It's those songs that I just bop around to, like last summer's hit on WKTV at home "A,E,I,O,U and sometimes Y," otherwise known as "The Vowel Song," just made me want to dance up a storm but there wasn't really any ulterior motive. Dancing makes me feel really good. I know I have a good time dancing, so let's say I went out tonight and danced to a great song, if I heard it tomorrow it would be even better—get my drift? When Denise Williams came out with the song "Silly of Me"—three years ago it made me feel really sad. It was the first disco (soul) song that made me really feel. Besides Diana Ross. Diana Ross has always been a part of my life because Dad has been playing her music ever since I can remember, but this was different—I discovered her by myself. What a sad song. That was my first connection with disco where I felt I could relate.

I noticed that I am mostly into female vocalists, maybe because I kind of feel a camaraderie with them. If somebody like James Taylor sang about a love affair that's ended I don't feel as close or understanding as I would for, say, Joni Mitchell. Sure I can relate to guys too in music like Steve Forbert's song about going home from someplace: he tries to find his friends and goes out and when he wakes up he tries to figure out what went down the night before while everyone at his house is at church. But men (I don't think) sing about less serious and/or personal experiences.

My dad turned me onto classical music unintentionally. We play pool in our basement every night after dinner. When he has had a bad day at work or if something is bothering him you can always expect classical on the radio instead of easy listening music. I used to hate it because I would love to talk to him but we don't if classical is on—that's just how it is. I started to open my eyes to it and took a particular interest in Baroque, especially Bach. My dad saw my interest and turned me on to some really good guitarists. I think I like this type of music in particular because of the beat that baroque music has. It's a kind of 1–2–3–4 kind of beat, kind of like rock'n'roll. I like to play it loud, so I can block everything else out.

"... if I were to cuss someone out right after church, what does my singing mean?"

Mabel is a nineteen-year-old African American woman. She is the daughter
of a preacher and was interviewed by a female high school friend.

Q: Okay . . . what is music for you?

A: Um, music to me . . . I love it . . . because there is a song for
everything. You know what I mean, all situations, all occasions. A song
can describe a person, a season, your innermost feelings . . . you can let
them out in a song. Some shy people . . . they're not able to tell you, in
words, how they feel. There are songwriters who can just put it down
in words. You know what I'm saying?

Q: So does music fit your moods?

A: Yes, very.

Q: How does it do that?

A: Sometimes, when I'm low in spirit, I can go in a room by myself
and really concentrate and start thinking about the problem and just
humming a song that fits it, um (laugh), because I do it all the time.

Q: What kind of music do you like, Mabel?

A: I love gospel music.

Q: Tell me about it.

A: Um, first of all, I am very much into the church so that's the kind
of music that's there. I'm very grateful and I have a lot of gratitude for
God sending His Son to die for me and the way I show my gratefulness
is singing. I uplift the name of Jesus and praise Him in songs. Gospel
music can never really be described because it's something that you have
to feel deep within. It's not like you can just jump up and sing "I Love
the Lord." Unless you do, it won't mean anything to you. You can sing
that the Lord has really been good to you in your life and unless you

know what He's done for you . . . you've got to realize that all these different little things He may have brought you through . . . it has to mean something to you and it does to me. When I sing, I never pick a song that I can't relate to, whether it's in my life or someone else's. When I sing, people sometimes give me requests because I sing various types of songs and they may say sing this song . . . maybe it's Amazing Grace . . . and because I know about amazing grace, which is God's love for me, I can really get into the song. Whereas if it was something about like, "Baby, you've been so good to me" or something (laughter) or "It hurts so good" (more laughter) . . . what would I know about that?

Q: Oh yeah, right! (with sarcasm)

A: No! It wouldn't be *me*! You know what I mean. It wouldn't be me expressing how *I* feel. Gospel music is really just something else . . . because you can have solos all right, we have quartets, which is four people, of course you know that, you can count (laugh) . . . and then you can have a duet. It's just different ways and gives you more room to express yourself.

Okay, with more people you can get over to the crowd, meaning they may enjoy it more because it's a choir and hear the different voices, different sections. For instance, if it was the song "Hallelujah" for twenty minutes it's just Hallelujah and you can really tear up the song because sopranos are really high-pitched. It just does something to you because Hallelujah is the highest praise you can give to the Lord.

If the sopranos sing it, you can hear the niceness of it and then the altos come in and harmonize . . . harmony is beautiful anyway . . . and then the tenors come in and that's quality because men can sing . . . and I like watching them sing! (laughing) So, it's just wonderful and I like directing the choir because . . . hmm . . . why do I like directing choir? I don't know . . . (quietly) . . . cut off the tape . . .

Q: Why? (leaving tape recorder on)

A: Leadership. Directing works hand in hand with leading people. In order to lead people, you have to have something special about you and I feel that I have leadership quality. Because I love singing, I can direct a choir the way I want to. I can have the sopranos sing three choruses by themselves and then ask the tenors to come in, forgetting about the altos. . . . I can do that.

Q: Okay, how do you feel when you're up there singing to the people?

A: I feel it's an honor and a privilege to be singing. I'm very grateful to the Lord for my talent. I try not to misuse or abuse the talent by being stuck-up because there's so many people that I know who would love to be able to sing. Everyone can to a certain extent, but to be able to have that quality in your voice that you'd like to have . . . everybody doesn't have that.

Getting back to your question, I feel very honored, I'm still uplifting His name and I'm also letting people enjoy it. If they're low in spirit, maybe a verse of the song or a word of encouragement to them to continue to be grateful. . . . Standing up there is just great. People are waiting for *me*! to open my mouth and to do something for them. That's what it really is. Like, I know if I was sitting in the audience waiting for a solo, they would have to win me over first of all. They would have to know what they were doing and do it right! (laugh)

Q: Does the music give you a sense of power?

A: It does! Because I control my voice. I feel the anointing of the Lord coming upon me because, in various parts of the song, you really get inspired to hit a high note and that's power, because as the people listen they're going along with me. They're saying, "Wow, Mabel is really getting into this" and, "Boy, she has a wonderful voice" or, "Boy, she really knows how to use her gift" and, yes, that does give me power. Of course, after, you're going to get applause and it would be kind of sad and empty if nobody clapped after I finished (more laughter). So that's power right there.

I go to various churches and different concerts. As I sing more and more, people get to know me as a singer and there might be a request for me to sing. If I hear anyone say, "Oh, Mabel, go ahead and sing," because they do that in church, then I think, "Well, wow, they must enjoy my music, there's something . . . me . . . that they want to hear me." Then, too, if I don't live anything after I sing . . . you know, if my life doesn't show anything or prove anything . . . it was worthless. You know, if I were to cuss someone out right after church, what does my singing mean? It doesn't stop or begin when I go in front of a crowd, it *has* to be everyday. Still, knowing that Jesus gave me my voice . . . and while I have it I'm going to do anything I can to sing . . . I couldn't really enjoy singing blues or jazz because that's not me. (pauses to think)

Some songs like Rick James, for instance, "Mary Jane" . . . what Mary Jane really is, is marijuana . . . and I could never sing about marijuana. What's the purpose? He's still making millions of dollars off Mary Jane and "she's my favorite thing," but Mary Jane isn't *my* favorite thing!

Q: So, for you to enjoy the music, or for you to even sing it, you have to be into it?

A: Right! I sing at weddings. I sing "You Are So Beautiful To Me."

Everyone seems to like that song and it fits the occasion and if I know the bride it's even better, and if she *looks* good its even better. (laugh, laugh) It just goes along with . . . like, I'm *not pretending* about things.

Q: When I see TV shows . . . like the Jeffersons or Flip Wilson . . . and you know how they have those people in church clapping their hands, saying Hallelujah! Is it really like that?

A: It's exactly like that!

Q: Wow, that must be quite a feeling. That must really get people going, the whole atmosphere.

A: I know, when I'm singing, I'm perspiring. I'm really getting into my song, and if the people are just going to sit there and stare at me, they're not really getting anything out of it. Some people don't show their emotions. Everyone shows it in different ways. Some people might jump up and start clapping, some others might just sit and smile and they're really enjoying it. But you have to show it some kind of way and in a Baptist church, that's how they show their feelings, that's how they praise the Lord.

Q: So the music really helps you to tell people how you feel?

A: Right! For instance, the song "I'm So Grateful" . . . I think about it a lot because I am. I've been through a lot of things in my life and I can think of songs for those situations.

Q: Like what kind of songs?

A: One song I know, its about healing. It says "Thank You, Lord," and there is one verse . . . "You heal me" . . . just those three words, "You heal *me*," just says a lot. I know, through my sickness . . . He has healed me. It's just there in the song and you can't help but feel emotional about it.

Q: I was going to ask you if it's just the music that makes you feel that way or the words, but obviously it's both.

A: Yeah, it does. Okay, a little beat to a song, it can get you swaying your body and clapping your hands, sure, but too many times I've sung without any music. It has to be in the words, you can't just go up there and depend on the music all the time because then you can just have the music. Am I right? Now, I will admit some instrumental pieces are inspiring, a note can say something whether it's low on the keyboard . . . that's sad . . . or if it's higher and a little bit jumpier . . . well, that's joyous. You can have that, but you really have to have some lyrics. In gospel music, if it's a song that everyone knows and nobody is singing and just playing on the piano . . . yes, it can become very emotional. There's one song, "Lord Have Mercy." It's so deep. I really can't express the song . . . it goes from one extreme to another as far as the keyboard is concerned . . . and how it jumps in the middle . . . everybody knows the song so they can't help but to respond to what they're feeling.

Q: Besides gospel music, what other kind of music do you like?

A: I like love songs because I think they're beautiful. When two people find each other out of nowhere and you walk into a store one day and he might say (lowly) "Hi, how are you?" (chuckle), and from there you started a relationship. It's just really sweet because love songs can go for years. You could be married for twenty years and your husband might say, "Remember our song?"

Q: Sentimental?

A: Yeah, it is, and I love those songs. They get you in the mood.

Q: What gets you in the mood, the music or the words or the tune?

A: It's a combination, but I think the music could get you in the mood. Certain tunes just say "Oh, this is so romantic" and you just think about candlelight with soft music. Then put some words in and you're in trouble.

Q: Why are you in trouble?

A: Because, for instance, if you're in a car looking at the moon and a song may come in and say, "Since I found you, I'm so very happy" and you start getting closer to him (laughing). . . . That's how you can get into trouble.

Q: Well, you just better be careful of those words, then! (laugh)

Q: What about mediated music like . . .

A: Like jazz?

Q: Yeah, what do you think about that?

A: I give them credit and my respect because they're definitely talented. Some jazz pieces are incredible. I tried to play a trombone once but I couldn't get my lips inside that little thing right.

I can respect and appreciate gospel music as well as opera as long as the person is putting themselves into that and really working at it. I can't see anybody just standing up there if it doesn't mean anything to them. You have to express yourself and music can help you do that.

Q: What do you think about rock, white folks' music? (laugh)

A: Rock and roll sounds to me like a whole bunch of noise but I have to give it to them because sometimes they have more than five chords in it. (laugh, laugh) You can tell these are talented people . . . they have gone to school for it. If they bring joy to an audience without words of profanity . . . why not!

Q: What about favorite singers, groups?

A: My favorite is Shirley Caesar and I had the privilege of meeting her. I talked with her and she's a crazy, fun-loving woman and she's an excellent singer. She can sing high or low. She's respected. Her name is known and I look up to her. She writes her own songs with words of her life experiences.

A L A N

"I'm not gonna sit there and worship someone."

Alan is nineteen years old and a college student. He
was interviewed by a female college student.

Q: What kind of music do you like?

A: Alternative music. (cough)

Q: Alternative?

A: Yeah! It's a new word, you know, 'cause I don't like to say new
wave 'cause . . . I don't. You can't classify music most of the time, you
know, I don't like new wave and punk and all of those other stuff, you
know, I don't believe in that.

Q: And what do you put in this classification?

A: You know, like, uh, the Psychedelic Furs, U2 . . . the Clash, stuff
like that. Like a lot of people say that the Clash is punk, but they're not
any more. Like supposedly they were but . . . you know, back in '76,
'77 . . . now they're not, you know? I just call it alternative. (cough)

Q: Why do you like this kind of music?

A: (pause) Like it's either, um, music's gotta, it's gotta like . . . hit you
a certain way like it's gotta . . . give you some kind of feeling like either
if you're in a depressed mood, you want to be, you know, it helps you be
depressed . . . 'cause . . . everybody has to be depressed . . . sometimes,
you know . . . and if you want to be in like an up mood, it's gotta be
able to do that . . . like, some music like the Doors . . . it just doesn't do
anything for me like . . . I never wanted to listen to it. It doesn't suit any
mood I have.

Q: What else do you like besides this alternative music?

A: I like fifties' and sixties' music too. There's a lot of stuff like, you
know, rockabilly. It's not that deep in meaning, most of their stuff, but
it's good music, it's got a good beat to it. And it's happy stuff, that's
what that is. But you're not thinking . . . it's not like you're in a thinking

mood, you know . . . it makes you like sort of want to bop around. Sixties stuff is good to listen to, like the words. I mean, the music's good too, it's more acoustic and stuff. I like early Dylan, he says a lot of stuff. He's got like protest songs and stuff like that. That's when you want to think.

Q: (pause) So you're saying you relate to music by the mood that it puts you in or stabilizes?

A: Yeah! It doesn't have to be political. A lot of people say songs have to be political. . . . Now they say if you're into new music, you're into political stuff, and that's not true. They say this because they say people who are into new music are against capitalism and new music's always gotta be against the government. It's always gotta be ragging on supposedly the higher class, because punk is supposedly for lower class people . . . that's who started it. And then they say new wave is all against politics and stuff . . . I don't think that's so, they're love songs.

Q: Do you agree with a lot of the lyrics?

A: Yeah . . . if I don't like the lyrics or if I don't like what they're saying . . . I probably wouldn't listen to it because I'm not gonna sit there and worship someone. That's what a lot of people do . . . everything that person does is great. Like Mick Jagger, people think everything he does is good because they like his music, but you're not supposed to idolize someone, you're supposed to like their music. You don't worship the person, you should listen to the music, feel the song, not the person just because of their political views on something. I don't think you have to be really into the person.

Q: Do you have anybody that you identify with though? Is there anyone you worship?

A: No, I don't worship any singer, because if you worship someone it's like saying you could never do what they are saying. Like I write my own songs . . . I don't write music 'cause I don't know notes and stuff, I play the drums . . . I think my lyrics are a lot better than a lot of other people's. So I don't worship anybody, because I know I could do better.

Q: I'm unclear about what you said about your music being political, can you clarify?

A: I agree with some political songs, what they're saying, but I don't think it has to be political. See, that's a changing move now. People are going back to sixties' music that people said was all political, all protest songs. Some were good, but it doesn't have to be political. It went through . . . like first in the fifties it wasn't, and in the sixties it went back to it. People were, you know . . . Vietnam and so on . . . so it was political again. Groups like Van Halen started coming out and stuff in the late seventies where it was going away from being political, and now supposedly it's going back. If people are into newer music, they think it's gotta be political, but, um, I don't agree with that. I mean some political songs are good but . . . it doesn't have to be. Like some people won't listen to a love song. I can see some of the ones on the radio, Top Forty ones, I don't like that much. You could make a real good love song, that's very poetic or whatever, that has a good tune.

Q: What do you think about the Dead Kennedys?

A: I don't really, like um their um . . . ha! They just . . . they're mostly just uh . . . you know, the world's dead! That's all they think, and I don't agree with that. But they're . . . that's what I mean . . . they're all political and their music's terrible. They don't play really, they just make noise, and there was only one song that I liked. They made a real good point quick but . . .

Q: What was that?

A: "Holiday in Cambodia." They make their point and it's cut short and it's good that way. But I don't like any other of their songs. I only have one album of theirs and it was given to me.

Q: How did you get involved in your record collection?

A: Uh . . . well, I always listened to . . . music. I started out listening to, you know, the same stuff people listen to today, like Van Halen. I started when I was in middle school. I started really listening in sixth grade. I bought records.

Q: What did you buy?

A: Van Halen's first albums and Kiss, Bay City Rollers, Kansas, Styx . . . this is more into middle school . . . along with C.S.N.Y., Eagles.

Q: Now you're into a totally different thing!

A: Yeah basically, because I got bored. There's probably like a year, around ninth grade, that I didn't really listen to anything. Then I started picking up college stations, a Syracuse University station that played the newer stuff. And so I started getting into that. And then I met one of my best friends and we started talking about music, and he listened to the same things. So we started going out to all the concerts, like the smaller concerts, the new groups, and then I just went from there. So . . . then I just kept buying records.

Q: A lot of people look at this kind of music as fashionable. Does that turn you on?

A: No, not at all. Some people don't even know what kind of music I listen to 'cause that . . . that's why it's fashionable . . . there's "a music scene," and I really don't think there is one. I think you make your own. Why, I first started getting into the fashion before there was one, you know? And when people started doing it, I just dropped it. So I guess I was kind of fashionable in the beginning but not anymore. I'm not into a fashion. It almost, it turns me off really. That's what I mean, you get a whole bunch of people who aren't listening to what they're saying, they're just worshiping the person, so they have to dress like them. I don't agree with that because that's not what the music's saying. I wrote a couple of songs on the scene, how there really isn't one, you know, uh, it's dead! It's a dead scene. Just a bunch of people going there and not caring about music just "Oh I'm being different" and they're worshiping these people. It's bad. Going to a concert there's just a bunch of people slam-dancing from L.A. People are just slam-dancing, hurting other people. It's so stupid, you know?

Q: Are a lot of your friends into alternative music?

A: My brother is and so is my best friend. We're the ones that go to all the concerts and stuff.

Q: How old is your brother?

A: He's two years older than I am. He's twenty-one. My friend is twenty years old. He influenced us a lot because he had all the albums, like U2, when they first came out.

Q: Why don't you like fashion?

A: I don't know why . . . it seems it just takes it away. A lot of times people get into fashion, and then they gain the masses, and then they play to them. They're not playing what they want. They're playing what people want to hear. Which is . . . it's a business, too, you know, so you can look at it like you have to make money. But you should still be playing what you want to play. And a lot of people don't anymore and admit it, too. Van Halen said, "I know our music's bad but I say nothing." People want to hear it. That's why I don't like him. I respect him for saying that, but I know it's not his music. A lot of the bands now say that. It's the American problem. That's why Van Halen can't make it in England. I don't think they have the best music. The people there go for the new trends. The people worship the people not the music and it's wrong. Like, say the person's homosexual, it doesn't mean that if you like the person you're one. That's how a lot of people think about David Bowie. He's homosexual and just because you like the music doesn't mean you're a homosexual. I don't like homosexuality and so, even if I liked him, it has nothing to do with it. If he had a song promoting homosexuality I probably wouldn't like it you know? That's what I mean by worship. Because that's the worst thing. You got to feel the music, listen to the words, that's what a good song is. It's not the person, it's the words.

Q: What does this kind of music do for you?

A: Well, when I put on U2's first album it's real high energy, it's up on the world you know? But if you put on their second album, it's positive on the world, but it's slow so it doesn't make your blood flow. There's this other group I listen to called Joy Division that's like real high energy. But I don't listen to it to get all psyched-up like some people do. I don't know how to classify the energy really, it just goes.

Q: Any specific experience you want to talk about?

A: Well, when I was in high school, I was into the Psychedelic Furs and I had never seen them, this was their third tour. It was really spontaneous. I was just hanging out in school one day, I didn't even know they were in Syracuse. They were giving a free concert up at S.U., someone told me that, so I hopped in the car, and ran out. It was a free concert, you know, and they were just . . . they weren't, they weren't dressed up . . . nothing like that. They were on a small stage in a park, there were hardly any people there, and they were just playing for like two and a half hours. They played just about every song on their whole album, and they had so much energy, you know? They were happy to be there. And there wasn't a huge crowd, they couldn't have been making much money. They must have been making something, but it was totally free so they would really connect with you. There couldn't have been more than a couple of hundred people there. It was a really big place so you had all the room you wanted. It was like you had them right in your own house. 'Cause, after, they stayed around and talked. It was . . . 'cause I like their music a lot, it helped drag me more into the music, the smaller bands and stuff. It just seemed so cool. It was a really good atmosphere. And now that's totally opposite. I went to see them again, they put out another album, I couldn't believe it. They're bigger now, a lot bigger. It seemed like they were a lot more distant from the crowd. Like they were just playing to make money or something. I see that happening like all the time now, so like that's an experience for me now because it keeps happening. I'm starting to feel like the whole thing's falling apart again, like it did when I was switching from middle school into high school. All the groups, it seems, are doing it. They start out good and then get bigger, then they forget about what they're supposed to be doing. It's not a positive experience anymore. I haven't seen many good concerts lately. They all have a bunch of people all over slamming. It's becoming violent or something.

ABBY

"It's about aggression."

Abby is a nineteen-year-old college sophomore.
She was interviewed in 1985 by her father.

Q: Well, we're on. What is music about for you in your daily life?

A: It's about aggression. (said with soft voice and mock-menacing smile)

Q: It's about aggression!? (semi-mock surprise)

A: . . . for a passive-aggressive soul. I use it when I wake up, and I'm not very sensitive to different things throughout the day. I remember a co-worker saying that some of this stuff he would never play first thing in the morning. He slowly rises with classical and sitar. But I find that I can listen to jarring danceable music, whether it's sweet danceable music or antiseptic danceable music, early in the morning, late at night, between classes, just to move around and wake up and that generally it gives me the same kind of happiness that being angry gives me. A kind of fierce feeling (whispered). Even with Aretha I get this kind of "yelly" feeling . . . "Here I am . . ." (shout-sings a bit of Aretha's song from her first LP for Columbia, *And It Won't Be Long*) . . . that kind of thing. It's a fierce feeling.

Q: So you use it to get charged up.

A: Yes. At this point. (whispering conspiratorially) It wasn't always that way. Even Elvis Costello . . . who's the only person who's not so danceable . . . has a lot of nasty, fierce lyrics. The same with Grace. . . . Well, when I think about it, it could be just where I am now. I wasn't always that way.

Q: Talk more about how you are now. Who is doing this aggression?

A: Well, maybe it's that I don't put it [aggression] anywhere else really. I mean, I go to my classes and . . . other things, but it's a way to move, and I do that a lot lately, with my housemates, especially Nora.

We'll get together when we're fed up with everything else and we should be doing work. We've been playing both this Motown tape and then another more modern, kind of antiseptic, Kraftwerky . . . more like the stuff that my brother plays a lot of the time like Depeche Mode and Ministry. It's like an anthology tape that we have with no more than one or two songs by each person. It's antiseptic, I guess, in the sense of not even pretending to be humanly created. You know, a lot of synth pop, a lot of repetition without much inflection. You know, like Kraftwerk: "She's a model and she's . . ." (singing in stiff, low tones) . . . or Grace Jones is very deadpan! And I like that about Grace Jones, too, actually. (sings) "Your sex life compli-ca-tions are not my fas-ci-na-tion" and "Nipple to the bottle never satisfied." That's a very nasty song.

Q: You say antiseptic because it's not human, mechanical . . .

A: I mean it's not like . . . I guess it's what you could call cold and danceable as opposed to hot and danceable, like James Brown or . . . and not very interpretation-oriented either. Although of course the deadpan thing is an interpretation. Grace Jones actually has a very strong voice but it's not very showy in the way that Joan Armatrading's would be.

Q: So it's dance music for aggression, hot or cold.

A: Hot or cold. And sweet or sour. I still love the Ghanaian high-life and that "Oh, papa . . ." (she imitates the guitar patterns with her voice) . . . so it's not necessarily just aggression although a lot of time it leaves me with the same kind of happiness that I get from feeling, you know, Arrgh (soft growl).

I think I would have more room for the Joni Mitchell, the lyrical cadence, if . . . I'm very irritated with Holly Near these days, and I think that right now I'm sort of emotionally conservative. It's at a point where I'm very cynical. When I used to be in high school, I picked fights with people and returned home all teary, so sincere and so gung-ho about, say, political things so that it really repelled people. No one should down someone like Holly Near who's trying to put forth good things in music, but . . . that irritates the hell out of me. I think some of it is my own cynicism, that I don't want music that is me—— . . . I regard it as almost propaganda again.

Q: Were you about to say medicinal? Here have a dose of politically correct . . .

A: Yes. She's been getting more sanctimonious and less eccentric. She used to have, like some weird songs that were more like the Roches, do you know them? But now it's more like her last concert had a lot of, you know. . . . There is something kind of self-righteous in these women singing "En Chile . . . en Chile . . . en Chile" (sung very melodramatically). What was another one? "Watch out . . . watch out . . . there's a rumble of war in the air." She was getting very into it and it was just disgusting. And it's not necessarily that her music is supposed to press a button and make people go out and do things and be socially active, but . . . I couldn't take much of it when we went to the concert. And Nora had the same feeling. Right afterwards, when we came back from the concert (raising her voice in mock hysteria) we turned on our boppy music and we . . . you know, we'd been dying to listen to something more, a lot more . . .

Q: Physical.

A: And not cuddly.

Q: And not correct.

A: Yeah. Yeah. Yes, in that sense I got lot more of a charge out of that. . . .

Q: So go back to Elvis Costello and Grace Slick . . .

A: Grace Jones, honey. Grace Slick? For-give me. Never in a million years.

Q: Are they satirical? Are they anti-political? What are they vis-a-vis Holly Near?

A: Costello is bitter, I'd say he's political in his way. Although he's trashing . . . he seems to be trashing just about everything in sight. There are a fair number of fairly misogynist lyrics. There's a fair number of . . . like "Senior Services" . . . anti-military lyrics: "If we run out of work we can always send you to Johannesburg," something about lives being cheap, all it takes is a whisper in Mr. Churchill's ear. It's like constant snideness, really rapidfire in the lyrics. They're really very dense.

Q: Sounds political to me. Or are you just giving me political examples?

A: They're not all political. He has put a lot of cynicism about gender relations that he puts in political terms. Like "Two Little Hitlers" (sings): "Two little Hitlers will fight it out, it's all so calculated, she's got a calculator, she's my little touch typewriter, and I'm the great dictator. Two little Hitlers. . . ." She's my touch typewriter and I'm her great dictator?

Q: Sounds very metaphorical-allegorical-intellectual.

A: Well, it's incredibly glib, smart-ass. He loves wordplay and sometimes it's really bad. And other times it's not. And I love his voice too.

Q: And it's all danceable? It all fits with your aggression-danceable category?

A: Some of it. Some of it is danceable. But I'm saying he's one person, that even when he's not danceable there's something I really get into about, also, this kind of snobby silkiness of delivery. He has very low . . . he has at least one of his voices that he uses most typically that is sort of tender and low when he sings horrible things. (said low and sinister) It's again (loudly) suited to the passive-aggressive personality! (singing) "Are you ready for the final solu-shun?" (laughs)

Q: Gross. So his voice contrasts with the content?

A: Sometimes. Or sometimes he does mockouts of earlier music, earlier forms, you know, whether it's . . .

Q: (interrupting) And Grace Jones is a similar thing? Her voice mocks the content?

A: Well, no, her voice is sort of completely . . . I'd say she tends to stay as close to toneless as she can. But sometimes she just sings melodically, say with a . . . I can't think of some songs that she does . . . (sings) "pull up to the bumper baby." She sings, sometimes it's just singing and strong, but . . . (sings a few phrases with pauses) I don't know, it's something, it's very . . . she's not incredibly embellishment-oriented. Just think of the way her head looks! She sounds the way her head looks, goddamnit. We're looking at a unified aesthetic. She looks like a couch. She sounds like a couch. No, that's not true.

Q: She looks sorta square. She sounds square. How does her head look?

A: Well, her head looks square, but the idea is something minimalist and robot-looking.

Q: This aggression thing, can we subdivide that? It's Grace Jones, Costello, who else fits in this?

A: I can even find it in Aretha, I can even find it in the sweet music, there's a kind of whooooo! (hooting) Even in the Pointer Sisters, even in inane songs like (sings) "He's so shy, that's why I love my baby," even in that. (mimics the instruments)

Q: So it's hot/cold or sardonic, and hot and sweet go together? Tell me more about the sweet/hot side.

A: That would be represented by the Ghanian high-life lately, by Aretha, by James Brown, the Motown that we listen to is fairly nice, you know, like "What I say, that land of a thousand dances" song, some new Aretha that's really oooo, and believe it or not there's a song by Donna Summer that I actually like, "Love Is in Control." I still like Rick James, those two songs, basically on this kind of hilarious mannerism, coupled with a pretty good beat. (sings) "I wanna talk . . ."

Q: Abby, as an anthropologist, an ethnographer of great skill, I notice that these catagories are "black" and "white," except that Grace Jones is somewhere in the "white" category.

A: I think there's a new antiseptic, and that some of the antiseptic from white things definitely derives from some sort of synth-funk. I mean, when you hear that new Chaka Khan thing, that "Chaka-khan, chaka-khan, I feel for you," a lot of that would definitely be classified as cold, in spite of . . . because even the vocal gymnastics . . . "Ooopa dop . . ." (etc.) are not interpretation so much as acrobatics.

Q: So the hot, sweet, energetic, aggression side is almost all black, but the sardonic, cold aggression is black and white . . .

A: I think you have your own ax to grind at this point, but . . . I think there's as much of it on the black side. . . . I'm sort of wary of what you're . . . I think you've got your own ax to grind.

Q: Those are my categories, not your categories?

A: And besides, there would be more sweet people if I were into gentle and lyrical, but Joan I think, is the only one that's sort of palatable in that way.

Q: But you don't use her to charge out the door in the morning.

A: Sometimes I listen to her in the morning, but it's more . . . I think of her more as an evening person, or as a lying around in the sun person. I tend to do it most of the day.

Q: So you come back to that like an oasis, like a resource?

A: I'm sorry. I do. I go out to dances where that's usually the sort of thing that's played too. Although sometimes they don't play such good music.

Q: When you say aggression, what were you into before, what preceded this aggression phase?

A: I think it's been aggression for a while . . . I mean, I know that I got a similar . . . I know that while I like the Police a lot . . . I still sort of like them, although now I like the Police in the same way that I like e. e. cummings, because, weirdly, images just hop into my head and I'm not sure why. I can see really detailed pictures and really detailed colors for some reason. But before, it used to be, again, the same sort of . . . I think it's partly image, associating a certain kind of mild controlled hostility with vitality and with being . . . together. Tightness. Some sort of authority or purpose. In just a very general sense, impressionistic. Yes. That sort of music made me feel . . .

Q: Purposeful, authoritative. . . .

A: Yeah. (sings instrumental beginning of "Bed's Too Big Without You") You know it is also fairly spare. That was also aggression. I was listening to that just around the time before I took off for Swarthmore. I was getting very ready to split.

*"Roger Waters is really it for me. . . . I honestly
feel that if George and I could contact Roger,
and have seven minutes of his attention,
he would take care of us forever."*

Rhonda was interviewed by a female college classmate.
She is in her early twenties.

Q: Tell me a little about yourself.

A: I was born in New York City, later moved to Long Island, and now I'm going to college here.

Q: We're trying to look at how music affects our daily lives. Have you ever thought about this?

A: Yes. It's simple. Without music, I would die. I would not exist. I couldn't. I don't see it.

Q: You wouldn't exist . . . meaning you wouldn't be happy in your existence?

A: I just wouldn't be. I wouldn't have a personality.

Q: You think it would take away from your personality?

A: It would take away from my entire existence. I don't think I could live. I am always listening to music. I am always thinking about music, even when I am not listening to music. For instance, I will always have a tune in my head. Sometimes, I look down so nobody can see me, and I groove to myself.

Q: Sometimes music can be found in the background of your life, sometimes in the forefront. What is music to you?

A: It is in both. I am one of the persons that has to have music on all the time. At night, I lie back to back, tape to tape, exactly what I want to hear, and the next tape . . . until I fall asleep.

Q: Is there a degree of relaxation to your music? The more relaxed you get, the more relaxed your music gets?

A: No. All my music is passionate and intense. I like to have good stereo equipment for this reason. I have begged for my equipment, for my eighteenth and nineteenth birthday, graduation, Christmas. My grandmother bought me a stereo. Even more important than my stereo is the headphones my mother bought me. They are absolutely perfect . . . digital wiring to perfectly conduct your music.

Q: So good equipment can help translate passion and intensity in music?

A: Well, when . . . take a disk to a tape to walkmans to headphones, you just connect. That bass comes through, and all that treble; nothing is distorted, even the softest lightest music. It is all crystal clear. Perfect music. That to me is Roger Waters [from Pink Floyd] . . . he gets that.

Q: So it has to do with equipment and the musician?

A: Yeah. Roger Waters is really it for me. My goal in life is to meet Roger Waters, my life ambition.

Q: Have you ever attended one of his concerts?

A: Yes, but only one. I would kill to see him again. I am addicted to Roger's solo albums. He puts together music you can't even believe is real. It actually hurts me to listen to his music. It just fills up every muscle and vein in my body. You feel so good you don't know what to do with yourself. That's why I have to meet him.

Q: Are there special times that you listen to Roger Waters? Does it make you dance?

A: No, it just intensifies my body, it fills me up with something, I don't know . . . it is hard to explain. I would put it on to go to sleep but it always keeps me awake. I can listen to it over and over again, and I would never get sick of it. They don't have many albums so it's good that it's like that.

Both *Dark Side of the Moon* and *Wish You Were Here* are perfect for those days when the sky is full of clouds in motion and gusts of wind push you along the walkways. The albums are so passionate and full of music, they make the earth feel healthy. I can feel it all around me and in me.

Atom Heart Mother makes the snow sing. They used a choir and a lot of horns for this album. They mix all the natural beauty of voice so that it sounds as if fifty people are all singing different melodies that all blend together in a big web of harmony with all the instruments and it's so great. The snow floats with the sound, and I don't feel as cold as I would otherwise.

Q: Do you think other people influenced the type of music you like?

A: My brother turned me on to Don Dorsey. We are really close.

Both of us will hear something and bring it in the other's life. George and I share the gifts of instantaneous communication and overemotion. We are able to feel, lock into each other's minds, and fuse together to produce energy on a level so high, it cannot be touched. When Pink Floyd's perfection gets involved with the scene, a triangular bond of such cogent power shoots through us that if we aimed it at something it would probably explode. Sometimes we are forced to do that to another person's mind, and it is really strange.

I honestly feel that if George and I could contact Roger, and have seven minutes of his attention, he would take care of us forever. As far as I can tell the need is mutual. But even if it was not, who would pass up the chance to meet people who have been mentally formed by their music? While there are thousands of Pink Floyd fans, there are not that many truly kind and peaceful addicts of their music. This is what George and I have to offer Roger. There is no way, if he knew about us, he wouldn't respond to us.

Q: Who turned you on to Roger Waters?

A: My dad actually. I used to beg him to put it on, and I used to sit in front of the speaker and say, "Dad, what is this vibration?"

Q: Degrees of music, do you like it soft or loud?

A: I need it full volume. That is why I like live shows. Concerts are the only way for me to get the full satisfaction from music. When something is live, there is such a feeling in it. The jams are longer, and the air is full with sound. Going to a Grateful Dead show is the best thing you can do. No one can do what the Dead do. Every song they play is different every time they play it. They don't have set patterns or line ups. They just play what they feel, and everyone gets caught up in it.

Q: Outside of listening to music, have you ever had music in your life from playing instruments?

A: I play guitar a little. I like to play a lot, but I wish I was better. I think I am at my plateau. I don't think I can get better. I just wouldn't know how to do it.

Q: Have there ever been any other instruments in your life?

A: I always wanted to play piano. I know very few songs. First, I play all the songs I know . . . about three, but I know them perfectly. I play them real loud when no one is home. I just practice these three. I don't know anything else.

Q: Do you regret this?

A: Yes, but I don't want to take lessons. I hate practicing scales. I just want the end result.

Q: Do you feel as if music has more input in your life than in other people's lives?

A: Yes, definitely. It's the kind of music I listen to. You can't help but be that way.

Q: So you're saying if everyone listens to Roger Waters . . .

A: Yeah, (laughing) everyone would be into music equally.

"It's hard to explain . . . it's all feelings and emotions . . ."

Gail is twenty-one years old and a student. She was
interviewed by a close friend who was a male graduate student.

Q: What part does music play in your life?

A: I guess I was sort of your stereotypical upper-middle-class girl.
Daddy always listened to classical music. All the kids played classical
instruments . . . piano, clarinet . . . I played oboe and still do. We all
started playing the piano at like six, although none of us were especially
good at it. I supposedly played the oboe very well . . . won competitions
and so on . . . and have and still do enjoy classical music more than any
other music. And the question is "Why?" or what does it do for me?
Well, it . . . umm . . . it's hard to explain walking to school with Bach
cantatas on and somehow being overwhelmed by it and enjoying it tremendously, envisioning yourself playing the oboe parts with a soprano
or alto singing the beautiful aria next to you. I guess it sort of . . . what
does it do? It makes me happy, generally, when I'm happy already, and
sad when I'm not happy.

Q: When you first said happy, I was surprised. I remember how sometimes you used to listen to Bach cantatas when you were really sad and
it would make you cry.

A: Sometimes it will. I think it's just incredible: the tones, the sound,
the chorus singing. I guess . . .

Q: What do you mean, incredible? That's one of those words that
masks a whole lot . . . that masks all the fine points.

A: Great. Wonderful. Overwhelming. Intense emotion, often melancholy. I'll cry listening, generally, to Bach cantatas. Bach is what I listen
to the most. And other times I'll be singing or conducting as I walk
along, enjoying it tremendously. I guess it's somewhat limited . . . and
you criticize it.

Q: You say that sometimes you walk down the street and listen to this stuff and it makes you incredibly melancholy and other times it makes you happy. I mean, what's the difference between the two? Is it the particular piece?

A: Well, it's always a . . . a dramatic and traumatic experience, but it has very little to do with the music itself, I think, and more to do with what's going on in my mind . . . whether I'm positive to begin with or negative to begin with. Because sometimes I'll hear the chorus and I'll just be like hooraaaay (waves) . . . there they go! Y'know? Singing and then the basses come in. And other times I'll hear the chorus and it'll just be like oppressive and dark . . . and I'll cry.

Q: You have two completely different reactions to it? For me, that seems to be counter-intuitive.

A: Yeah, maybe that would be the case with certain pieces, but Bach cantatas are generally interpretable either way. At least for me. It's not like you're listening to songs by Mahler which are really depressing— *kindertotenlieder* . . . you can never feel happy when you hear about all those kids dying. Mahler is generally not happy, and the music can't be interpreted any other way.

Q: Do you ever listen to music like that? What else do you listen to besides Bach?

A: Besides Bach cantatas? Not a lot actually. I used to listen to a lot, but it takes time . . . it's always such an involved process. You can't do something else when you listen to it. You can't have it on as background music. Or at least I can't. If I have it on, I have to listen to it. With a full-time school schedule your life is sort of limited . . . so mostly Bach. I don't know why. Maybe because I *enjoy* being overwhelmed. I like losing myself completely, or fantasizing.

Now that I think about it . . . the period in which I was frequently crying to music . . . y'know, when we lived at Clavin [her first apartment] . . . the one cantata I'd listen to continuously was number 140, and I think that a lot of that [crying and listening to Bach] had to do with leaving home and being reminded of home, reminded of my father in the living room with Bach cantatas on Sunday mornings. And all that . . . old feelings and thinking about being there . . . missing my parents, missing my family.

Q: Why, if you're homesick, would you listen to music that makes you sad that you're not home?

A: Well, maybe I'm homesick, and I listen to music that I grew up with and like to listen to and, at the same time, it reminds me of home and makes me feel sad. It still does that sometimes. Certain pieces that I listen to (she is getting choked up . . . watery eyes) . . . it's so weird that

I'm so attached to that . . . to the family scene through music. Y'know? Through the music that I've grown up with.

Q: Music attaches you to your family, or to your father?

A: Well, that's another weird thing I was thinking. I'm always talking about my father, my father, my father . . . and the music he listens to. My mother has like no musical interests at all. She's never played a musical instrument, doesn't listen to music on her own. She turns on the radio station that usually plays a lot of news and jokes. And if she listens to music, like if she wants music to be played—for guests or on a festive evening like when my parents are having a bottle of champagne on Christmas eve or something—it's usually German pop songs, or Canadian or French. Strange how I've so acquired my parents' tastes in music. That one woman singer, Edith Piaf, and Harry Belafonte are the two things that I heard frequently, other than classical music, and the two things that, if I hear now, I can enjoy. My brothers didn't do that at all. Maybe as a female I was much more attached to my parents. In general, females—I may be pushing a bit here—tend to be more emotional. I spent more time with my parents, I spent more time at home, I spent more time going to Europe with them, more time in their presence, more time being influenced by them in tastes. But at this stage it's sort of irrelevant, because it seems so natural . . . I don't feel as if I've been forced, or told to like a certain thing . . . not allowed to like something else. Well, I've been influenced . . . conditions have made me like the music I like but it's like that with everyone. (They put on Bach's *Magnificat*.)

A: Isn't that just great though?

Q: Why is it so great?

A: I have no idea.

Q: You have no idea why this is great? Why you like it?

A: It needs more bass. You have the treble all the way up and no bass. Turn it up, it needs to be booming! (pause . . . listening) Don't you think it's great? No, right? (laughs)

Q: It doesn't move me incredibly. I get a vague feeling of the overwhelmed and total that you mentioned before.

A: Don't you see why this is a happy one? It's so force . . . it's so going forward, y'know?

Q: And how is that different from a sad one?

A: I don't know. A sad one . . . usually I'm sad when altos are singing. I'm sure that it's *somewhat* due to the music . . . because I'm never sad to this.

Q: What do you mean by "going forward," I don't understand those musical terms.

A: That's pretty vague . . . it's not a musical term there. I don't know . . . impetus . . . forward . . . positive . . . (she makes forward-moving gestures).

Q: What is it about *the music*?

A: Okay, the music. I'm sure . . . well, I'm not really sure, because my musical history is somewhat lacking, but it seems as if it was written for a festive occasion. Maybe an Easter ceremony.

Q: I understand that. I understand the positive, festive, but what is it in the music that's doing it for you? You say it's festive but why?

A: Okay. I don't know, I guess . . . maybe the key—major versus minor—lots of instruments versus a few, quick music versus slow. Things like that.

I just think this is great. . . . I don't know why I like it so much. And some of them I've listened to so many times that I sing along. (laughs) Like "Here Comes Jesus" in German.

Q: But why is it so great?

A: I don't know.

Q: Well, you have to tell me.

A: It's hard to explain . . . it's all feelings and emotions . . .

Q: You gotta tell me why, though.

A: I don't know why. (annoyed) Just like you don't know why your music is a particular way . . . even if I tried to tell you a million reasons, you know, like it reminds me of home or because of the key . . . even if I say all those things . . . (she stops and gasps as a new part of the piece starts, an oboe solo). Now this part is *sad*. (listens for a while)

Q: Why is this part sadder than the other part?

A: (glares) I'm getting annoyed.

Q: Why?

A: Because the fact is it *is* sad. It evokes certain feelings. It has and it probably always will. Why? Well, I don't know why. I could talk about the notes or the voice or the oboe.

Q: Well, go ahead then.

A: But I feel no . . . I mean, I feel somewhat of a . . . maybe I just want to enjoy it, I don't want to explain it. I don't want to start describing "what" and "why." I just like it and like to hear it . . . like to be moved by it. I feel no *need* to explain it . . . you can't explain why. I don't know, it makes my epinephrine levels decrease. How's that for a scientific explanation? We should measure my blood . . . take a blood sample and analyze it everytime I hear this part of the cantata. And then we'll know what hormonal reason. Maybe it's programmed into my genes so that a G sharp really knocks me out.

Q: Okay, okay. . . .

A: I think it's unexplainable. Maybe the problem is that there could be so many different reasons and since I don't know the reason . . . I mean I could . . . for example, I could say: the relationship I have with my dad is a positive and close one and he listens to it and I have feelings toward him . . . positive feelings toward my family and my home. Or I could talk about the technical musical aspect and how the music is intentionally designed to evoke certain feelings. Or I could talk about my high school experiences playing the oboe . . . experiences walking through gothic cathedrals, spending the afternoon listening to Bach cantatas, and how architecture . . . and these singers in the front and the little chamber orchestra. And maybe it's partially all of them. Or maybe it's absolutely none of them. I don't know and I never will know. . . . It's not a scientific experiment. And I'm glad, because I don't want to know. . . . I don't want to know. I don't care.

VICTOR

"They feel it more because they created the instrument."

Victor is a Bolivian student who is attending university in
the United States. He was interviewed by a female classmate.

Q: Is there any specific kind of music that you like?

A: I like all kinds of music. It doesn't have to be mellow.

Q: What do you mean by mellow?

A: Music that puts you to sleep. Like music on easy listening radio
stations. I don't like the music that was a popular rock and roll song,
and they put it to an orchestra . . . like they do for restaurants. I don't
like that.

Q: Do you like rock?

A: I like rock. I don't like particular folk music, but I like vernacular
music. I like rock and roll and vernacular music.

Q: What is vernacular music?

A: Vernacular music is a music that you play with traditional instruments from any country.

Q: Like Bolivia?

A: Well, yes. But all countries have their vernacular music. You have
your sitar from India and the guitar . . . music that has been created by
people without any influence from other music.

Q: Traditional?

A: Yes, modern music is influenced by many things . . . rock and
roll, jazz.

Q: You don't think traditional is influenced though?

A: Vernacular music comes from a certain region. Maybe it can be
influenced by small towns around from radios, but it is not influenced
by external music. I have many tapes of this music . . . just pure sounds.

I prefer music from my own country, but I have some from other countries. It takes a while to get used to it. If your ear is not trained, you don't like it because you don't understand it. Like for classical . . . the same is true for vernacular music.

For example, we have an instrument like a flute called Quena. It is made out of wood. It's similar to the flute but not as refined. Usually they play the instrument to imitate the wind. You listen to it and imagine that maybe you're in the high mountains.

Q: Does this "wind" feeling make you sad or happy?

A: It depends on my mood. Sometimes I listen to it and it makes me think about things I would like to see again. For instance I remember friends gathering and we were listening to the same music. It made me happy.

Q: Do you use music to suit your moods?

A: Maybe I do in a way. I don't think I do it on purpose. I listen to music to enjoy it more than anything else. Just like when you want to read a book really badly, you don't read it just to make yourself really happy. You want to know what it's all about.

Every time I listen to a song I'm consciously or subconsciously concentrating and I will try to listen to all the sounds that an instrument will produce. Next time I listen to the same song I will try to listen to all the sounds that another instrument will make. After ten or twenty times I can listen to all of them together. I like that.

Q: When do you do this? Always? Sometimes? When?

A: I don't do that all the time. I do it especially the first time I listen to a song. And then, after, I like to listen to it again, like right after maybe, to let it stay there for a while. I never do this to examine myself. I can't tell you right away but if I sat down to think about it, exactly how I get involved with music, I can maybe tell you a bit more on why I do this.

Q: Name some of your albums or tapes that you have and really like. Give me your favorite album.

A: I have many. Rock and roll is the Beatles. I started liking the Beatles when I was five years old.

Q: What song did you like then? Do you remember?

A: I think the album I remember most was *Sgt. Pepper's Lonely Hearts Club Band.* I remember the cover. My favorite song was "Lucy in the Sky With Diamonds."

I think I liked the tune itself because I couldn't understand the lyrics and now I can understand literally what it means but I still don't know exactly what the composer wanted to convey. But I have an idea because back in those days they were influenced by many things. I didn't know itself what rock' and roll meant until I was twenty-one. It was just music to me. The melody, beat, and rhythm.

Q: What did that do for you?

A: Make me like to dance maybe, or just relax. Or be with friends. Usually rock and roll is not something you can enjoy, you have to have the right mood to listen to it or to dance.

Q: Do you listen to any music from your country?

A: Yes I do. There is a whole variety of different types of music. Not only one like rock and roll. Some of it I like for parties and other ones are very mellow and sad, or just melodies that make you feel good. I like to listen to those.

There's one particular group that I like who's name is Wara. It's a name that means something like earth in the Quechua language. They play sad songs, happy songs. The sound they make with the instruments is really great.

Q: Do you ever get homesick?

A: Yes I do.

Q: What do you listen to then?

A: Bolivian music. Sometimes I'll want to listen to a particular group and they play both happy and sad music. I try not to dwell on my homesickness because then eventually I would be really sick. Not only mentally but physically. It doesn't happen to me that often. . . . It used to before. Now I have more friends. One of the good things about pop music is that it's accepted everywhere.

Q: Could you fall asleep to music?

A: I can't. I've tried many times but I just keep listening and listening.

Q: Is there any music that you hate?

A: I don't think I hate music. Sometimes, like last summer for example, I was in California and for the first time I was exposed to heavy metal. I didn't like it, but my cousin played it all day and my ear got used to it and then I liked it, but not all of it.

Q: Is there any music that you would never collect?

A: Disco, I think. I don't like to collect it, but I like to listen to it. I think it is my bias. I don't collect it because I think disco is played because you want to dance. I don't think you can sit down and listen to it as you would other types of music. I don't want to dance all the time. If I do go to a disco, I'm really happy because I can dance.

Q: What about country music?

A: American country music? Mmmm . . . it's funny, but to me it's kind of mixed. They do not use what I call vernacular instruments. To me, that kills it. You know, sometimes I cannot distinguish a country song.

Q: What is an American vernacular instrument? A banjo?

A: Ah . . . yes. It's made of some sort of animal skin, wood . . . yes. But now they have electric banjos. That ruins it. See, the difference is, when you play vernacular music, you master the instrument in such a way, you can create sounds that nobody else can create. Just you, because you developed that skill. When you have an electrical instrument, the sounds you make can be duplicated or produced by anyone who knows how to play with the controls. Maybe I'm wrong, but many artists who play vernacular music, they develop a certain style that is their own. They build their own instruments themselves, and it's so personal. They feel it more because they created the instrument. I like that. That's the main reason.

CHAD

"It is not just the making of sound . . . it is how one nation expresses its opinion."

Chad is from Ethiopia and drove a cab for a while in
New York City. He is a twenty-six-year-old student.

Q: What is music about for you?

A: Music is a reflection of culture to me, to be frank, part of which
reflects a tradition. The way people live, the way people celebrate. It is a
reflection of sorrowness, of sadness. It is not just the making of sound.
It is how . . . ah, it is how one nation expresses its opinion. Not only
about love, but how they live and how they survive. That is what music
is all about.

Q: What kind of role would you say music plays in your personal
world?

A: In my own life? I can really enjoy . . . happiness. It just takes my
mind away from other things. A lot of daily things. It's not the way a
guy sings. It just takes me away.

Q: It's like an escape?

A: Yeah. You just escape from your own frame of mind. You just
become like . . . daydreaming.

Q: Does that happen to you all the time when you listen to music?

A: I'm not that fond of music. I enjoy it when it comes to classical
music. Maybe I'm an old-fashioned guy. The word that comes out of
music sometimes makes quite a lot of sense . . . even though music is
about love.

Q: So you think music sends a message?

A: Of course. That is really what music is created for.

Q: What sort of message?

A: Usually political, or love, or even religious feeling.

Q: What sort of message do you usually pick up?

A: Usually about love. You know . . . how beautiful the lady is or how beautiful the guy is.

Q: So do you think music revolves around sex a lot nowadays?

A: Oh, yeah. I would say about eighty percent is about love or a relationship.

Q: What do you think about this influence?

A: Well . . . that is the center of daily life today. It's a healthy topic but I don't think one has to sing about two people loving each other or, ". . . will you go to bed with me?" We do preach about love a lot.

Q: What do you mean?

A: By singing songs about it. Two people loving each other or getting crazy about each other . . . stuff like that. But the way we change reflects on how the music changes. Maybe an older person would not want to listen to music about love. He would rather listen to something like . . . ah . . .

Q: Something like ragtime?

A: Yeah. Something like that. Something that has no message about love at all.

Q: So the music today is based around young people?

A: Music today is like a business enterprise. It's got to attract a lot of buyers. It has got to market to those who can afford to buy. Most of the famous musicians today are also young. They have to get the attention of the young ones. The only way they can get that attention is if they sing only about love. So I would say people at the age of fifty, or in their late fifties, would not appreciate today's music. It's a business. You have to come with the sweetest voice that say, "I love you." Few popular bands nowadays sing about politics. But even if you do sing about politics, you have got to be super sexy to make a sale. It has to be music that can wrap you around so somebody will get up and dance the hell out of it.

Q: What do you think about dancing?

A: I think it is very sexual. Once you think about it, it's like . . . "Why am I out on the floor with this lady, shaking my booties around?" You know, it's like I'm crazy.

[Interview was briefly interrupted.]

Q: So do you think that the American type of dance has the biggest sexual messages in it?

A: No, dance has been around since the beginning of time. It has always had a sexual connotation.

Q: What is music like in Ethiopia?

A: About sixty percent is about love.

Q: What's the other forty percent?

A: I would say it is about fear or anger or hate or praising. A lot of politics. We are not a stable country.

Q: How does the actual music sound?

A: We are composed of about two hundred tribes. Different tribes have different music.

Q: Do you belong to a certain tribe?

A: Yes. We have different dialects and different culture. It is like a melting pot.

Q: What is your musical culture like?

A: A lot of our music is played on the sitar. There's a type of violin too. Instead of having it on your shoulder, though, you have it on your lap. It is like a violin in the early stage. Maybe the violin was a creation of us. They make the string out of horse hairs. This is a traditional instrument. The drums are also very common. They are covered with animal skin.

Q: What is that drum called?

A: We call it cabaro. It also used to be used as a means of communication.

Q: What about dancing in your culture?

A: Like I said, each tribe has it's own unique style. It's like Italians have their own style. We use our dancing more to communicate. Much of it would not be called dancing by Americans. A lot of it is just hand movements that express certain emotions and say different things. Dancing is more important to the people in Ethiopia than it is to Americans.

Q: Why is that?

A: Because we can trace certain dances back to the roots. It is just more of a tradition.

Q: Do you ever listen to music that is from Ethiopia anymore?

A: No. My brother has a few tapes, but I never listen to them. I find no reason to. When I do listen to music, it is usually on the radio or at a bar. I enjoy most music at bars. It seems to set the right mood for me. It makes me more talkative.

Q: Do you like to dance to it?

A: No. I'm a terrible dancer. I'm getting old. I'm usually too tired to dance. My feet are too sore from working all day.

Q: Doesn't dancing relax you?

A: No. Not the type of dancing at the clubs I go to. I just enjoy having a few drinks and listening to the music.

Q: How about when you're alone at home?

A: Well, I usually don't listen to much when I'm home.

Q: Do you prefer sharing music or do you prefer listening in private?

A: Music is something that should be shared. You have to listen to it with other people to enjoy it. Sometimes you wonder why people walk around with headphones on. You can't talk to them.

ADULTS

NEIL

"Music is just part of life, like air."

Neil is a heavy truck salesman, selling dump trucks,
over-the-road semis, and special equipment. He was twenty-three years
old when he was interviewed by a female classmate.

Q: What does music mean to you?

A: Music is just part of life, like air. You live with it all the time, so
it's tough to judge what it means to you. For some people, it's a deep
emotional thing, for some people, it's casual. I turn on the radio and it's
there in the morning; it's there when I drive; it's there when I go out.

Q: If it isn't there, do you miss it?

A: No.

Q: So you're not really aware that it is there?

A: It's like a companion, or a back-up noise. Just something in the
background. A lot of people turn the radio on and they're not listening
to it for the most part, but it's there to keep them company; it's background noise. It's like the TV: they leave the TV on all the time, although
it never gets watched. But it's background, people use it just to feel
comfortable with.

Q: And music is background noise for you?

A: For the most part.

Q: So you could turn on the radio and not even be aware of what is
playing?

A: Right. Many times . . . I drive a lot. I put five or seven hundred
miles on a week . . . and in the car, it can be on, it can be off, and if
I'm thinking, or whatever, I don't listen to the radio. Very rarely do I
consciously listen to the radio.

Q: Well . . . what kind of music do you like?

A: Mostly I like Top Forty. I like country and western . . . at times. I
like rap. I like *some* jazz, mellow jazz, if it's really laid back. I don't like

classical. Probably because it seems you have to work to appreciate it. It's nothing that I am accustomed to. And to appreciate the quality of music that it is, you have to really concentrate while listening to it, I feel. Personally, I don't put that much energy into music.

Q: If you were to go out and buy an album, what kind of album would you buy?

A: I would buy Top Forty. No. No, I wouldn't. I think I would buy more country and western or jazz, because I don't think it would outdate itself quickly. Or an oldies album—fifties or sixties. Most of that music goes on forever. Most of the music today is, if you will, passe. It's here today and gone in eight months. They wear out so quickly. It's not a wise decision.

Q: Do you own many albums?

A: (laughs) No. I have about fifty albums; maybe ten cassettes. The albums are mostly older, Dick Clark stuff, because that's the stuff I like to listen to all the time.

Q: Do you go to a lot of concerts? Do you like live music as opposed to recorded music?

A: Well, I really can't say. I don't go to a lot of concerts, so I really don't know. I've been to one or two. Um . . . I went to Kenny Rogers, and . . . I really can't remember who else.

Q: That memorable, huh?

A: (laughs) Yeah.

Q: Do you like to dance?

A: Oh yeah. I like to dance. That's just about the only time I really appreciate, listen to, the music. You have to concentrate on the music to get the beat of a song, because it's always changing. It's not a steady 4/4 pattern.

Q: So what kind of music do you really like to dance to?

A: Uh, Top Forty. The newer stuff. I can't really think of who offhand. They are just played all night. I don't know who does a lot of stuff but I would know all the words. If a song was playing, me and my friends would know all the words, what comes next. If the music were suddenly to stop, we would know the next couple of lines.

Q: Do you ever sing?

A: (pause) In the bars. When we are dancing to the music, we will sing along with the words.

Q: So you just sing when you dance?

A: No, when we are in the bars, just standing there drinking, we will all sing at the top of our lungs to the music. Nobody really cares, we don't bother anybody. Everybody knows us there, we have our own group. It's just like "Cheers" with Norm. (laughs) They have an oldies night at the bar I usually go to.

Q: So, you like *Big Chill* music?

A: Yeah. *Big Chill* music. I guess that's what it is called. I like it, though it's before my time. My mother listens to it. She's just nineteen years older than me. I grew up . . . she always listened to music much in the same way I do now, casually. It's just always there. I always grew up with what was in style at the time . . . Top Forty. As time goes on, you just get accustomed to it.

Q: Do you like new wave music?

A: No! It always seems so . . . harsh to me. In all honesty, I really haven't given it a fair shake. Music isn't enough to me to have to really work at something. I may someday start to drift towards it, but other than that, that's it. I'm not one to work at liking something.

Q: Does your mother like new wave?

A: No. (laughs) No. We just never hear it. It's not usually on the radio stations that we listen to. We are not accustomed to it. It's like driving a Porsche. (laughs) We aren't used to driving one, you know? It's the same with music. It's the same with all my friends. I have this kind of clique of friends. We all like the same kind of music, for the most part. There is the occasional one that likes country and western more, or new wave more, but for the most part, we are all the same in our taste in music.

Q: What do you think of MTV? Do you ever watch it?

A: No. Not more than ten minutes here or there in the past couple of years. It seems like they are always grasping for concepts. I think MTV, for the most part, is a very poor attempt to make something spectacular. Some are good but, most of the time, they seem to be grasping for a concept. They are just too abstract. But MTV isn't for everyone's enjoyment; it's marketing. It's to sell products. They have so much more advertising now than they did when they first started out.

Q: Do you feel music is something to get you going?

A: Oh yeah. When you wake up in the morning, instead of just waking up by taking a shower, you have something to listen to. It just seems to get the mind going a little bit, which, in turn, gets the heart going a little bit. I like to ski, and I frequently use a walkman. I can ski faster and better if a good song is on.

Q: Can music affect your mood?

A: Oh, sure. Absolutely. If you're down, upset about a break-up or something, put on some country and western music. If that doesn't make you cry, nothing will. It's all the same thing; she cheated on me, I got drunk, she died. (laughs) That will put you right out.

Q: Is there anything you would like to add? Any profound statements about what music means to you?

A: No. Nothing really profound. Like I said in the beginning, music is just there. It's like the air.

"It's a kind of critiquing . . . an enjoyable critiquing."

Ralph is thirty-three years old, an experienced truckdriver who was working as a busdriver for a city transit authority when he was interviewed by a male friend.

Q: What is music about for you?

A: Well, gee . . . where can I start? What is music about for me? It's a kind of critiquing . . . an enjoyable critiquing. It's hard to put a finger on. Music is just so many different things. I like all kinds, with the exception of opera. Well, "Madam Butterfly" is okay, but that's the only one I really appreciate. I basically like all forms.

I could start by saying that I was first introduced to music by my mom. I remember her singing. I was brought up with the forties' and the fifties' hits. Mom and Dad loved to play them on the old 78-RPM records. We'd do little minstrel shows. They thought we were cute.

There's some great music I've noticed in the cartoons on television, just great musical scores on some of those . . . like Tom and Jerry. There's quite a bit of classic, a bit of current music . . . as in the forties, y'know . . . jitterbug, Fats Waller, things from that era . . . but you also have things like Liszt's "Hungarian Rhapsody" . . . just some fantastic scores with those cartoons. Wagner's "Flight of the Valkyrie" becomes Elmer Fudd's "Kill the Rabbit" . . . an example of a classic piece put into a contemporary sketch. Does it take away from it? Does it add to it? I don't know; things change every decade or five-year period or so. If Wagner was alive today, he might sound like Abba.

Y'know, the masters are gone; it's a dead musical subject. You can still appreciate it though. I haven't heard of any orchestral movements being written lately, with the exception of one; but I haven't heard it yet. You don't see any new operas; they are all called musicals now. Opera is dead. Why those Italians still listen to it I'll never know. I don't understand . . . I mean Tuscany. . . . You got to be crazy to play that joint. The roar of the boos if you hit a wrong note! . . . you are scarred for life in that country. One off-note and they want your head! They are worse than British soccer fans!

And speaking of Britain . . . I should analyze what the British do. They take American music and throw it right back in our face after it's been out previously for three years, has died down; like with the disco craze . . . they came back in the late seventies, early eighties, and threw that back in our face. Then all the kids are buying it; you know it's all disco scored, but it was cool because it was "British." Black musicians had put this stuff out years before, but it wasn't cool then because it wasn't English. The Beatles syndrome . . . if it's Continental, it's chic . . . which is just ridiculous; but who am I to dictate taste? But that's what the kids want; they want their all-white rhythm bands.

I also find polkas outstanding. A Polish polka is . . . well, I don't know. I think there were Jewish influences on these things. Around 75 A.D., they were cast out. The Romans just came in and threw them out of Israel, and they all headed north. They hit the Soviet Union; they hit Poland, Czechoslovakia, Hungary, your Slavic-Ukraine countries. I think that definitely had a major influence on the polka scene, with your German oom-pa-pa band or Bier Haus bands. Polka's a little bit in the same vein. You can draw the line; it would probably end around France. Never made it to Scandinavia; it didn't travel into those countries. You find it mainly where the large Jewish settlements were.

You had the beat! I like the polka. I remember the polka hour on Channel Eleven out of Hamilton. Every Saturday I used to catch it. Some of those people were so dorky but I really dug the music. It's music to get loaded by; what can I tell you? I've been to a couple of Polish weddings . . . fabulous! We just polka the night away. My all-time favorite . . . "Polka Twist," "Who Stole the Kishka?" And then there's Big Steve every Sunday on the radio . . . "Big Steve's Polka Hour"; it lasts from 11:00 until 2:00 in the afternoon. I like that. I usually get up for work, when I have to work Sundays, and put on Big Steve.

I've been crisscrossing this country for about, oh, I'd say, ten or eleven years. I've spent a lot of time on the roads; I've heard a lot of radio stations. It's really hard to define one area . . . what they generally like . . . except you get into the western parts of Texas and it's really hard to find popular music stations. It's all country-western basically. There *are* some interesting stations out there and—it's because there's so few of them—they'll break it up. They'll have a pop, a heavy underground hit—you know, whatever, an underground group—and then they'll have a country group, then a 1940s swing group. They mix their format like that because there are so few radio stations in an area. They cover a huge segment so you're getting bombarded by all these musical forms all at once out of this one station; that's interesting.

And you go to the ultra-liberal state of California. I used to listen to one station all of the time when I was in San Francisco, and they try to portray a witty, well-run radio station. They used to have daily traffic reports by Timothy Leary, which were interesting. It was interesting hearing him comment on weather and traffic report: "Just everybody float your car four feet over and you'll get to work on time."

And then you go to a market like Los Angeles; it's ridiculous, it's so big . . . well, same as New York City. Buffalo is also a pretty big market. But the more you go through the country . . . well, you might pick up a rare gem every once in a while. Like in Dallas they have an all blues twenty-four-hour station, which is a short band. You can only pick it up so far, but it's a fantastic station; and the same way in New Orleans. I mean you pick up gems, but you have to look for them; because all the rest is just crap. Just a Top Forty format or middle-of-the-road Jell-O music. Easy listening. But you can find your underground stations; there's some really interesting ones out there. That's what I've picked out when going cross-country.

There's some AM stations in Colorado that are unique; they're playing underground or punk or whatever on AM radio stations out there. There used to be some stations in Buffalo that were that way; but unfortunately the sales weren't there, and they had to close their doors. It's changed now . . . the call letters are different. Before, it was a phenomenal radio station. It was things you never hear on AM radio; that was years ago. It probably closed down in about 1975.

I've adapted pretty good. I was weaned on the music of the fifties. My musical taste began to form in about . . . well, my first record album was Chubby Checker's *Let's Do the Twist* . . . that was 1961. I begged my mom for it. I saw it up at a grocery store here; I had to have it. So she bought it for me. I really dug that.

I still really dig those old rhythm and blues bands back then. I was mainly a product of the Beatles–Rolling Stones–Dave Clark Five era. You know, I never really cared for the Rolling Stones when they first came out. My big group was the Dave Clark Five. I thought they were it until I heard they died in a plane crash somewhere in France, which was a big rumor of the day; but two or three weeks later we found out they didn't die.

I was a Beatles generation kid. I can still remember most of the lyrics of most of the songs they put out. It's a result of constant repetition of it being drummed into my head constantly . . . just as I'm sure that like somebody who was born in the seventies . . . David Bowie . . . I'm sure that a teenager in the seventies would know the words to his songs—"Ziggy Stardust," the early Bowie stuff.

Did the Beatles direct me? Yes, they had some influence on my life. I hate to admit it, but they did. They always painted a rosy picture when I was growing up. It was all love and peace, the flower-child movement. But at that time someone who had a big influence on my musical life was my big brother. He was bringing home stuff like the Supremes at the A-Go-Go . . . blues . . . which I really think is the Lord's music. Today you can't find it anymore; there is very little of it coming out, if any.

Today's music just depresses me; it's like the doldrums between 1973 to about 1978 . . . before the new pop or new wave scene arrived . . . the punkies, the pop stars. I can see things leading that way now too with all this techno-pop. Basically I was into jazz at the time; that's when I got my jazz influences with Monk, Bird, and Coltrane. I used to listen to those people heavily back in the early 1970s. I really loved groups like the Mahavishnu Orchestra. I love jazz fusion and Jeff Beck, but there's some people I really don't care for . . . Pat Metheny. I never cared for him; why, I don't know. Maybe he has no character in his guitar. It's like a bland speed shuffle. Whereas people like Larry Coryell and John McLaughlin and Jeff Beck, Jan Akkerman . . . it's just so distinct . . . their own personal signature. But guys like Pat Metheny and that guy who played with Chick Corea, Al Dimeola, they just don't sign their work; it's all just mumbo-jumbo to me. Other people like them; they sell, right? I don't know; that's my personal taste. I really appreciated any band with a truly outstanding guitarist, somebody you can say: Ah, now this is *him* . . . I really appreciate that, the signatures.

I like to hear music that I'm not going to hear anyplace else; judge it for myself. Another phase of my life I went through, I really appreciated the blues. From about '67 to '72 was really my blues era, when I was in college. Of course, a lot of people were blues addicts then. Everybody was getting drafted for Vietnam . . . the blues were very popular back then. You had a lot of English blues groups coming out, like the original Fleetwood Mac, Peter Green . . . who I thought was a phenomenal blues guitar player, phenomenal! . . . different groups like the Hedgehogs. A lot of groups shucked it off and went commercial; that really turned me off to them. I also happen to like Beach Boy music . . . all a rip-off of black history, all a rip-off of black music . . . but white fun . . . black fun translated into white fun. Surf music was big around '65 or '66. I'll admit it; we were punks.

Ah, let's see . . . punk. Where did punk start out? Malcolm McLaren? Malcolm McDowell in *Clockwork Orange*? . . . when he played the ultimate punk, Alex? Was it Richard Hell in 1974 in New York City with ripped t-shirts and safety pins? Punk is kind of a quaint way of expressing yourself. It hasn't come to murder yet; I wonder if it's gonna come down to murder-rock? You've got savage beating and stuff like that; I wonder if it's ever going to get there. It'll be interesting to see where it goes in the future . . . looking ahead.

These days I like to go into a bar with a quality jukebox . . . go in there, dump some quarters in the box, and listen to the old songs.

"... I can't wait to come home and get back to my Neil Diamond."

Betty is thirty-six years old. She is the mother of two and works
full time in her husband's office. This interview is one of the
original interviews done by Carol Hadley [see introduction].

Q: Okay. Just tell me everything that you want to tell me about
your record collection. Just talk. Think about what you'd like to tell me
about it.

A: We've a wide variety of music. I grew up on classical music, playing an instrument, and as I got older, somehow that all got behind me,
I guess. Family . . . godparents who were in the Philharmonic offered
the tickets and things, but I've never kept up my interest in the classical music, and I'm now into what I call soft rock, which is mostly a
form of poetry set to music for the purposes that I use it for. I use
particular songs at particular times. When my tape deck was working
I would spend hours, literally hours, recording various tapes for a particular mood. Okay . . . one tape is sensuous, uh . . . a tape of songs
about rain . . . a tape of "down in the dumps" . . . a tape of favorites. I
once went through two hundred albums and made tapes. I limited myself to no more than two cuts from an album. I made up custom tapes
of music that means a lot to me.

I just *really* do use music as many things . . . as a companion, as a
stimulant. It can pull me out of a mood . . . if I'm in a reflective mood
or if I'm in a slightly down mood and just . . . ride it out. You know,
there's certain kinds of music you can do *that* with, not to get you more
depressed, just ride a certain mood out.

And I love sharing it with my children too. My son does not particularly care about it, but my daughter has a lot of the same tastes that I
do, and knows the words to so many current songs. We'll be walking

through a department store, and she'll say they're playing Neil Diamond, and it'll be some extreme version of a song that I haven't even picked up in my subconscious, you know. . . .

Q: Do you remember the first record you got, when you first started?

A: (laughs exuberantly) Yes it was a ridiculous 45 by a black group, called "Get A Job." (more laughter) And it came with a brand new record player that I got from my father. I was a teenager. The first LP that I remember that I really, really loved—that I had any kind of choice in getting—was the original Broadway cast of *The King and I*. (laughter) I played that into the ground.

Q: How old were you when you first started with these things?

A: I must have been about thirteen. We had some records, and back then my interest was mostly classical. I was playing clarinet and going a lot to the Philharmonic, and I remember we got a set . . . I can see what the covers looked like . . . green cardboard covers, and it was like one of those sets that you pick up a record a week at the supermarket, of classical music played by famous orchestras. And that was really the basis for a musical library for a long, long time.

Q: So where did it go from there? Can you take it from there to where you are now?

A: Do you mean chronologically? I can't do that without losing a few years, because of what happened in my personal life—upheaval, and not being at home, and things like that, okay? But speaking then from maybe the time I was sixteen until I was eighteen or nineteen, on my own and going to college, I was not as much into music then as I have been, and I was away from it, I would say, until I was about twenty-four or twenty-five . . . and then started picking up on some of the soft-rock sound that was coming out: Neil Diamond, James Taylor; Bob Dylan back then but I don't listen to him any more . . . but a lot of that kind of thing. And my ex-husband was mainly into classical and I was getting into this modern type of thing, and so there wasn't a whole lot of music played in the house at that time. So I think I really, really cued into it when we split up nine years ago. I *really* got into music heavily then.

Q: And at that time then, had your tastes changed completely from classical?

A: Oh yeah, yeah. Pretty much completely from classical. I can still enjoy it now and then. If someone else put on a classical record I would really enjoy it, but I would almost never walk over and pick up a classical record. It's really strange.

You know, it's funny because back in the sixties, when I was a teenager growing up, the rock was stuff like "Get A Job" or "Purple People

Eater" or "Who Wore Short Shorts," or those kinds of songs—and they were *great* songs and I can still remember them fondly, but they weren't poetry like it is today. I really feel today that it's poetry. Some of these people that are writing are so talented.

Q: What do you think you're drawn to the most, the music or the words, or isn't there a distinction?

A: I don't think so, because there's no particular type of music that I would like; what I'm trying to think is if there's a song with really tremendous words but doesn't have music that I like . . . would I really listen to it? But I really can't recall that happening. I would tend to think that for one reason or another . . . if it's a well-enough-put-together song, I don't think too often you get something that's really good poetically and yet has crummy music . . . or something that has gorgeous music and says nothing. It doesn't seem to happen too often and maybe that's a function of how good the writing is. If the writing is that good the person is probably that good musically.

Q: After you got divorced, you definitely got into your own kind of music, and that's the way it's been ever since?

A: Um hm. I'll bet we've got about three hundred albums.

Q: What kind of music do you play?

A: Mainly what I call soft rock, no hard beats, no metal guitars, no loud-mouthed noise. I like something that has different rhythms in it, and I'm certainly not averse to strings. I don't care for synthesizers too much. There's a kind of standard guitar, piano . . . I . . . I call it soft rock; I hate to say just rock because that isn't it.

Q: Your entire taste is soft rock?

A: It's all I would buy.

Q: There's no kind of jazz or blues or country or any other conceivable kind?

A: A teeny, teeny bit of country by Willie Nelson. Three or four Willie Nelson albums snuck in there, and a . . . I suppose a little bit different category too, we both like Liza Minelli.

Q: You would never call that rock?

A: No. No.

Q: Why do you collect these categories? What is there about each one of these?

A: Because *I* can relate to it. Because it relates to me. I can relate to the style of music . . . the music itself, and the beat can move me. The poetry is relevant to me and my life . . . it can make me *feel* things, and it can make me *think* things.

Q: What kinds of music *don't* you collect?

A: I would, under *no* circumstances ever have acid rock, or punk rock . . . the hard, hard rock sounds because I find them too blaring, and too intrusive and driving. I don't think you can really listen to them. You'd be very unlikely to find any disco music in my house.

Q: Why not?

A: Because I think disco music is mindless. (laughter) But that's not *quite* it. I think it's light and airy and emptyheaded and I've never heard a disco piece that I thought had any substance. They went with a beat and got stuck in it for a long time . . . the same beat, the same kind of thing, and a lot of people who had been doing different things tried to get *their* lyrics and *their* style to fit that particular beat. It was impossible, and so you ended up with nothing.

Jazz I know nothing about, so I really can't say that I would never own it, but I have none . . . and country also, except for those two or three Willie Nelson albums, and that was mainly because of the lyrics.

Q: Why wouldn't you buy country?

A: It strikes me as corny; it's too direct, there's nothing subtle about it. There's not much interpretive about it either, as I think about it now. That's one of the things I think about the complex lyrics of the music I listen to. There's a lot of interpretive quality to what I listen to.

Q: Why did you get those Liza Minelli records you mentioned?

A: Because she's such an extraordinary singer. Again, if I was listening to her sing, it would be more for the quality of her singing and treatment of the song than it would be for the artistic quality of it.

Q: How do you use your records?

A: I have never used them for just background music. I'm not the type of person to put them on and have a lot of noise and not be able to listen to them. I'll use them sometimes for playing backgammon on Saturday night because I can listen and still move pieces. I'll use them if I'm alone in the house and doing something . . . but I don't like to have them going on when there's another activity going on. For example, I'd never sit down and play a game with the family and turn my records on, because of the type of records that I have. I like to listen to the words. It would frustrate me that it wasn't being appreciated. And occasionally, when I really want to relax, I'll put on the headphones and turn up the volume, if I'm here alone, and really crank up the volume.

I also like to share them with somebody, if I can find somebody. My sister and I could come over here and put on a Neil Diamond album and crank it up to full volume; John would be out for the evening, the kids would be in bed, and the two of us could sit there and we could practically cry over songs together and share things with songs together, and it's really a great experience. There's nothing like having a song that really, really means something to you, and sharing it with another person.

I had another friend who used to be a nurse, who also loved Neil Diamond and told me . . . she was as familiar with his stuff as I was, and told me when she got married she would love to have her opening dance with her new husband at her wedding be one of Neil Diamond's songs, but she hasn't been able to find anything. And I said, "I've got exactly the song. You don't know it because it's so new," and it was from the brand new film *The Jazz Singer*, and I sat down and played it and that's what she used. It was a great feeling because she has the same appreciation for him. It was a glorious song; it was perfect for the situation. It's probably one of the most beautiful songs. She would have known it if it had been out longer. I was just more familiar.

Q: But you knew right away that was *the thing*?

A: Oh, yeah.

Q: I think in the beginning we mentioned some of the moods you used music for: sad, happy, what-not. You don't have anything to add?

A: Sad, happy, sexual. (laughter) I don't mean to imply that when I'm sad I listen to sad music, and when I'm happy I listen to happy music, and if I'm sexual I listen to sensual music. I may use it in opposition too, you know, or to intensify; really, depending on the mood I'm in, which is really nice, I think. I mean there are some days I would listen to anything, to any of them, you know, and there are some when I'm feeling a little bit blue and I would just as soon get up and going, and then I'll play something that I know will get me up.

Q: Is that always the same type of thing that'll get you going and get you up?

A: Pretty much. There's one Neil Diamond album that really gets me going . . . a good album, and interestingly enough it contains a jumble of those moods.

Q: I don't remember how you replied when I asked you about categories or types. I think you right away said soft rock, but Neil Diamond plays a big part in your musical life.

A: The biggest! Absolutely the biggest. And his female counterpart would be Carly Simon. I think the two of them have a great deal in common but I listen to him more than anyone else in my entire collection and have consistently for many years now. I have every record that he's ever put out and a lot of his sheet music.

Q: What degree of feeling do you have for this music?

A: Maybe I can give you a feeling for that answer if I tell you that when we go away a week every summer, by the end of the week, I can't wait to come home and get back to my Neil Diamond. I really feel a lack when I don't have it for a solid week. I don't miss television. I don't miss radio. I don't miss papers. I miss . . . music.

Q: Neil Diamond is soft rock?

A: Yes. And I do believe that's a legitimate term by the way. I do believe that that is a term that's used for a particular classification of music, into which falls people like James Taylor . . . Barry Manilow, probably the Carpenters—or maybe they would go with the popular, you know, that kind of thing—but America, probably the Eagles—the Eagles for sure—Peter, Paul, and Mary.

Q: I think of all those as ballads.

A: Except that they're not all; a lot of them have a rock beat, okay? If they were all strictly ballads, then you'd be talking about folk music.

Q: You didn't mention folk music as a like or dislike.

A: I had forgotten about folk music. When I was younger I liked folk music, not so much any more . . . when I was younger, about seventeen or eighteen.

Q: Do you know why?

A: I think the era. You know I graduated in '65, and really that was the time of Dylan and, oh my God, Joan Baez (laughter) . . . and Pete Seeger, and there was a whole group of them.

Q: They're still around, though? Still doing their thing?

A: I . . . don't even know.

Q: How do you store your records?

A: *Very carefully* . . . I say, with a stack of about eight of them to be put away. You'll never find a record lying out, you'll never find a turntable in this house that drops records on top of another record. You will never find a dust cover put into a jacket so that the open edge is exposed because then you might as well not have a dust cover on. It drives me crazy when people do that. You won't find too many other people operating my stereo.

Q: Are all your records in one place? Do you have a special place for favorites? Are there any in a spot that are harder to reach than others?

A: They're all alphabetical, and they're all within six feet of where I am right now. (laughter)

Q: I see some there but if you've got three hundred records, that's certainly not all.

A: Yes, those are overflow . . . when I pull them out and don't have anyplace to put them, you know. But this whole thing is full, from one window to the other (indicates a long cabinet), and then there's more in the bottom of that, filled all the way across.

Q: Oh, two whole record cabinets!

A: Yeah.

Q: What song or group would you zero in on as most important? Which single thing is most important with your emotional identification?

A: *Songs of Life* by Neil Diamond. I would say 75 percent of the music I listen to is Neil Diamond and the rest is . . . (laughter)

CARL

"I can't give it up."

Carl is thirty-seven years old, married, a father, and a jazz guitarist.
He was interviewed by a female college student.

Q: When and how did your involvement with music begin?

A: It started off when I was about seven years old. I started with accordion lessons. I can still remember how that all came about. There was
a local businessman named the Cactus Kid. He had a local TV and radio
show in which he would dress up as a cowboy and play the accordion at
a campfire. My father thought *this was it*, that is the best.

Cactus Kid also owned two music stores at the time and was re-
cruiting students for lessons at his music stores. I can remember him
knocking on our door one evening. My father just about dies, "Look
out there, it's the Cactus Kid!" He had come to see if he could get
someone to take music lessons. He brought in an accordion and this big
colored album with pictures of smiling little kids with green teeth sitting on accordions, or holding saxophones. My father just thought this
was wonderful. "Well, what do you want to take? Sign yourself up." So
I said, "Drums, I want to take drums." "No. No, too much noise, no
drums," was my father's reply. So I thought saxophone would be nice.
He said, "No." I said, "Trumpet?" He said, "How about the accordion?
Sign him up for the accordion." It all started out on the wrong foot because I despised the accordion. It was really all my father's decision. He
signed me up for the accordion. Six years and probably $2,000-worth
of accordion lessons later, I quit the accordion.

Although the accordion can be a difficult instrument, and in many
ways it's a nice instrument, it's an ethnic-oriented instrument. You can
play Italian or Polish music on it. It's not really a contemporary type
of instrument and therefore it's not something a lot of young children
really take to. As I was growing and getting to be a teenager and listen-

ing to the popular records there wasn't anything I could relate back to the accordion. I took lessons for six years and actually I did quite well with it, but I never really liked it. Finally I quit.

I guess I always liked music. I got a tape recorder for Christmas one year and recorded and bought records. I started guitar when I was fourteen years old. I was a freshman in high school. I met this guy there and one day a couple of us were at his house. He had a guitar, he was taking lessons. He sat down and played a couple of things for us. I thought it was really neat, a different sound. I didn't necessarily think about playing guitar at that point. When I thought of musical instruments I thought of the accordion and it just turned me off. This seemed to be so different. It sort of stuck in my mind. Within another year or so the Beatles came out. I was influenced by the Beatles just like anyone else that age in 1964 . . . fourteen and a half or fifteen years old. I started the guitar. The Beatles were a big influence, there was a lot of public awareness [of their music] and a lot of kids were getting brought into music.

I started out with a rental guitar. It was a little acoustic six-string called Stella, that's a brand name, a very common rental guitar. Really it's a piece of junk. It's awful, it's strings are very high on the neck and difficult to press down. I had a half-hour lesson every Saturday morning at 9:00 A.M. A friend went with me. His lesson was at 8:30. We both took lessons from the same teacher one after another. Not sounding modest, but I had a lot more ability [than my friend] and even after a month I could see I was pulling away from him already. I really liked it and could do a lot with it. I was a fanatic, right off the bat. I was an immediate fanatic.

I played that guitar for about six months. Then I really wanted an electric guitar and an amplifier, the whole shot. I remember waiting and waiting for my parents to agree. Finally my parents said, "Okay, we will buy you this guitar but after the accordion if you blow this one don't ever ask for anything else."

I remember I got this cheap electric guitar and then it was totally opposite of the accordion. My father would come into my room at 11:00 P.M. and literally yell at me, "Put it down, it's late! Tomorrow is another day. You can practice again tomorrow." I practiced every day, the amount of time varied but I practiced every day. I can remember the senior retreat when I was in high school. We went for three days to a retreat house. I had been playing the guitar for a year and a half at that time and those three days were the first days since I started that I did not pick up the guitar and practice. For a year and a half I practiced every day, even Christmas, Easter, and the Fourth of July. I remember one Christmas day . . . it sticks in my mind because I had a lesson I thought was kind of difficult . . . we were celebrating at our house, all the relatives were there. I went to my bedroom, locked the door, opened the guitar and practiced. My father had to come and say, "You have company here."

I think if you talk to a lot of serious musicians their stories are very similar. You just get obsessed and it goes from there. I was a pretty decent athelete but I didn't do anything [with sports] in school because it would take too much time away from playing the guitar. That was the choice I made. Maybe, in retrospect, sometimes it's almost an unhealthy obsession.

It all happened pretty fast. The summer before my senior year in high school I was offered a job to teach. I was really in no position to be a teacher. It was a job at the music studio level. There are a lot of young people who teach young children at music studios. My teacher felt I could handle it. He said I was his best student. He was teaching at two different stores and sometimes had conflicts and couldn't make it. He recommended to this guy that I fill in for him. I ended up working there three or four days a week for twelve years.

The psychology of it is interesting too. I remember starting out in high school. I was sort of a shy, fat kid, not unpopular but not necessarily the most popular kid, an average kid, a little withdrawn. After about a year, when I started teaching, I was getting into a band. We were *the hottest band* to hit school. All of a sudden it was like night and day. I mean everybody knows who you are. If they weren't your friend before, they want to be your friend now. I was at Springville High School but the kids I grew up with in West Valley, N.Y., were at Franklin D. Roosevelt High School. Most of the guys I hung around with were in that school system. We played a lot of their dances. We even made the school year book as "The Band of the Year." It's interesting to watch the development of how you're treated by other people. I'm sure half of that process is just getting a little bit older. One day you're just a little fat kid . . . nobody really pays attention . . . then all of a sudden you're lead guitarist in this hot band.

I got into the Beatles and watched some other bands. I pick up stuff from watching other people. Then I got into listening to different rock guitar players. Remember the group Cream and Eric Clapton. I started playing all this Eric Clapton stuff. He was like a god. At seventeen I didn't necessarily feel that I could play like him, but pretty darn close. I thought, there's got to be something more than this. I felt I was pretty good, but I didn't feel I was any world-class protege.

There was a Jimmy Smith song, "I Got My Mojo Working," that got some air play on pop stations. It was a commercial hit on a jazz album. I liked it, so instead of buying the single I bought the album. On that album was Kenny Burrell . . . a jazz guitar player. It's a whole different way of playing. I really liked it. Then I got an album that was probably the *biggest influence*. It was a Wes Montgomery album and my life was never the same! I mean that was it! He knocked me out! I mean, I was out of rock, that was over. From then on I was buying jazz albums. I was totally immersed in jazz.

After high school I wanted to go to the Berklee School of Music in Boston. It is a jazz-oriented school, one of the better regarded schools for players rather than educators. But it wasn't an accredited college and this was back in 1966 and Vietnam was on. So I couldn't go . . . because I would have been drafted right out of it. Also there was parental pressure. They said, "Music is wonderful but do something respectable." I didn't want to go to Vietnam. So, I ended up at the University of Rochester getting a 2–S draft deferment. It shifted to 1–A a couple of times and I got nervous. I happened to be able to get into the National Guard. If I had it to do over again I don't know what I'd do. Maybe I would try to find a way to put in my two years and then get out of the service. I probably would do that and then go to school afterward.

At Rochester I had a minor in music and a major in psychology. I wasn't overwhelmed by the music program. I mean it's like night and day now compared to what it was. Even when I was in high school a band consisted of playing for fifteen minutes three times for the senior play. It was nothing like what's available to kids today. Almost any high school today has a good music program. Part of the change in formal education is because the teachers, instructors, and educators are a lot younger. They're from my generation. They were determined to do something when they got into the educational system. So the whole system has changed. Sometimes . . . it is frustrating because I'm either five years too young or maybe ten years too old. If I were forty-five or twenty-five I'd have it knocked! But I'm thirty-seven and it didn't work out that way.

I worked my way through school primarily by teaching and a little bit of playing in clubs. I was in the National Guard and was on a lot of weekend guard drill. I would be gone from Saturday morning until Sunday evening. I might have lined up a job for Saturday night. I would have to pass on it or try to get out of Guard duty. Sometimes I'd get permission to leave, so I could go play, and then come back the next day. But sometimes they would give permission and sometimes they wouldn't. It really cramped my style for the six years I was in the Guard. That's probably one of the reasons I didn't go into a full-time music career. Sometimes I get really frustrated thinking about it.

Q: Did you ever consider going to the Berklee School later?

A: By the time I got out of the Guard it was already 1974. Allison and I got married in 1970. I was working so I really didn't think about going back to school. I was in various jazz groups through 1973 and then I started at Allstate where I'm [employed] now.

At that point music was at a low ebb as far as I was concerned. There wasn't much of substance or quality, and there weren't many places you could play. If I were going to go and play music that really didn't turn me on, I might as well go and work a normal day job. I mean there was just no sense doing it. It was just like putting in a day job.

Q: Could you tell me about your music "education" through 1973?

A: I just got more into playing the instrument. Then in 1970, when I got out of the Army [National Guard] active duty, I went to study with J. K. He's a jazz guitarist, probably one of the premier players around. That was a whole different thing than taking lessons on Saturday morning. What happens, when somebody gives you something conceptually in a half an hour and you walk out, is that you're really going to take years to assimilate it. When you get into a high level of playing, someone can throw a concept at you and you can carry that concept as far as you want. Years later you'll still be building on that. When you get into these more advanced types of lessons, they aren't with any regularity. A lot of teachers say: "When you feel you want a lesson come on down." There are techniques that you learn and you've got to apply them to the instrument. You strive to learn all the material . . . then "forgetting it," assimilating it. You might get to the point where you've taken a certain concept to where you've a good understanding of it and you're well on your way to doing what you want to do with it. This is where you get into the psychology of playing . . . just letting everything go, "forgetting," not thinking about the technical aspects but just thinking about the music and nothing else. It's not that easy to do. There are different aspects to playing: good ears, good time, a lot of these are inborn. For example: I have a friend who has studied for years, and in many respects is a good pianist, but he's got lousy time. I mean he always rushes. You have to make a concentrated effort to keep him under harness. It puts everybody else in a strange situation, he's always rushing away.

Some musicians are better listeners than others. There's a spontaneity of playing [in jazz]. The better listeners hear what everybody else around them is doing and get off on that. There's an element of humor,

I mean the audience laughs. I heard a story from a friend about George Shearing which illustrates this point. It was a summer night in Paris and a police car went by with a European siren on. George Shearing heard it and just worked those two notes right into the song they were playing. The audience just broke up laughing. It's incredible to be able to do that. He didn't fiddle around for a couple of notes, he knew what they were. This is an amazing example of listening, having "good ears," perfect pitch.

Q: You indicated that by 1973 you were at a low point in music. When did you get involved again?

A: From 1973 to 1978 I played but without any kind of consistency. I had almost gotten out altogether. I was frustrated with what was going on in music. It hurt too much to stay involved. The kid came along and it was tough.

Then in 1978 I started playing bass in this wedding band. There were four guys. The saxophone player had experience in commercial work, the piano player was more of a jazz musician, and the drummer was a typical Polish wedding weekend warrior type.

In 1980 I had the guys down for a pool party at the house. The saxophone player also played a little bass so I got the guitar. I sat there and played guitar and it really sounded terrible, at least I thought it sounded terrible. This was driving me crazy. I had things to do, my day job took a lot of time, but I just couldn't let this wither and die. After the party I told my wife, Allison, starting tomorrow I'm going to set aside a minimum of two to three hours every night for practice. I'll do anything, cut the grass, anything, but at 10:00 P.M. that's when I practice. I did that for two years.

Q: You practiced for two to three hours? Where did you hide out?

A: I would come down here [the family room]. Allison would be in the living room watching TV. I would put the headphones on and sit and practice.

Q: The headphones?

A: The headphones on the stereo. I was copying music off records. By listening you get something to build on. There are different ways of picking things up. You listen to what other people have done and try to copy various parts of their style. Hopefully over a number of years you can build on that, use bits and pieces of what you've taken from somebody else and then add your own ideas. You can sit down and read music off a piece of paper, play it a few times, and put it away, or you can say I'm going to look at this concept, shoot for this objective. It's like learning anything else. I see what I want to go for and give it intense practice. Practice might be reading, a certain technique of playing, or just listening, developing your ear.

It was not always that productive. There were a couple of times that I actually fell asleep. Allison would come in and wake me up. I was so mentally and physically tired a couple of times I didn't really get anything accomplished but exercise for the fingers. It was frustrating because you should be awake. I figured the law of averages: I'm blocking off time, this is mine, world you've got the rest, this is mine and that's the only way. Within two years I was asked to play with the Philharmonic. I did it!

Q: The Philharmonic?

A: Well, that's another thing I regret. Lukas Foss came back to town to do a "Tribute to John Lennon." There were three concerts. I got a call from the Philharmonic contractor. They had a rehearsal the next morning at 9:30 and another Friday. Of course I was working. Looking back on it, Allison says I should have called in sick. But we had this critical sales meeting. If only it had been any other day of the year except that one. I called back and said I couldn't make it. I recommended a very close friend of mine, an excellent guitar player. He did the job and he's done a bunch for them since. He's pretty much the guitarist on call for the Philharmonic. I probably should have taken the job.

Now there's a lot of work I don't get for the simple reason that I'm working full time and a lot of other guys are not. When a guitarist is needed they say: "Well let's call this guy because Carl is working full time." That really gets frustrating but I can't blame people for doing it. It does get frustrating to work yourself up to the point where you have the ability to do something and then there's another reason why you can't.

Q: Do you ever want to take a chance? Sometimes do you get the urge to just do it?

A: I'll make one statement. There is not a day in my life that I don't get up and think about doing music. Allison still worries about that everyday. She says, "That really scares me because I'm going to wake up some morning . . . some guitarist got sick, and somebody, he doesn't know you from Adam, says let's give this guy a chance. You call Allstate, tell them you're not coming in and you're off to New York." It's not going to happen. I'm happy with my life and family.

On the other hand, if I should get a promotion at work, and if it's really going to involve giving up music, I'm not going to take it. If they're going to transfer me and I'm not going to have access to music, I'm not going to take it.

Q: But have you thought: the children aren't always going to be small?

A: Well, that's why you try, and that's where frustration with time comes in: you've got to keep current, you've got to keep everything together, styles change, you've got to keep on top of it. You can't let it die. With the job I have now there's no way I should even be thinking about playing because there's really no time for it. Yet, I can't give it up.

Q: Have you thought about another full-time job, one closer to music?

A: I've seen people over the years love music and aren't necessarily players. They stay involved. They are D.J.s, or recording engineers, or they own music stores. Allison once said: "Well if you don't like the insurance job we could open up a music store." I could do that. I might be closer to it, but it's really academic. Owning your own store is going to take a lot of time. What I'm really driven to do is play . . . all the other stuff is not really important.

Q: What have been some of your recent high points in music?

A: There's this local place at 77 Cambridge. It's an old club that started many years ago. It's not in the greatest neighborhood. The first time I went to a jam session there I sat in the car with the doors locked and waited for somebody white to walk in. Somebody did and it turns out he was the only other white guy there. You go up these big long stairs and ring the buzzer. The people there are just unbelievable.

I can remember one particular night. There must have been about a hundred people in there. Ninety-five of them were musicians and the rest were avid music appreciators. It was just a ball. There was this one old black guy, his name's L.H., he died this last year. He had played with Dizzy Gillespie and all the big guys. L. would just sit at the end of the bar and have a couple of drinks. If someone played something that he really enjoyed, he'd get up and walk over to the bass. It was almost like the *supreme compliment*. I was there playing and all of sudden L. got up and decided to join us. I thought, "Oh, I've made it!" He was a master. A lot of guys would come in just to be with him. There's a spirit of camaraderie. Those things are great.

Recently I've been to a Sunday night jam session at another club on High St. I did about a dozen songs with great musicians. They were all fantastic. Other musicians can really inspire you. We did this one Charlie Parker song and I did a solo. Everything came out. I could feel myself playing and it was all working out. The more I played, the better it was. I was playing this chord solo on the guitar, and the funny thing was I didn't realize until it was over that there was all this applause. Everyone was applauding and there were flashbulbs. Somebody was taking pictures. The other guitarist said, "Oh man that was fantastic! Where did you get that chord thing? It was great!" Well it just worked out well . . . sometimes it does. That carried me for weeks.

Q: What's going on now?

A: Well, now I'm tied up with the kids in Little League. They are both on different teams, different nights, just about every day. So I pretty much told myself: I'm not going to do much with the guitar for the next couple of weeks. I'm just going to leave it on the side. I'm not even going to worry about it, just get these other things out of the way. When they get done, then I'm going to go back with a full head of steam. You have to psych yourself up that way. There's an article I read by Larry Coryell. What he says is: It took him twenty-five years to figure out that the striving is better than the arriving. You never really arrive, what keeps you going is that you just keep striving.

"To be the creator of it is to participate directly in that point of coherence of the earth, of the universe, of humanity, of meaning; all else is darkness."

Charles is a thirty-six-year-old music teacher and composer.
He was interviewed by one of his male former students.

Q: How do you identify yourself?

A: Well, I am a practicing musician. I am a composer of music and a music teacher. That about says it.

Q: What is music about for you?

A: Why that question? Well, anyway, regarding the business of music on the radio, that stuff is some sort of commerical industry. It is meant only to sell products that people don't even really want. Usually it's just totally fabricated . . . those people playing only for money. Don't tell me there's artistic expression involved in a radio station. It's only to sell products pure and simple; that's the only reason it's on the air. And most of the people who listen to it don't really even know what they should be thinking anyway. That whole industry is just geared to first of all create a market and then exploit it. But then again maybe I'm assuming that the sensitivity of some people is so low that they really have no real aesthetic perception in the first place. That could be true, so I can't really. . . .

To ask somebody who is willing to spend a whole lot of time . . . with all of the study and work that goes into seemingly a vacuum . . . to ask somebody a question like "What is music about?" . . . you're asking for a pretty severe type of answer. Really, I mean . . . I could be making a lot of money instead. I could have a Ph.D. in Biochemistry or something, you know. I am more mystified by what it means than other people . . .

what it means to me . . . to tell you the truth. Like for instance, why a person would want to learn to play a song . . . I have no desire to do that. I've been practicing for twenty-two years, and I still don't want to play a song. I end up having to do it, for other people. A Beethoven sonata, they're nice; they are great! My wife plays them all the time. I've even played them myself; but that's all secondary. And listening is a funny thing too. What are you listening for, what are you listening to music for? I mean I sometimes hear things that are just unbelievable, like these Griffis preludes. Charles Griffis . . . I don't know if you know him . . . he's an American composer from the early part of this century. Just amazing! Now there was something there. This guy speaks to you directly. . . .

Plotinus said something about the glowing of the eternal through the art work. Plotinus . . . I don't know if you know about him . . . he was a mystic around, well, just after Christ, somewhere right around there, around 150 A.D. But there's another way of looking at it—music as an artwork, which is the relation of the parts themselves unto the whole. You'll notice that this is a very objective way and it would be used in any good definition of an artwork. Any good artwork would have to have a coherence of parts to the whole and to themselves. In other words, the coherence of the parts themselves and to the whole will happen in any great artwork. Some people consider that to be the definition of the great artwork itself. I happen to know a certain composer who believes that is absolutely true for his definition of artistic beauty. Personally, I don't go with that at all. I have to see that glowing of the eternal behind this veil, this force.

Now what this has to do with commercial music is a complete mystery to me. And why another person would even hear anything in that stuff is, like I say, more mysterious and does not even interest me. It's just, I don't know, it's incomprehensible from that standpoint. Now you may ask what about music for enjoyment purposes, just to enjoy rather than having to see the eternal glowing, glowing from the heart of this magnificent piece. Well personally I'm not sure if I enjoy any other kind. If you can use the word enjoyment for experiencing such beauty, it's almost like hearing the voice of God . . . that's a funny word too. It's more like the point of humanity; the consciousness of man becomes concentrated in a bright point, and then there is the coherence of the universe because you are only conscious of that. There's nothing else that is going to mean anything to you.

As far as your awareness concentrating on this bright single point . . . the entire coherence of the universe . . . a great artwork brings that out.

That's the way it's been; that's what makes a classical piece or a great painting. It's always there; there are none that do not have it. It's a lot like being in the woods. For me, nature . . . it's the same thing. Maybe that's why so many great classics are rooted in nature: their subjects are natural. It's more difficult to see in something as abstract as music, of course. You can talk about Mozart symphonies or Mozart string quintets or even Bartok's string quartets, a little newer; it's always there. You'll find those pieces; they'll sneak up on you too. You won't know where. The great classics, of course, have been time-tested and sifted through by millions of people. That's why it's easy to find the absolute great wonders. But even modern things, I'm not talking about the category which I mentioned earlier; but, well, there's a market created, geared towards kids mostly who don't know what they want anyway. Boy, you've got to take some heat for that.

Every day almost, well an awful lot of the time, I'll be working steadily away because I know at this point what I'm trying to get out of music, what it means to me, and I work steadily along that path. But people come and say to me, "Can you play 'Stairway to Heaven'?" A Led Zeppelin tune I'm sure you know. Well, yes, I can play it but why in God's name would I ever want to, and why would you like it? You see, even Jimmy Page . . . no matter what he thinks about his religion, his devil worship and all that stuff . . . that bright point of humanity coming together, the coherence of the universe, etc., comes through even in rock 'n' roll solo playing. Jimi Hendrix too, a guy of course who would be considered by any organized religion as Beelzebub incarnate.

It is far better to create music than to listen to it. There is nothing better than an improvisational flight, a truly inspired one; they happen occasionally.

So anyway that pretty much sums up what music is about to me. To be the creator of it is to participate directly in that point of coherence of the earth, of the universe, of humanity, of meaning; all else is darkness.

"I like mood tapes, subliminals, and new age music. That really sets me free."

Karen is thirty-seven years old, has operated her own cleaning
business for seven years, and has raised several children.
She likes antiques, flea markets, and spiritualism. Karen and
the interviewer have known one another for a long time.

Q: What is music to you?

A: A release from the rat race. I love to sit down and just listen, and
go off into my own little world. (brief pause) I can be in a very stress-
ful situation, a tension situation, and I can go upstairs and turn on the
radio or put on a tape, or whatever, and just zone out for a little while
and I feel better.

Q: Is there any particular type of music that you listen to?

A: I've been listening to . . . I like mood tapes, subliminals, and
new age music. That really sets me free. I really like all kinds of music,
there really isn't any music that I don't like. There's some I'd rather not
listen to.

Q: What types would that be?

A: Punk! (both laugh) Heavy metal . . . I don't understand it. Some of
the beat in that is good, just some of them, it doesn't really do anything
for me.

Q: What kind of feelings do you have when you try to release yourself?

A: Well, when I do get in a situation like that, when I have to go
some place and listen to the music, I come back calmer, I feel calmer . . .
I feel that I can handle the situation. So I guess it's like a tranquilizer.

Q: So then if you were in a really angry mood and you put on something soft and quiet, it would change your mood?

A: Mellow out, mellow out, yeah . . . very easily. Just by listening
to music.

Q: Is there anything else you use music for?

A: Oh, I use it when I paint. I have to have the radio on when I'm painting or decorating. I have it on in the car all the time. I usually have it on in the house all the time and I go to sleep to it at night. Now that I'm into the new-age stuff, there's certain tapes that I'll listen to every night. Sometimes I listen to the whole thing and then flip it over and listen to the other side because I can't wait to hear the rest of it.

When I'm listening to the radio, there are certain parts in the mood tapes that take me off. If I listen to ocean surf, all of a sudden I'm back in Florida collecting shells. There's one we've got upstairs called *The Back-yard Stream* . . . you can hear the bees buzzing and the birds singing and the crickets chirping, and you can just put yourself in that situation and you're just right there with it.

Q: Do you prefer sharing music or do you prefer listening in private?

A: Well, certain times for each. I like to listen in private when I need to listen in private, but I like to share. If I find something that's very interesting, I want everybody to listen to it. I like to hear their opinions, like with the mood tapes. I usually share, I don't wear headsets around when I'm listening to it. When I have it on, it's on.

Q: Is there any music that you are protective of, that you feel, "This is my music," and you'll share it with your close friends, but if someone came in from the outside and said, "Oh, I like that," . . . would you have a negative feeling?

A: No, that would be all right with me. Because you take it or leave it, it doesn't make any difference to me. If you like it, I would appreciate you saying you like it. If you didn't like it, I would probably turn it off, if it was offending to someone, or if they really just didn't like it.

Q: Can you remember your first musical experience?

A: Probably in the sixties when I was in high school and the Beatles came out. That was just it, then all of a sudden, no matter what song came on the radio you had to listen to it, because they were either as good as the Beatles or they stunk. There was no in-between. That's probably when I started really getting into music, using it for relaxation, and stuff like that. I used to turn on a couple albums that I really liked, and they would be the ones I studied with. There were certain albums that I would do studying with and there were certain albums that I would just turn on to listen to.

Q: Are there any times that you experience music in a particularly powerful way?

A: The mood tapes. I've astral-projected with some of them, because of the visual effects it has played on my mind. I have gone with it, and I know I have. It's just like . . . like the mountain stream, or the backyard stream tapes. Nature. I don't visualize myself walking some place . . . I am there. I know I'm there. I've done that with certain people, not with just mood tapes, so I know that when I'm with a mood tape and I think I'm there, I really am there. I'm not thinking it. It's true.

Q: So then it evokes strong emotions with you?

A: Yes, I would say so, certainly the new age music does. It gets you inside yourself. I've learned to love myself, and since I've learned to love myself, I've learned to love other things. It never really meant anything to me before, like nature, like my fellow man . . .

Q: Do you sing?

A: In church. (both laugh) Not professionally. I sing a lot when the radio is on. I'll sing along with tunes.

Q: You don't strike me as the type of person who would have any inhibitions singing in front of anyone else.

A: No. Unless I had to do it by myself. It doesn't bother me if other people are around and I'm singing to the radio. I can release a lot of tension that way, too. (sings) Just before you came over I had the hymnal out and was playing hymns on the organ and Cathy was yelling out the names. . . . Some of the hymns are beautiful, like "In the Garden." If you really listen to the words in that, it puts you in a completely different perspective with your religion.

Q: Do you listen to music more for words or for the music? The voice or the sound?

A: It used to be words, but since I've gotten into the new age and the subliminal, I'm into the harps and the flutes and it's really beautiful. The harps and the flutes are the peaceful, relaxing stuff. Other than that I like to hear people play the guitar. I like to hear a little group, or a band or something together, especially when they're just starting out, because I like to hear their mistakes and see how they correct them.

Q: Do you remember any kind of music that you had never particularly liked before suddenly touched you or made sense?

A: Well, I was just talking about this. Last week I was watching TV and they had a commercial for the classics, a lot of Beethoven and Mozart. We were listening to it and I said, "Gee, that would be nice to use as a mood tape. I could really get into it." It really surprised me because I used to think it was really boring. So I guess I'm mellowing in my old age and opening my horizons, so to speak, to like different things. I guess my age has a lot to do with that.

"As I developed from childhood to adulthood, the music developed with me."

Keith is originally from Jamaica and is pastor of a church. He was
interviewed by a female student who was a member of his congregation.

Q: What does music mean to you?

A: (pause) . . . a form of entertainment.

Q: How is that?

A: Classical music is a form of relaxation after a hard day's work;
gospel for inspiration; and culture, a type of entertainment.

Q: What does classical music do for you?

A: Okay, since you're going on like that, rock music aggravates me. I
hate rock music. Rock is wild, violent, and everything that I don't want
to hear. I don't classify rock music as music, it's noise.

Q: So now only classical, gospel, and cultural music are music . . .
everything else is noise.

A: Certain cultural musics are. Rock music is a cultural I don't care
for.

Q: So you've got your own music.

A: Yeah! . . . Okay. Music is an expression—an expression that can be
appreciated by people of other cultures. It's a universal language. You
don't have to speak English to understand music. It breaks the language
barrier.

Q: (Interviewer snaps her fingers) What do you call this?

A: Snapping your fingers.

Q: How would someone from another culture understand it?

A: That don't make no sense. A dog will wag his tail. That's about it.

Q: Do you mean that there has to be an instrument with an ordered
melody to make music?

A: Certain musics have certain rhythm, but I wouldn't define that as music . . . because . . . yeah (singing and snapping fingers, stamping feet), you can snap your fingers, stamp your feet, in a certain kind of rhythm . . . but that's not music in itself.

Q: What is it?

A: That's *not* music . . . the music is in the individual's head, you see. Like what I just did, I created a rhythm but not solely by snapping fingers, I also stamp my feet. If I go over there and bang on a drum, I'm not making music. I am making noise. But playing the drum at a certain interval with the cymbal, it helps to create music.

Q: So there must be uniform music with the piano, drumset, played in the right key to make music in your ear. But tapping your foot means the music is in your head?

A: That's correct.

Q: Why?

A: Because that's my definition.

Q: Your definition is a combination of instruments played in a melody.

A: If it's in the right melody, together . . . in the same keynote . . . those instruments can create music. As I said, the music is in the individual head. Now take an artist who writes a song. . . . The artist composes a song. He wants the song this way, then he uses the instrument to make his music.

Q: Do you have a music?

A: I would say I have a concept of music that's acceptable to me, yes. If you want to say it's in my head, it's in my head.

Q: What's your acceptable music?

A: It all depends. I make my own music at times, with music I'll play to myself in my head, of course. I find this very amusing and entertaining. There are times when I'll take a certain beat and put certain words together and create my own music. The beat I usually use is reggae . . . a culture which I grew up with. Now the words to the song are religious but the music is reggae.

Q: To make your music, you've got the help of a cultural music.

A: It's my music because it's my culture. Yes, I'm creative; I create my own music sometimes, but it's naturally reggae.

Q: Well, then, reggae is your music. How did it get in your head?

A: Nobody put anything in my head that wasn't there. Reggae evolves. From the first time I heard it, it started developing. You see, reggae wasn't put in my culture . . . it developed. As I developed from childhood to adulthood the music developed with me. So it wasn't put in my head, it evolved. Reggae evolved from what's known as ska.

Q: You mean your mind has comprehended the music around you in a possessive way.

A: Yeah.

Q: That's heavy.

A: That's culture.

WANDA

"... *if I don't think of music in terms of dance, I'll think of it in terms of colors.*"

Wanda is a forty-year-old Polish American woman who teaches dance in a suburb of a
northeastern industrial city. She was interviewed by a female graduate student.

Q: What is music about for you?

A: Well, music is something I use in my business so I'm always listening to music . . . because I want to know what I'm going to use for
a certain dance and I'm looking for the beat, the melody. I always think
of music in terms of dance. It's funny, what I listen to at dancing school,
I don't like to listen to at home. Not the music with the big strong
beat . . . it upsets me . . . it makes me feel that I have to keep moving. . . .

Usually I visualize to the music . . . it's very visual. I think of colors
and dancers. Even when I'm feeling in love and happy . . . I think
of people dancing and I play appropriate music. Times of feeling very
noble, trying to accomplish things . . . I'd listen to "The Impossible
Dream" or Broadway shows.

Q: When you're feeling noble . . . you like Broadway show music?

A: (laugh) Yes. Things like *Man from La Mancha*. When I have an
idea and some people don't think it's too great, I like to listen to music
that supports my feelings.

When I was feeling depressed, in times of divorce (laugh), I'd listen
to serious classical music. I haven't listened to that in a long time, so I
haven't been too depressed lately.

I also listened to country music with the different lyrics. I don't particularly like country music. But when I was depressed and I listened
to the down-to-earth lyrics (laugh) . . . that sort of seemed soothing.
(laugh) Now, I don't listen to it at all. . . . It was at a time when I was
getting divorced and they have all those lyrics about the man leaving

you and sort of down, low music. That's probably the only time in my life that I listened to it.

Q: So now do you hate country music?

A: No, I just don't bother putting it on.

Q: Would it make you feel depressed if you heard it again?

A: No, it really doesn't have too much relevance in my life. . . . I don't care for it too much.

Q: So when you're depressed you want to stay in a depressed mood?

A: Well, I don't think I should talk to other people and burden them. I want someone to understand me . . . if you put on music that is depressing too, it seems like the music and you agree. I don't listen to it for a long time . . . you get over that period . . . you stay in it for a while, but then get on with it and put on happier music.

Q: You said before that music is very visual to you. What are some of the things you visualize?

A: Okay, if I go to a concert, I can't just sit there and listen to the music. First of all I start by watching the musicians and actually think about what's going on. But before long . . . maybe because I don't know that much about the different instruments . . . if it's a soft sound, I'll start thinking of people dancing and I visualize colors. I sit there and think of my own type of ballet. And it changes right away to a dance . . . and it becomes very interesting to me.

Some people will ask, "Oh, weren't those flutes great?" or "What about the drummer?" By that time I'm already into my dance and I probably didn't know that it was the drummer doing it. . . . I might think that part was great for a ballet duet. I don't realize what the musicians are doing. Maybe everyone does this . . . I don't know. I've often wondered, what do people do when there's no dancing going on?

Q: Since music is so much a part of your work and since you don't like this period in your life . . . it's all work, work, work . . . do you think of music as something you don't even want to listen to?

A: No! It's not that. Music is associated with my work, that's fine. But I've been doing things that I hate to do, things I don't consider artistic. I've been so concerned about paying bills, and other things . . . not artistic things. Those are so unmusical things, so when I'm thinking of those things, I don't play music.

I like music for when I relax or when I have the time to feel depressed or happy . . . then I'll play the music.

I like music that I teach to . . . sometimes I'll play some music that I work with when I'm doing other things, like washing dishes or dusting, because I don't have to think about that activity.

If I'm paying bills or something, I don't like to play music because I get too involved with the music.

When I eat, I play nice music because if I play other music I feel like I have to chew faster. (laugh) Music makes you feel like you've got to get involved.

Q: When you said you listen to music that you teach around the house . . . it's not like a dividing line between work music and music for relaxation?

A: Yes, right. There are certain songs at dancing school that I don't like to listen to a lot. I don't care for some music we use in jazz class. It's funny . . . music that would be good for jazz class with a good beat but that I don't have any ideas for it . . . I won't listen to it at home. If I'm doing a dance to it and I have ideas, I listen to that music and I'll think of different dance steps like, "Boy, that sounds like they're really turning here."

If I hear a song that I can't think of any ideas for . . . the music becomes very aggravating to listen to. Shut it off.

Q: You said before you think in colors. Can you give me an example?

A: Well, I was also an art major in college. I think of music and colors. I think people may stereotype . . . like a soft song may go with cool colors, maybe blues. But that's not necessarily true.

I think of it in terms of painting . . . colors blending. When you hear some dynamic music . . . you may think of blobs of red, then it's mixing with yellows. It's kind of like finger painting, taking different colors and throwing them on with water in the background and all other colors swirl together. As the music unfolds, you see the colors moving and blending. They aren't just sitting there. It's like they are reacting with one another.

Q: Kind of like the instruments interacting with each other?

A: Yes, like when different instruments come in . . . a different color will come into the picture and blend in. So, if I don't think of music in terms of dance, I'll think of it in terms of colors. And then it seems like I'll see the whole scene . . . the colors become the lighting on the stage or the dancers in different costumes. It makes an interesting picture.

I used to teach art class for an eighth-grade homeroom for one year. I really didn't like it too much. I had kids that really didn't want to be there. But a few times I brought in music or things related to dance and had them do action drawings with music in the background and that worked out great. It affected the way they worked. They really captured the action.

Then we did stuff with mixing different colors to music. So music is useful for many things. Like quieting down a class, wild little kids in a tiny tots dance class, and it also quiets down an audience before a show is about to begin.

Q: You don't like rock music?

A: I wouldn't put it on for myself. I don't like the lyrics. I guess I'm sort of reserved. I'm not opposed to love and sex but I don't like those things openly stated. It seems like they are pounding those ideas into you.

Q: So that's what you don't like about the modern music?

A: Yes, the overstating and forcing of those ideas. If you listen to that music all the time, you're always looking for the highs, everything has to be on a spectacular level. There is no balance. And life isn't like that and you may be disappointed. People should have a variety of things . . . what you read, what you listen to.

Q: So music is a nice balance in your life, if you like variety. You said you listen to lyrics. Do you listen to the music more or the lyrics more or both together?

A: I don't know, sometimes I don't even get the lyrics. If I like the music, then I'll try to figure out the lyrics. Either both together or the music more.

In some Polish songs, I really like the lyrics, they really go well with the music and it's interesting. Or from certain Broadway show tunes, like from *Chorus Line* . . ."One" and "What I Did For Love." They need both lyrics and music, sort of like a marriage.

Q: When you said earlier that you visualize to music and you have your own perceptions of music . . . but on MTV they would visualize for you . . . does it bother you?

A: I don't like that. I'll be watching it and I'll see the different characters and I'll think, "Gee, I never thought of it that way," and they sort of destroy it for me. It's like they're trying to sell you a package. This music has to go with this idea. I want my own idea. I like the Michael Jackson videos because I think he is clever with his dancing. But even there you feel limited because, if you want to make a dance to the song and you don't do what Michael Jackson does, people think you are doing something less.

Oh, another thing I didn't tell you about music that I use is Polish music . . . a lot of that music, I really like to listen to. I find I'm listening to music now that's very old-fashioned with very strange instruments. And they'll use archaic words that I don't really understand but they're appealing to me. Generally Polish music aggravates my family— my kids—and my other guests so I'll play that when I'm alone.

Q: Can you tell me why you started getting into Polish music?

A: Well, I thought, here's a part of my background and culture that's just being lost. I started teaching my own kids a few songs and explained what they were. I was going to send them somewhere else to Polish folkdance but I thought "I want to do it myself." I started to learn about the different regions of Poland and their different instruments, it was interesting and fun to listen to.

Then I started to read about the history and listen to Chopin. Now I like to listen to the folk music and see what else I can discover. The music demonstrated the spirit of the country and the majesty. Different instruments go so well with the type of character and the jokes they are singing about. A lot of the lyrics are sort of sexual, but it's not very openly stated. You have to figure it out. It's very interesting.

People will mention to me about different composers and I feel I should know more about them, like Chopin. This is what I'll listen to privately.

Q: Kind of educational?

A: Yes, I feel like I'm learning things. I think you should be open to different kinds of music and discover new things.

STAN

"... if I don't know it perfectly, I won't do it."

Stan is in his thirties. He is a married man with children and was
interviewed by a female friend who was once one of his employees.

Q: Why don't you tell me a little about yourself, anything that you
feel makes you a little different from anyone else.

A: Different, huh? God knows I've been called "different" enough
times. Well, my name is Stan. I am a food and beverage manager. I've
been in the restaurant business most of my life, even though I keep saying it's not really what I want to do. I've done a lot of traveling, most
recently Poland, France, and a few parts of Italy. I lived in Florida for
five years. Now I'm back in Buffalo, for a little while at least, but I'm
thinking of renting out my house and doing some traveling or building
the recording studio I was telling you about.

Q: Please tell me about the studio again.

A: At first I was going to remodel the basement into another apartment. Then I was thinking of remaking the basement into more offices,
but I can barely rent the ones I own now. So I was talking to one of the
guys at work, and he was talking about moving out of the house and
asked if I was interested in renting out any of my places for him to live.
He didn't care if it was finished or not. We talked a real lot about music;
he was in California working for a real recording studio for the past six
months. Anyway, he's got me really interested in the idea of building
myself a recording studio in the basement and buying some equipment.

Q: I hate to sound stupid, but what does one do with a recording
studio in one's house if one doesn't record? Is this going to be like
the baby grand that you bought because you liked the way it looked?
Remember, you don't even play piano!

A: I told you, I'm going to take lessons. I still mean to. You just don't
find baby grands for $800 these days. A baby grand is a gorgeous thing.

Besides, it kind of means something to me to say I own one, kind of like my house or my Mercedes. With the recording studio, I was going to rent it out to some local talent: bands, singers, whatever, to cut demo tapes. Besides I might use it myself someday.

Q: I'm glad you brought that up. Tell me a little about yourself musically.

A: I play the violin and give violin lessons to children. I always say I'm going to quit and this year I really meant to, but one of my kids is really good, shows a lot of promise. I'd hate to leave him hanging. I might just drop everyone but him after the next concert is over.

Q: When and how did you begin to play violin?

A: I think I was about eight. My parents initially forced me into it, and I loathed it for the first few months. I swore then, if I was a father, I wouldn't make my kids take any kind of lesson at all that they really weren't into. But . . . now I really am glad my parents made me stick it out because I'm still really into the violin.

Q: Your musical background goes much further than that, though. Tell me about your different choirs.

A: Well, right now I only belong to two. One is a church choir and one is affiliated with the college. Originally, I started singing in them for the money . . . we get paid for concerts that we put on, and for singing in church. But now, I don't know; I still really enjoy it, and the people have become some of my closest friends, but I hardly ever make it to all the practices that I'm supposed to, and I feel guilty just showing up to sing, and collect the money. I probably will have to drop one, but I don't know which one. Probably the church because I really don't like our new director. Although I've been saying I want to find another church to sing in, so I'll probably be right back where I started from. Probably worse, because the church and people would be unfamiliar to me.

Q: Would you have your son or daughter join in a choir?

A: I don't know. I had an experience last week that would make me say no.

Q: What do you mean?

A: (silence)

Q: Do you not want to talk about it?

A: Well . . . I don't know. I had a solo last week that I really didn't prepare for. I was so embarrassed. People said that I did great, but I know that I didn't.

Q: What makes you feel that you didn't?

A: Well, first of all, I have to say that I hate making mistakes. I won't sing or play violin in front of anyone, family, friends, anyone, unless I know that I won't screw up. It really pisses me off to make mistakes at all, let alone in front of anyone.

Q: So you mean if you haven't done it flawlessly at home, you won't do it in public?

A: Of course. I won't make an idiot of myself in front of all those people. If I don't know it perfectly, I won't do it.

Q: But what about the time leading up to the point where you do it perfectly? Obviously you are going to make some mistakes somewhere before you reach the point of perfection.

A: Yeah, I suppose.

Q: How do you feel if you make a mistake while practicing?

A: God, then I feel terrible enough. My wife and I were just talking about this the other day. She's an amazing flutist. Well, she practices in front of me all the time, and I think that is just great, but I won't play in front of her unless I have something perfect.

Q: Really? You are embarrassed to make a mistake even in front of her?

A: Of course. I won't practice in front of anyone. In my old apartment, I would only practice during the day when I knew my neighbors were out, so they wouldn't hear me make an idiot out of myself.

Q: That's the second time you have used that phrase "idiot." Do you really think that if you make a mistake it makes you an idiot?

A: Of course.

Q: Why do you think you have such a hang-up about people hearing you?

A: I really don't know. I don't mind performing in public at all as long as I don't make any mistakes doing it. I really don't think it has anything to do with the public. I just think it has to do with my father, from when I was a kid. He used to really piss me off. I would be upstairs, and he would be downstairs watching TV or something and . . . wouldn't you know it . . . every goddamn time I made a mistake, no matter how small or how loud the TV was, he'd scream up the stairs, "You screwed up again. Do it over."

Q: Do you think that someone will yell at you if you make a mistake?

A: Of course not. I know nobody will yell at me. I mean, I'm an adult for God's sake, but I just don't need the hassle or embarrassment.

Q: Do you think all of that affects the way you perform in public?

A: Probably. I'm sure that is why I am such a perfectionist in everything I do, not just my music. Because my father was always on my back, any time I messed up.

Q: Do you think you will ever reach a point where you won't mind making a few mistakes in front of someone?

A: Probably not.

Q: Do you feel more at ease singing in front of people than you do playing the violin?

A: Not really. Why do you ask?

Q: I was just wondering if your experience with your father listening to you practice the violin rubbed off on your singing.

A: I don't think so. I really don't feel comfortable making mistakes in front of anyone regardless of what I am doing, be it work, or playing a sport, or whatever. I really don't think it has all that much to do with music or my family. It just has to do with me and the way I am, the way I was raised.

Q: Remember you telling me that you were going to start taking piano lessons to justify buying the baby grand? Well, at some point during your lesson, you will probably make a mistake because you will still be learning. Your teacher will be hearing your mistake. What will you do?

A: I will probably just make sure that I am really prepared for my lesson, so that I don't make any mistakes . . . or at least not a lot of them.

Q: You must have made mistakes when you were first learning to play the violin during your lessons?

A: Yeah, but even then, I remember just about every one of them, and I went home and made sure I had them real polished for the next time I had a lesson.

Q: I'm getting the feeling you are ready to change the subject.

A: Gee, how could you tell?

Q: Lucky guess. Anyway, you've always told me how important your heritage is to you. You have intentionally stayed in a Polish neighborhood, you speak Polish, and you like Polish food. Does any of this carry to your musical taste? Do you associate yourself at all with ethnic music?

A: Probably. As a kid, I had to take polka lessons. I really like polkas; they are a lot of fun. I won't dance, though.

Q: What do you mean?

A: I hate to dance. I won't dance in public. I think most guys look like jerks when they dance except the really good ones, and I'm not stupid enough to think that I am really good.

Q: Have you ever tried to dance in public, and had a bad experience?

A: No. Like I said, I won't dance at all in public, so I've never had a bad experience. It works out kind of nice that way.

Q: Do you think you feel the same way about dancing in public that you do about making mistakes in public, that you would feel like a jerk?

A: Oh, I am sure I would, but I'll never find out because I will never dance in public. Ever. People always say that no one pays attention, but that's not true because I always watch the people on the dance floor, and I notice who looks like a jerk, and who looks fairly normal.

Q: Well Stan, thanks for the interview.

A: Hey. Do I get to read this thing, and edit out all the parts that make me sound stupid?

OLDER ADULTS

"I actually become what I hear."

Richard is white, in his late forties, a hospital worker, and was formerly
a professional dancer. He was interviewed by a male foreign student.

Q: So, what is music about for you?

A: Well, it is a . . . I suppose, a kind of tonic or a medication of sorts.
It enables me to feel better usually, even if it is a small piece or sad piece.
I feel some sort of relief when I'm listening to music. I can be trans-
ported or get out of myself or my immediate surroundings and . . . take
a journey on the melody.

Q: Does music affect your mood?

A: I'll say. In fact, sometimes some selection can make me cry . . . you
know, a sad sounding piece in a minor key . . . or, say, sometimes the
words are very sad, combined with that type of music. I actually become
what I hear. It affects me greatly. In fact, I very often . . . when I'm upset
or I need to feel calm . . . I won't put any music on the radio that's loud
and irritating. I will play something quiet, slow, so I can channel that
quiet music, or old-fashioned music . . . . (laughs)

Q: Can you clarify to me what you mean by "old-fashioned music"?

A: Yes. Old music for me will be music from the twenties, thirties,
and forties. And when I was a young boy, I was able to memorize a lot
of lyrics and melodies I heard then. My grandmother sang a lot. And so
from her I learned to sing, and I learned a lot of lyrics that cannot be
found anywhere—songs that are probably little known to England. So,
obscure and old music as that. And to me, new music will be from the
1950s on. I learned less after the fifties. I absorbed more before, when
I was a younger person. And I find out . . . to the fifties my interest
was lagging. I didn't care for a lot of music that was played, so I started
creating music on my own that I like to do.

Q: So how do you start creating music on your own?

A: Well, I suppose that I became somewhat bored with music that I had been playing, or that I had heard so much for so many years that I decided that it was time that I would try to make up some lyrics or melodies of my own from the mass storehouse of information that I had gleaned through the years. And I just wanted to express myself instead of expressing the ideas of other people. I would just sit and strum a certain chord on the guitar and let my thoughts go rambling and jot down the ideas or the stream of consciousness and then add some melody with it or create a melody as I went along. And it turned out quite nice. I found that people enjoyed it, and people often thought when I was playing in a night club that I had learned the material from someone else, or it had already been created. But what I was able to do was create on the spot . . . melodies, you know, just to ad lib, and I feel that I was much more satisfied with the feelings in the moments with the music that was in my soul as opposed to someone else's ideas or musical flow.

Q: What is the significance of the "1950s new music" to you?

A: Well, I suppose it's the coming of the Beatles. They changed everything, I feel. You know, the total feeling of music became more lively, or more personal, and I really have to say that it had some life to it. It was like a brave bold step in a new direction. The fifties was a very exciting period, and everything became more upbeat. Rock'n'roll, of course, developed with Elvis Presley. And I really have to say that it was fabulous and wonderful. He was very exciting. He, all his tunes, were generally upbeat, and he used his body to express the song. And that added to the things that he sang. In fact, it added greatly. It was like an exclamation or a very emphatic way to thrust his music into the public . . . . (laughs)

Q: Do you have a favorite music?

A: I certainly do. I find it a . . . a singer named Billie Holiday, who sang the blues, affected me greatly when I heard her sing. And she wrote a lot of the songs and even had some of the melodies herself . . . you know, developed the melodies of her own. And she sang the blues, and I could relate to what she was talking about. And she sang a lot of love, and how great it is, and how painful it is, in the final analysis.

Q: You could relate to what she was saying?

A: Oh, I could relate to . . .

Q: To your own life?

A: Yeah, to my own life having something like the loss of love, you know, having been depressed over a loss of someone. She sang about that sort of thing. And so I had the blues. And then I naturally listened to the blues, and I always select to hear a song that she would sing to accompany my suffering. . . . (laughs again)

Q: Did you ever notice how music affects other people?

A: Oh, I certainly do. Because of the kind of work I have been doing these last years. And I see that, if we play pleasant music for people, they sit calmly, and they're very sociable with one another. But if you're playing something that is very harsh or loud, like fast music or rock'n'roll or something, I notice that a lot of times people will become agitated and also with one another. Sometimes people will then get up and start walking around and talking aloud, as in competition with the loud or fast music. And I'm talking about the situation with the mental hospital. I work in the mental hospital. So it's very important what kind of music you play, let's say, in a disturbed ward. . . . (laughs) Music calms the savage beast.

Q: What do you think about the MTV channel?

A: Yes, well, Music Television is very exciting. I've become addicted to it. I prefer now to sit and watch Music Television for hours. It has a certain quality to stimulate my own imagination. And a lot of the videos they show accompanying a song or the singers or the players of the musical instruments are just like a dream, oftentimes like having a nightmare or some fantastic flights of imagination. And so, it's very stimulating. And I think MTV will grow more popular as time goes by.

They show a wide assortment of groups. On MTV, they have rock'n' roll artists, and they have singers who sing slow songs or blues. I notice, though, a lot of rock'n'roll on MTV. And rock'n'roll is very stimulating and exciting. I mean, it seems like the performers do a lot of crazy things. They throw their bodies around and fall on the floor, and they climb on top of furniture, and they smash things, and they scream, and they holler, and they tear their clothes off, and it's so incredible, and they shake their booty.

Q: What performers do you like on MTV?

A: Oh, my all-time favorite is Tina Turner. She's a very famous black singer of rock'n'roll. She's like the mother of rock'n'roll. She's very great. She moves her body so well, and she sings with great passion, you know, sexual passion. And they have close-ups of her face where she is breathing deeply and sighing, and telling everyone how hot she is.

Oh, yes . . . (laughing uncontrollably) T-i-n-a-t-u-r-n-e-r! She brings tears to my eyes. She's hilarious at times because of her movements and her facial expressions. She wears tight leather pants and very, very, you know, tight jackets, and she fastly moves her lips around, and she's oftentimes, how would you say, sticking her lips a way out, you know, and it looks like she's ready to eat you. . . . (more laughter) She's very seductive. I mean, her facial expressions are very intense as I said before, and the thing I noticed is that they give a close-up of her and come right very close into her lips, and her lips are very large, and they are painted with a very bright red, you know, and I feel completely captured and enveloped with her, with her lips as she sings the song.

And so the words at that point become very important and I can actually become excited just listening and looking at the music television there. I'm always especially looking for Tina Turner. She sings songs of unrequited love. Or one of her latest songs is "You Better Be Good To Me," and another one is called "What's Love?" But I mean, she's absolutely amazing. She's forty-six years old and yet she looks like a very young woman, and she dances very well too.

Q: Do you think that modern American music has any redeeming quality?

A: Oh, yeah. It's quite beneficial for people to have something to fill the void, I mean to feel about. And a lot of times certain songs are presented in such a way that they give hope to people, you know, they make people feel better, or they have some kind of religious message or just a friendly message, and it can help the general populace. People can be affected by the lyrics of a particular group singing about particular things that pertain to the everyday person. And, generally, music is fun and light-hearted. The majority of MTV music is even laughable. I mean it contains all these different elements that enables the persons to enjoy themselves, to laugh, or even to sing.

Q: Do you think music can be a tool for other people?

A: Oh, it's definitely a means to an end. You can get an idea across in music without actually saying anything . . . just the feeling in the music. It conveys a message. Oftentimes it's subliminal, and, well, they use music to sell products on television. It's a very powerful tool for people to convince others whatever they produce is good and to get people to buy their products. So it's one of the best tools for the commercial industry in this country or anywhere in the world.

"... *country and western is the only ... adult music.*"

Stella left Greece when she was eighteen, and has lived most of her
forty-nine years in the U.S. This interview was conducted by her husband.

Q: What's music about for you in your daily life?

A: My daily life? Music is a huge imposition. My son plays the drums
whenever he gets a chance. My husband plays the drums, plays the
thumb pianos . . . and everybody, EVERYBODY, considers it a great af-
front if I don't particularly feel pleased with the music they play. So on
the whole it's an assault.

That's why I love listening to music in the car when I am there because I have to choose from what is there. So I turn to the Continuous
Country, or if it is not that stupid jerk in the morning on the campus
station . . . those silly things . . . I may find some nice jazz or something.
Or something in between those two stations.

Q: So the only place that you really have music of your own is when
you get in the car?

A: Yeah. But I sort of see that as an accommodation, because the car
does not have much choice, and there is a lot in the car that I don't like.
Because right now the music I don't like very much is the kind of music
that's there. So that's what's happening right now.

Q: So that's your current daily life. Daily life is the assault inside the
house from your son and your husband, and having some music that
you like on Continuous Country in the car.

A: Yeah.

Q: What would you say is *your* music? If you had your choice?

A: (whispering) I don't have anything that I consider "my" music.

Q: What about Savopolous and all that Greek music?

A: Well, it's not mine, it's a couple million other people's.

Q: Tell me about what you like on the Continuous Country.

A: In the Continuous Country, John Conlee.

Q: Why do you like John Conlee?

A: Well, I like him a little bit for the same reasons I like . . . (pause) Frank Sinatra.

Q: You like John Conlee for some of the same reasons you like Frank Sinatra?

A: Yeah! Conlee has a very nice attack. He has very nice expression. He is very leisurely. He sings meaningful, corny songs. That's it.

Q: Nice attack . . .

A: Well, you know, he has very nice timing, so he sort of starts at the right place, he says it in the right way, he expresses himself. I mean, I can hardly imagine that guy singing anything, and not just doing it right. I mean it's just a very nice, absolutely . . . you know, the expression, and the *way* he sings, and the inflection, and the note treatment, and the timing, and the music all go together, and the lyric, and they are out to wipe you out!

Q: What about the sound of his voice?

A: Aaaooooww! The sound of his voice sounds like sixty! Like he's sixty years old. And I saw him, and I still can't remember him as he was. He's short, fat, and about twenty-nine or thirty years old. I keep thinking of him like I thought of him before . . . sixtyish, a kind of ravaged, seasoned old man.

Q: Yeah. Who else do you like on Continuous Country?

A: John Conlee I love the most. Otherwise, I like many songs, but I don't remember them and I don't remember who sings them. The one thing I know, I don't like what's his name . . . I don't like Nelson. Willie Nelson I hate. I think his approach is . . . I hate the kind of songs, the kind of rowdy, male-bonding songs, eeeyagh, I don't like. His voice is expressionless. That kind of controlled twang just says nothing. There is nothing about him that I like; I think he is a waste. Oh, I like Charlie Pride a lot. A whole lot.

Q: For some of the same reasons you like John Conlee?

A: Yeah. Charlie Pride is a great artist.

Q: So within the country and western thing you know who you like and dislike?

A: Oh within the country, yeah! I know which things I like. I think country and western is the only music that's an adult music. With words, okay? Frank Sinatra and those guys are essentially singing the teenage and twenty-year-old kind of concern sixty years later . . . so that's no big deal. But country and western is really written for adult people with adult concerns. It has to do with achieving, or usually non-achieving, at work. It's about evaluating yourself around the thirties, the forties and the fifties. Facing death. Facing failure. Facing repeated failures. I like it! (both laugh)

No, it's about real life! I think all these intellectuals are leading country and western lives, but they all up their noses at country and western music and they like other kinds of music, but I don't know what the hell they think they're doing. So I find that country music is about the only one that I know right now really trying to be a music and lyrics for mature people, dealing with midlife crisis, and everything a decade up and a decade lower than the midlife crisis. That's important.

I don't see it . . . like some smart-alecks say it's depressing. I think, and I consider this a very good percentage, that I usually like one-third of the songs I hear there, on a good day. One out of three is a good average, songs that have something, a very good average for turning on the radio. I mean some of the stuff I hear there is atrocious. I think the bonding kind of party songs are awful.

Q: The male party songs?

A: Those songs and some of the other things are absolutely hackneyed. But on a good song, when the cliches are given reasons as to *why* they became cliches, that kind of meaning, you know, worked into a paradigm, they are very powerful songs—about the only ones that say anything about my life, and where I am. Kids, work, middle-aged love, betrayal, limitations in terms of body and past history, hopes, starting new, all kinds of things. That's what it is for me. The radio.

But aside from the male party songs, I still usually listen to the men.

Q: Why do you suppose that is?

A: It's a kind of sexual . . . it's a sexual music. In the same way that I think teenage music is sexual music. It deals with the sex role type stuff.

Q: So you feel more sung to by a man?

A: Well, no, I hear some good women too, but John Conlee and Charlie Pride and some other guys are just very impressive, in ways that I haven't heard any really impressive women singers. Sometimes you hear very strong women, with that kind of catch in the throat that rips your heart apart, very good timing and stuff. Once in awhile you hear an extraordinary woman singer. Dolly Parton is good for a nice rowdy song, but she doesn't have much subtlety either. And I haven't been hearing Loretta Lynn and those guys lately, at least on the radio. Maybe they are even playing more men. You see my thing is just from listening to that station. You see I don't play my own songs, because if I play the songs, I usually *listen* to the song. I can't listen to the song and do other things. So I don't play songs mainly when I'm by myself. Maybe I should do that.

Q: For awhile there you were playing Savopolous and a . . .

A: I played Savopolous for something like six months, the same songs over and over again. That was just an unusual passion.

Q: That was last spring, before we went to Greece.

A: But I don't work when I have that music, I think about the music. That was kind of a special situation. I don't remember listening to songs like this, unless when I was a kid.

SALLY

"It can make you cry, and then other times it can really perk you up."

Sally was about fifty years old when she was interviewed
by a female graduate student.

Q: Why don't you tell me a little bit about yourself.

A: Well, I was born in 1938, so I was a teenager in the fifties, the famous fifties. I have four children. My husband has been dead. I'm self-supporting . . . uh, an average person.

Q: What is music to you?

A: Well, when I was growing up music was never . . . nobody played an instrument, it wasn't really important to anybody . . . until we got to be teenagers. Then my sister and I used to go to a place where they used to have the High Teen show, so my sister and I used to go to that. We saw the people that were popular back then, like Bobby Rydell, Gogi Grant, and things like that . . . things that you've probably never heard of. It was a teen show . . . something like Dick Clark, only not on that big of a scale . . . a place for teenagers to go, and they went and we danced.

There was live bands and there was music. That was the beginning of the real exposure to music, probably when I was twelve or thirteen. Then we would listen to the radio all the time, my sister and I, in our room or while we worked around the house. Music was just something that was always there in the background.

Sometimes I really like quiet, just quiet, so I'll put on an easy listening station or a tape. Sometimes I like a lot of noise. I like a lot of fast music, especially if I've got a lot of work to do and a little bit of time . . . because, if I play fast music, I find that I kind of pace myself to the music and can get a lot more done. It's funny, at Christmastime, I can't bake Christmas cookies unless I have carols on, because they put me in the mood. (laughs)

At work, sometimes they have the radio on . . . the easy listening station JOY on . . . and it kind of puts you in a relaxing mood and then sometimes I wish they'd just put it over the whole PA system, so that the people in the rooms could hear it too. It seems to have a relaxing, calming effect on some patients.

Music can make you do a lot. It can make you cry, it can make you laugh, it can make you stop . . . really stop . . . and listen, it can make you think . . . well . . . now you see this can relate to this, or this could relate to that. When you really sit down and listen to a song like "Abraham, Martin, and John," you think, "Well, why did they die?"

There's a new song now, I haven't heard it yet, but the girls at work were talking about it, it's called "Yesterday's Child." They said, "Wait'll you hear that one; you're going to cry." The song is all about old people, and I work with old people. They said that "you're going to see a lot of your patients in that."

So sometimes you'll hear a song that will remind you of someone who is dead, or remind you of someone that you knew and don't know anymore, or maybe it'll remind you of a situation of time that was and isn't anymore. It can make you cry, and then other times it can really perk you up, and lift you up.

If I was to sit down and write a song, the mood I was in at that time is going to be in that song, but if you're not in that mood when you hear the song, it's not going to mean the same thing to you. So I think music . . . when you write it or when you hear it . . . it's a very private, very personal thing.

How do you interpret hearing it? I mean five people can hear the same song and get a different interpretation of it. So I don't think music . . . as you asked before: does it have to be a private thing for you? No, because if I listen to music and it makes me cry . . . I'll cry . . . it doesn't bother me. If you can't stand to see me cry, that's your problem. If it doesn't move you, fine, something else will that doesn't move me. Or sometimes you'll just say, "Oh . . . isn't that pretty?"

Lots of times you'll listen to a song and you'll say to whoever you're with, "I never realized that song was about that." Then you can talk about it.

Over the past two or three years I've gotten involved in religion and spiritualism. Lots of times you'll hear a song and you'll say, "You know, you could interpret that song as very spiritual . . . ." There's a lot of songs like that.

Like I said, everything depends on your interpretation of a song, the music, the music itself. Sometimes the music is enough, sometimes the words are the thing. That's how I feel about music. It's almost always a part of my day. I can't think of one day that I've gone through without listening to music in one way or another.

Q: Are there any times that you experience music in a particularly powerful way?

A: (long pause) Hmmm, yes, okay . . . I would have to say if I'm in an upbeat mood, and upbeat music is on, it doesn't really make any difference, I'm still in a good mood. If I'm in a sad mood, or if I'm in a bitchy mood, or just . . . you know . . . this bluesy music that comes on . . . that's going to bring me down. Whereas, if I'm in a bitchy mood, and good music comes on it's not going to make a bit of difference either. I'm going to enjoy my bitch, so just leave me alone, because I earned this here self-pity period, and I'm going to have it and when it's over with . . . why . . . then everything will be fine. Music can't bring me out of a funk. It can make me go deeper into one where I can really enjoy it and luxuriate in it, you know, and you think, "Oh, this is great."

At Christmastime I think music really adds to it, because it's the holiday music and just knowing that EVERYBODY around you is in the same mood. Listening to the same music makes you feel better, makes you feel like maybe there is some hope for this old globe after all. Maybe there's some cohesiveness after all. That's it, I don't know if that answers your question.

Q: Does music work on you in any stimulus-response, cause-and-effect ways?

A: Yes, like I said before, if I'm already in an up mood and there's good catchy music on it'll get me moving more. I'll be more cheerful. It will cheer me up . . . more so if I'm in a normal or more cheerful mood. Not that I'm depressed. I'm very rarely depressed, but when I am, I feel like I've earned this . . . so I'm going to enjoy it. And then I don't want to be cheered up.

It's something that comes from inside you and music can enhance it, but it had to come from inside you to begin with. If we were a nation of people that music could drastically change our moods . . . gee, that would make a good book, think of the potential there. That would be like being manipulated by the government, being manipulated by outside groups, by other groups that want to control your mind.

Q: Do you think the media manipulates people's musical tastes?

A: I don't think it manipulates them. I know there is MTV and the video hits show. I think it caters to and encourages couch potatoism. I don't have MTV at present, and I won't get it. Summer is coming and if you're sitting around on the couch all the time . . . come on! Go outside and do something. Blow the steam off, take a walk, play baseball, play basketball, do something outside. You shouldn't have to sit twenty-four hours a day in front of the radio or TV watching these jerks. I used to like Michael Jackson. Now I've had him past my eyebrows. I don't care if I never see him again. He doesn't even look like himself anymore. I'm tired of hearing him, and seeing him on TV commercials. That may be the only thing that I would say would be manipulative, that would be to have somebody that kids look up to sell a certain product.

Q: Do you think it's scary, in a way, that these people kids look up to are not necessarily good role models?

A: Yes, because he is a perennial Peter Pan and he's refusing to grow up, which is feeding on to a lot of kids now a days that are refusing to grow up. They're not facing the world head on, they're looking for other ways out. No, I don't think he's a good role model at all.

I, honest to God, can't think of one pop singer that's a good role model . . . unless you want to go for somebody older. There's one group—Earth, Wind, and Fire—that does not allow drugs or alcohol to be used by any of their band members. I was very impressed when I read this interview with them. I was very impressed, I thought that was great. Maybe it would reverse the peer pressure . . . like Ozzy Osborne, and all those other guys, that says . . . well, "you've got to eat rats to be popular."

Q: Do you play any instruments?

A: Only the radio. (both laugh)

Q: Well, do you dance?

A: Only with the baby. I grab the baby and dance around with her. Not really.

Q: What do you use music for?

A: I should say relaxation, but, really, background noise. Sometimes I like it real quiet, sometimes I use it as a crutch to entertain the baby. When I put her down for a nap and I put on soft music, it kind of lulls her. I use it to go to sleep at night, I use it to relax other people around me. I use it to set a mood . . . a background mood, just to make them relax more. You might use it for upbeat if you're having a gathering. Instead of sitting around looking at each other in silence, at least there's a little background music to provoke conversation.

To set a mood and relax. To enjoy. Sometimes I'll just sit down and listen to an album because it's a favorite of mine. Sometimes I'll put an album on just so I can forget what I'm doing, especially when I'm ironing. I put music on just so I don't have to concentrate on the fact that I'm doing the most hated job in the world. I just listen to this music and what I'm doing with my right hand doesn't have any bearing. That's about it.

". . . the type of music that sells today is for that age group that really doesn't care about the words."

Frances is fifty years old, was born and raised in
Londonderry, Northern Ireland, and came to America after
World War II. She was interviewed by her son, a student.

Q: What is music about for you? What role does music play in
your life?

A: Well, music has always played an important part in my life. Because I find it's probably . . . one of my deep loves is the love of books,
the love of words, the written word, and music would play the same
role. Because if I didn't feel . . . if I were very low and didn't want to
read, then I would play a particular piece of music, or turn on one of
the FM stations. And if I were feeling a little lugubrious I'd put on some
Chopin, or some Beethoven, or Bach, or Mozart, or something of the
classical type of music. And if I was feeling very up and cheerful and
bright, then I would love something more jivey or rock-and-rolly, or a
romantic love ballad, so that's how music would . . .

Q: (interrupting) So are you saying your mood dictates the music
you listen to?

A: Oh, most definitely. For all, I believe, for everyone, I think one's
mood is the type of music, you know. I think music can make you feel
happy and gay . . .

Q: But would it ever be the other way around?

A: No, I would not naturally put on or choose a piece of music . . .
but if it came on and I was feeling in a happy mood, and say it was a very
pensive type, a very sad ballad of unrequited love or something, then I
might think, oh what a sha— you know, how sad, I could relate to the
words. Perhaps that's why in modern music today a lot of the songs . . .

their elocution is so poor that you don't understand what the singer is trying to say, unfortunately, so you . . . you don't know what they're actually singing about.

Q: Because of your great love of words, is that what you listen to in most of your music?

A: Yes, I would definitely have to say that the words and the emotion of what musicians try to put across in their music is very important to me. You could have a wonderful piece of music, and yet if the words were meaningless. . . . It's very difficult in today's music to really find something that has wonderful music and interesting lyrics.

Q: Why do you think that is?

A: Because the type of music that sells today is for that age group that really doesn't care about the words. Much of it is just meaningless, and I've noticed that they often repeat the same line in the vocals. Whatever the written sentence is they'll keep repeating that through the entire song. So it doesn't take much to write a song today. (laughing) It's the same sentence over and over again; pick up anything at all and you'll notice that each line is not different. It's just maybe the beat that makes the rock-and-rollers go out and buy it, and that's what makes the music world go 'round . . . the bottom line is what counts . . . dollars and cents.

Q: Why are lyrics so important and what do you get out of them?

A: I think that sometimes the lyrics can be interesting, depending on who's writing them. I think the country and western singers seem to write more about everyday occurences, I don't know why, but I think their type of balladeering, their type of music, is more about life's experiences . . . working on the farm. Dolly Parton wrote about the coat of many colors that her mother gave her. People hearing those songs know that they're real things, that really happened, not just someone sitting down and trying to write a hit. That's why I think you'll find all country and western music is sentimental . . . more so than hard rock, which has to do with the occult and drugs, which are certainly not very uplifting topics to write about.

Q: Obviously much different from the music you listened to when you were growing up.

A: Well, when I was growing up, generally the songs that you fell in love with and remember reminded you of when you met some very charming guy and you danced and that was your favorite song. I remember, for instance, when "The Last Time I Saw Paris" had come out, which was a beautiful piece of music, and I had been to Paris just three weeks before. I had a very good time and met some very interesting people, and I remember . . . even to this day, all these years later (laughing), when I hear (sings) "The Last Time in Paris," it just immediately takes me back in time, and I have fabulous memories, what can I say? (laughing giddily by this time) So I do believe even in today's world that you can still relate to boy meets girl . . . dancing . . . a favorite song . . . I don't think that has changed, feelings don't change.

". . . if I were home cleaning by myself during the day I might put Pavarotti on and have it shaking to the rafters!"

Violet is in her early fifties and married. Her children are grown.
She was interviewed by her future son-in-law, a graduate student.

Q: Who are you? How would you describe yourself?

A: Probably the average person. I don't lead an over-exciting life. I work, take care of a family. I'm quiet.

Q: What does music mean to you?

A: Music means a lot to me, believe it or not. (laughs) It's been around ever since I was young. I used to sing in the school choir, for instance, and I enjoyed music, you know, at that point in my life, when I was in grammar school. So it had to be . . . what . . . ten, eleven. I used to sing a lot before that.

Q: What, just around the house?

A: Oh, yeah. (excited) Oh, yeah! When I was a kid . . . you know how parents will read to kids? My mother would buy songbooks, and we would always sing. You know, my brother and I would sing all the time instead. Also my cousin in New York is an opera singer. And as a young person I would go there for the summers, and she would always be practicing and singing her . . . her music. And I would sometimes go to her master with her. So I got the opera influence.

Q: Did your parents listen to music?

A: Oh, yeah. Oh yeah, my father loves music. My mother likes music. My father especially likes to sing, and you know we used to have hi-fi . . . no, even before the hi-fi, before stereo and everything now. (laughs) As a matter of fact I had bought myself a hi-fi when I was still single. Now that goes back quite a ways.

Q: Did you buy records and stuff?

A: Oh, sure. Different types, different kinds that were popular at the time. Um, and then because my father did like to sing, I bought Al Jolson and Mitch Miller and, you know, that type . . . sing-along type, popular music.

Q: What kind of music was popular music when you were growing up? It wasn't the Beatles, eh?

A: Oh, no! No, no, no, no, no . . . . (laughs) Well, when I was growing up it was the big bands. Um, as a matter of fact I used to go to Crystal Beach to listen to the big bands.

Q: Live.

A: Right. My brother played instruments. The sax. Though I never did, I've always loved the piano. But it was too expensive for me to get a piano and play. I had always wanted to take piano lessons.

Q: Is that why you have a piano here now? (gesturing to piano in living room)

A: Exactly, yeah . . . . Oh! Another thing, my grandparents owned a piano player, a piano with the rollers. I used to go there as a kid and just pretend I was playing the piano and you know I'd do that all the time. Both of my grandparents owned one of those.

Q: As you were growing up did your musical interests change at all or not?

A: It changed . . . I'd have to say . . . for instance, I didn't think I even liked western music, but my husband liked western music when we first got married and I got introduced to that type. And I learned to appreciate that. I like all different types of music. I think I'm a mood person for music, it depends on what mood I'm in. In the morning, I like very soft type music; if I'm alone in the house doing housework, I might put something on that's got a nice beat to it to kind of spur me along; and in the car, I have another type music.

Q: Well, you were saying that you got interested in western music . . .

A: Not that I'm that great on it. You know, I'm not thrilled over it, but I can appreciate it. Yeah, I can. I can appreciate it. And I remember . . . going back to growing up . . . when I was still a teenager and the jitterbug was very popular, and there was a lot of that going on and I used to like that.

Q: Did you like to dance?

A: I've always had two left feet, but I love to dance. (laughs)

Q: You said you used to go see big bands. Did you like live music over recorded music? Was there a difference to you?

A: Because I was young and single, the whole thing was Crystal

Beach. You go on a boat, you go over there with your friends . . . it was the whole thing . . . a night out. And you'd go and stand around and listen to the band. There definitely was a difference. You were just all around it. Or I should say it was all around you. And, yeah, yeah . . . I like, as I said, I like all kinds. I like dixieland . . . even growing up. I always did. It goes from one extreme to the other. I like all kinds at different times.

Q: Well, wait a minute. How about your kids' music?

A: (pause and laughs) Rock'n'roll? I've learned to tolerate it, and sometimes enjoy it. It depends.

Q: I heard you went to a Bruce [Springsteen] concert once.

A: Well, yeah! Oh, that was Bruce. I had to find out what he was all about. (laughs) It was kind of exciting. It was an experience. (laughs) I've never gone to anything like it. But that's today's . . . today's age, today's music, today's kids, you know? Loud and, you know, different.

Q: Would you say music has gotten worse?

A: Different.

Q: Just different?

A: Yeah, I don't think it's ever gotten . . . you can't say it got worse because probably years ago people thought music was bad then. And you have the same thing now. I mean, today's music we'll appreciate tomorrow.

Q: So, most of your music listening is . . .

A: Usually on a weekend. Say, uhm, that . . . you know, if . . . if I want to just listen to music on a weekend I don't appreciate the weather/news, you know. On the weekend I like nice soft music first in the morning, and then, as I wake up, I might change my mind about . . . I might change my music pattern.

Q: What's this "nice soft music?" Could you describe it more? Is it strings or . . .

A: A blend of things. It definitely wouldn't be rock, you know, your rock'n'roll. It would be more your string instrumental, you know, soft, nothing . . . oh, okay, 102 FM . . . is that it, here? Or it's 107.9 now, I guess. That type. Or even, it could be vocal but it would be . . . Frank Sinatra, that type. No (laughs) . . . no rock! De Tah De Tah De Tah . . . no bouncy! (laughs)

Q: Did you ever get into the Sinatra thing?

A: You're talking about way back? Frank Sinatra and Bing Crosby were rival enemies . . . when they first started. The bobby-sockers liked Frank Sinatra and, uh, so . . . I guess they got along fine, but it was this camp and that camp. I guess I really didn't side with one or the other.

Q: I don't see you as a person who is very open with music or likes to share it with other people. Is that true or not?

A: (laughs)

Q: Do you share your music with other people?

A: No, well, I keep it to myself because my husband has taken over the music in the family. (laughs)

Q: Do you resent that at all?

A: Yeah, yeah. Because I've got my opera records in there which I never played. (laughs) I don't think that anyone else is interested in my music . . . what I like. Everybody has their own likes.

Q: When you're home alone, do you ever sneak to the stereo?

A: Oh, yeah. I used to . . . yeah. Not so much now, but, yeah, lots of times I would . . . you know, if I were home cleaning by myself during the day I might put Pavarotti on and have it shaking to the rafters! My husband wouldn't be home to say "put it down," or "put something else on," or "do you have to listen to that?" Because I . . . for some reason, when I listen to that type of music I like to hear it loud. (laughs)

Q: Do you have music in your head at all? You know, a tune going on in your head?

A: (pause) I did. You know, when my kids were growing up, I didn't always think of them, but I'd make up little things. And a couple of times, they came out now, when I'm older. So, I kind of get a funny look from them . . . . (laughs) So, I don't even go on with that.

Q: Does a song on the radio ever stick in your head and you can't get rid of it?

A: Oh, yeah. Oh, it drives me crazy! When I'm working, that's all, you know, I'd think about a tune, and it would come out and it would just go on, yeah.

Q: Some people say they have music always going on in their head. They sometimes just tune in to what's going on in their head. But that doesn't happen to you.

A: Oh, yeah!

Q: It does?

A: Oh, yeah, lots. I . . . I can catch a tune or a part of it and it could even be at church, you know you hear some music there that doesn't want to . . . but it can be anything. And . . . and I think about it often and it just keeps going.

Q: Is there anything you wanted to add about music in your life?

A: I think we'd be kind of lost without music, no matter what kind it is. I think it gives everybody an upbeat in life . . . . Whistle a happy tune! (laughs)

"Regardless of what it is, somebody likes it."

James is a black man in his early fifties who was interviewed by a
male neighbor. James works as a mechanic and is a Vietnam veteran.

Q: So what's music about for you?

A: Relaxation. Entertainment. It washes away the trials and tribula-
tions of the day. If you're feeling bad, I guess, a little music can change
the mood for the day. But I like *good* music. I don't know what you'd
call the latest fad; I don't like that too much, but I do like *good* music . . .
regardless of who's playing it. I don't have no preference on that. Good
hard jazz. Some rock and, ah, old blues. I'm not really hip on some of
the latest stuff. Maybe I don't really come into contact with it.

Q: Yeah. One of the reasons I came to talk to you is that we're about
the same age, and I figured, you know, we'd get slightly different per-
spectives on some of the same stuff.

A: Well like, you know, when I go to work in the morning I listen
to one or two stations, an FM station and an AM station. I was listening
to one FM station and that was with Joe Rico in the afternoon. Well I
don't know what happened, but he used to come on at four o'clock so I
could catch him on the way home. And the guy played all the old jazz,
back like, say, from the forties and fifties and into the sixties. And then
something happened to the radio station, I don't know . . . just don't
play now, so I lost out on that.

Q: What? The station just stopped broadcasting?

A: No, no. The station didn't stop broadcasting, but Joe Rico is not
on there any more. I don't know what happened to him. Plays a lot of
good music.

Q: That was like the main thing that you were looking forward to?

A: Yeah, in the afternoon coming home. Cause, I don't know man,
like, if you hear too much of one thing it burns you out. Like a lot of

the guys that I work with they may be into . . . the kids are into the hard rock stuff; the older cats are into country and western; and there is only a few down-to-earth jazz cats that, don't make no difference which way it goes, they'll listen to anything as long as it don't burn them out. So, it's kind of refreshing when you sit down in your car in the afternoon and hear something that you really haven't heard, or you don't have at home on a record or a tape, and you hear it, and it brings back memories of something.

Q: So what do you do with Rico off the air, in the afternoons?

A: Well, I still play it, man, because . . . I don't know what it is, but they play good music. They got something, every now and then they drops a little something that I like.

I'm not into nothing loud. Like . . . I like . . . Grover Washington down there. (gestures downtown) They had "Pieces of a Dream." "Pieces of a Dream" were for the benefit of the younger set. Grover was nice.

Q: So music for you is relaxation, entertainment . . . and what was the third thing? Shifting a mood?

A: Yes, sir.

Q: Let's take each one of those, one at a time. Relaxation. How does it relax you?

A: Ah, well, I don't know. For me, I mean I could probably go over there (points to stereo) to the box and show you. And I could play anything that I want, anything that I'm thinking about.

Now normally, with my job, you wouldn't think that I would be into music. I work with a young fella named Jack. And we used to play . . . I can't remember what station it was, but at that time they allowed us to have radios. We'd put us on some music and we'd step through any project that we had on the job. They took the music away and it was just like putting us out on the field again, you know. We don't have radios on the job anymore. The guy we work for says "no gettin' down, no dance hall" . . . just doesn't want music at all.

Q: You think you were producing more when you had music?

A: You know, I read something about GM someplace one time said that they would pipe in music and they had more work done. And you see this with a lot of heavier manufacturing places, you know, where the noise level is not that great, they have music.

Even if you dial up some of the repair shops and stuff like they have around town . . . hey, if they put you on hold, the telephone even plays music. There's gotta be something to it. But this cat he just don't like music. I don't think he likes what he's doing either.

Q: Tell me more about you and Jack, you said you were stepping through things.

A: Oh, hey, we could step through anything, it didn't make any difference.

Q: What music would you have on when you were doing that?

A: Just plain jazz. I forgot what station it was.

Q: This was a couple of years ago?

A: Right now I don't believe you got too many real good jazz stations in town.

Q: There were better stations with better music back then?

A: Yeah, I think so. I really believe so. You know, they play some nice music around; I don't get a chance to listen to radio that much. And that's why I say drive-time in the morning and the evening for me is about the only time that I would listen to the radio. The record player in my house, with my two grandkids here, each one of 'em has got different preferences in music; one's got a stereo set in the back, and if you played it right now it's all bumpty-bumpty-bump, you know? It's like one of those bump and grind shows because the music all sounds the same. It's all the same beat. There's no variation to it. That's bump and grind music 'cause that's all they're doing back there you know.

Q: What do you use to relax with? What's the first thing that pops into mind when I say relaxation?

A: Okay. All right. To play a little relaxation music, I could go with Stephane Grappelli. You understand? And if you really wanted to swing, I could probably say, ah . . . little Groove Holmes or something like that. A little organ music. It's not gonna be really loud or nothing like that, but you know, you could set a nice groove and just go on about whatever you wanna do! You see, the record player is only gonna play one thing. And the Akai that I had, the kids relieved me of it. It would play . . . go to the end and stop and reverse, and come back and play again. Now I don't have that so I'm just limited to what my box will play.

Q: You mean you can mellow out only twenty minutes at a time?

A: Yeah, well, then it plays the same thing, but with the tape on it would just go to whatever you want to have. But, ah . . . hey, listen, I heard some Etta James the other day. And I was trying to ask my wife . . . because it has to go back, I don't know if it was Etta James or Etta Jones . . . but I know someplace up in the attic . . . if I just happened to have the time, I was gonna go up and dig out some of those old records. I mean *old* records. I got 'em in the attic and upstairs, y'know, got to keep 'em away from the kids because they don't have no value on these sides. If you went down to the record store and tried to buy some, you can't get 'em! I tell ya, I went to get a Stanley Turrentine the other day, and I can't remember what it was right now, but they sent me a note back in the mail. Just says, no longer, not available. So you hear stuff like that and if you don't have somebody that's got it already, or you can't tape it or something like that, you just don't never hear it.

Q: For entertainment? What's good for entertainment?

A: What artists? I like to see someone like Brazil 66. Someone else I saw that was fantastic as far as what it takes for them to *make* music, and the way they done it . . . . 'cause really, I just have my attention to watch these cats *do* it . . . now I went over to the . . .

Q: The minute I say entertainment you think about seeing something, as well as hearing it.

A: Right. Seeing and hearing. Because if you hear it on the radio, or you play a record, you don't really realize what these cats have to do in order to make this terrific sound. We went down to see an old vocalist; it was Betty Carter. And she had three younger fellas with her, and you just couldn't imagine that these young guys could make this much music. Outta sight man. And this I enjoy doing. I don't like to get dressed up, 'cause I want to relax when I go. I enjoy going down to the Tralfamadore. And sometimes I catch some shows at Shea's. And in the summer I really like Artpark. Now, I try to make as many as I can; and I think the biggest trip I had this summer was with my wife, and somebody else, and I missed getting good tickets inside and I went out on the grass for the violin player, Jean Luc Ponty? And I'll tell ya, the girls, the older ones, they had never seen nothing like this, this was really nice. (chuckling softly) Get your basket, get your blanket, and get out on the grass and let the cat perform, going into whatever he wants.

Q: So the relaxation and the entertainment overlap? You wanna go someplace where you can relax and be entertained.

A: Yeah! Right. Now I have to say this about Buffalo. In the early fifties there was a lot of places you could go. It was like a strip. You could go on the West Side into a couple of places. You could come on the East Side and on Fillmore, they had a couple of places. And downtown . . . they had Jan's, you had Balfour's. I can't really name them all now. When it comes time to think about it, if my mind really made up to think of the old names . . . there were so many groups and places with a *lot* of entertainment. Now, I would imagine that you would have to say this was class B entertainment as far as the groups. And then you had the Royal Arms, you have guys like . . . well, you could catch Jimmy Smith different places in town, all kinds of groups.

Maynard Ferguson used to be at the Dellwood. Chubby Jackson. A lot of sidemen from Kenton would come to the Dellwood ballroom which was at Main and Utica, and you could dance upstairs! Well, that's long gone. There ain't nothin' up there now, probably just fall in the floor, but it used to be the best dance hall and they had dance bands and stuff that would come up there.

There was so many things that you could do. You know every joint that was in town at that time . . . like Mandy's would have a lot of blues. Mandy's was strictly a blues joint. You could go down there and hear Big Maybelle, or, ah, any blues artist like that. You go up to the Zanzibar and Dinah Washington was there. What's the trumpet player's name? Cicely Tyson's husband? . . . Miles Davis. People like that would be at the Zanzibar.

Then you come up on Michigan Avenue and they had a place was the Cotton Club, you run into class B outfits. Then you could go to the Pine Grill which was on Jefferson Avenue, and you still have class B joints.

Now I mean class B places. Jimmy Smith started coming in there. They had a guy named, what's the violin player's name? Richard Otto, and his wife was on organ. You know there were a lot of groups, a lot of groups. This place used to be fantastic for entertainment. Then you had the local guys who played like at the Anchor Bar. The old standby cats, the musician's local down on Broadway. They had Sunday afternoons. But now we're talking '49, '50, and early '60s.

Now Buffalo just ain't got any place for them to come. Just look at the unemployment and everything. An evening out, man . . . a guy can't talk about no $25 tickets. Or if he spends $25 for just the tickets, him and his wife, he ain't got much more. I don't feel there's that much money around. I mean even though you see the younger kids . . . like out at 2001 where they jump up and down and all that, those jump-up-and-down joints. But I don't know . . . somebody was down at the Tralfamadore, some other violin player, and the early show was all the older people. But the second show, it looked like Ringling Brothers was comin' to town with all them clowns, y'know. Oh, hey, it was time for me to leave then.

Q: But what do you mean clowns? Everybody dressed up funny?

A: I don't understand it. Course I might be old-fashioned. But (chuckling) I ain't kidding you, man. I enjoy sitting, watching them. But everybody seems to know what they want to listen to, and that's the way they go. I don't knock 'em for that at all.

Q: So for you the entertainment thing is like getting out there, being able to relax, and being able to go to a club, go to a place and see how the music is created. See as well as hear.

A: Right. Yeah. See what participation will do. But, see, the thing about it is, you go over there and turn the record on, but all you're doing is listening to the music. You see this guy like Stanley Turrentine will come down to the Tralf and bring in . . . I don't know the names of all the side men, but he always has a nice group behind him. And watch the people get involved; and watch him set a mood in the crowd; watch everybody coming down. And you're sitting there watching around the room and you see the room change, y'know. From each individual piece that he plays. Everybody don't understand everything that he plays, but sometimes during his set he's gonna hit something that everybody wants to hear.

I saw Bobby Bland when he was down there, and it was an entirely different crowd. Everybody that comes out brings an entirely different crowd. David Clayton Thomas was down there one night and a lot of people don't know nothing about David Clayton Thomas, but if you know anything about Blood, Sweat, and Tears . . . you gotta know him. Ya understand? But you never really paid no attention to him. Now this guy has gotta be a local cat, I believe he's from either Toronto or some place close by here. And he filled the house up. With an entirely different crowd. And you'd be surprised who comes to listen to who.

This is another thing (chuckling) that amuses and amazes me, because I just like to go out and see! Who *is* going to be there.

Q: So you're curious to see who your fellow fans are. What surprises you when you go to hear somebody and see a different crowd than you expected?

A: What surprises me . . . ? Just how much effect these people have on people. How they get the message that they want to send out . . . out to the crowd . . . and they really take care of business.

Q: So how about the mood change part. You said relaxation, entertainment, and to change your mood. How does that work?

A: I don't know. I guess I'm getting old; sometimes things bother me. If I feel like things are getting down a little bit tight I can come and play something that I know I enjoy hearing. It ain't no high as far as say getting high off alcohol or something like that, it just change me, and I don't have that feeling no more, down or nothing like that.

Q: Who will do that for you?

A: I really like Bill Withers. I like Bill Withers for years. And nobody really says anything about him. Course lately, he's had a couple of hits. I dunno, I guess I kind of grew up with Bill and I just like the way he takes care of business, nothing loud, ragged.

Q: Is there any music you positively hate?

A: None.

Q: Even the bump and grind kids' music?

A: I'll take it. I don't take it steady, but I'll . . . I always been brought up like this: Regardless of what it is, somebody likes it. You don't have to be in love with it or anything like that, but just be aware of it. And everything that you hear comes from some kind of ethnic background, and from somewhere. So why do you want to be narrow? Hey, I went to Europe, they had brass bands in Germany with the oom-pah thing. If you couldn't drink no wine or beer and sit out there in the park and listen to them, what else was you gonna listen to? You weren't going to hear Kenton or nobody.

Even when I was in the Far East. I didn't know nothing about their music, but in Thailand and Korea, in Japan, everywhere I went there was something different about it. Thai music is outa sight. There again, it was like religious or something; I wasn't hip to what it was, but these gals would dance and you could never touch these chicks. They would do a very good job. And the music was just something different.

You hear a lot of guys saying, "Oh, I'm a country and western buff." Like the guys at work. I get to looking at 'em. Now all these kids say they're born here in Buffalo, or Niagara Falls, or the surrounding community. What the hell do they know about country and western? They don't know nothing about bluegrass, except what they hear on the radio. But if you go out on the road as a driver or something, this is mainly all you hear, because that's gonna go from coast to coast. But as you get to Chicago, or the midwest, you get some midwest jazz, or east coast you got that. But jazz, you're either going to hear it early in the morning, or you're going to get lucky and pick up an afternoon station for an hour.

Q: But country you can pick up anywhere?

A: Just to tell you how it is. Charlie Daniels is a swinging dude, and so is Willie Nelson. And these guys don't only play bluegrass, or down-home, or whatever your country and western is. They play anything. This makes me know the cat is a well-rounded musician. This is good. Willie Nelson will knock you out in a live performance. And I always thought that, if I had the chance, I'd like to go down to that birthday party they have there down in Texas. But I don't know if I could cut the crowd. A whole weekend with so many people, that ain't my meat. I don't think I could make that.

Q: So a common denominator running through your music is the skill of a person? Across race, creed, and national character . . . ?

A: It don't make no difference. If they've got the skill . . . I can talk with them.

"I would say thirty percent of what I know about life today was gleaned from songs."

Steve is fifty-seven years old and works as a salesman.
He was interviewed by his daughter.

Q: Dad, what does music do for you?

A: What does music do for me? Well, music relaxes me. In order for me to explain, I have to go back and give you an idea exactly how my whole life was affected by music. For example, when I was five or six years old, my mother and father had come from Poland, so naturally all music played at home was ethnic music. This established my ethnic heritage. I had a love for Polish music. Later on in life, like at Polish weddings, they played mostly Polish music . . . since we lived in Cheektowaga and there is mostly Polish people and a Polish parish. My love for Polish music gave me enjoyment when I was growing up and it carried on all these years to the present time.

But naturally as I got educated in the English language I started going to the movies. I was raised during the depression and, at that time, the biggest form of escape was musicals . . . people like Dick Powell, Ruby Keeler, Eddie Cantor, Al Jolson and Shirley Temple. These were big stars of their day and in order to relax and forget your troubles . . . we all went through hard times . . . everybody enjoyed musicals, they were the biggest thing at that time. A lot of musicals were shows from Broadway so, as I was growing up in the depression and watching movie musicals, I was also getting acquainted with hit tunes that came from Broadway. In that era, Tin Pan Alley was an expression for the place where all these song writers used to write and compose music, and these songs became the hits in the musicals.

Later on these writers went to the movies and it seemed as if every month there was a new hit song that everyone was singing. Some of the writers, like Irving Berlin, Gershwin, Jerome Kern, Harry Warren, and Sammy Kahn . . . some of these songs are the prettiest songs that were ever written. Even though I never played a musical instrument or was a singer, I was like hundreds of thousands of people in my era who loved music. In fact, radio was very popular at that time, so you heard music constantly on the radio, in the musicals, and all my life I could sing a song all the way through, knowing the tune *and knowing the words.*

Later on in life, when we get to W.W. II, music used to inspire patriotism, and also to bring you closer to home when overseas. For example, one place that just meant music was the Stage Door Canteen in Hollywood. All the stars of the movies and musicals used to volunteer their services and entertain everybody. Later on, as these stars went overseas and performed for the G.I.s, I had a chance to see a lot of these stars in person—stars that I really enjoyed, seeing their movies and listening to their music. So it was like bringing home to overseas. Of course, there was a lot of patriotic songs that stirred us . . . we were young . . . say, the Air Force song like "Praise the Lord and Pass the Ammunition." There was sentimental songs like "There'll Be Blue Birds Over the White Cliffs of Dover," "I Heard a Nightingale Sing Over Barkley Square." But it was actually music that helped you through tough times like W.W. II, the way music helped you feel better during the depression . . . in days that I was younger.

When I came back from overseas . . . now I'm entering the romantic part of my life, in my early twenties . . . it was the era of the big bands. One of the greatest events in music history were bands like Glen Miller and Benny Goodman, the Dorsey Brothers and Sammy Kaye . . . big bands were popular at the time you used to go to local Candy Kitchens and play the jukebox, and, just like some of the songs said, it was a wonderful time to be with your friends. Good clean entertainment; you listen to the jukebox, dance on the dance floor.

In the big band era, we get into the popular singers who used to sing with the big bands. They went on their own and the era of the ballads was born, and to me this was my favorite era of music in my life. I'll mention some of the big singers just to give you an idea of what I mean—singers like Bing Crosby, Frank Sinatra, Doris Day, Margaret Whiting, Jo Stafford, and Perry Como.

The time of your life when you meet the "girl of your dreams." I was fortunate that we had the Canadiana. It was just like the Love Boat of its time. They used to have a band, and you used to be able to dance on the dance floor. If they didn't have a dance band that night, they would play records, and you could listen to music riding on the lake at night under the stars and moon. It was unbelievable, that particular part of life. It's a shame the younger people of today couldn't experience, not only the boat, but a lot of the things we went through. We thought it was tough at that time, but it was the music that really made things a lot happier and the reason why it's so easy for someone like myself to hear a song and just place myself back in time, at exactly where I was. Was I in the Philippines, or Tokyo, or on the boat? What were the songs that were playing when I first met my wife, what were they playing when I was a young recruit in the Air Force? All I have to do is hear the songs and it'll just take me back in time and I will relive a lot of the parts of my life and, of course, you only remember the good parts! (laughing) You don't remember the bad.

Music to me is very important. One thought that I wanted to mention, about going back in time: when I was just five or six years old, my parents, because they were from the old country, played Polish music, so that when I did meet the girl I was going to marry . . . every couple has a favorite song and ours was one that was very popular at that time . . . it was a Polish song to which they put American lyrics. The song was "Tell Me Whose Girl You Are," and I think it was because my wife and I came from a Polish background that Polish music was still a very important part of our life.

Q: What music really did for you was to make you get through bad times and made you think of good things mostly, right?

A: Well, yes, and I would say that music became part of my personality. I use music to not only relax, I use it to relieve tension. About thirty percent of the time I am singing, and it has become part of my personality because it has given me a certain amount of assurance. Not only does it relax me but I think it also bolsters my confidence in being a salesman where you have to always be up. You can't be depressed. Otherwise, you're just going to waste a day. I think music to me is also something that bolsters my spirit.

Q: Does music amplify your mood or does it change your mood? For example, when you're in a depressed mood do you put on something slow or something happy to get you out of that mood?

A: Well, when I was single, if my love life wasn't going right, I used to play sad songs. Well, I guess like most young kids when their love life isn't going right they turn to sad music. I know that after I'm married and have children and more experience, if I get in a depressed mood then I switch to happier music to change the mood.

Q: What do you think about today's music?

A: (laughing) I could give you enough swear words. . . . No, seriously, I will answer you. I can do it right off the top of my head because I was in a restaurant this morning and I heard a song being played on the radio, which was supposedly a big hit by a new big star. Supposedly this fellow is just as big as Michael Jackson. I think his name is Prince, singing "All Night Long" [Lionel Richie], and, my God when I heard that record where they kept repeating the words over and over, I said to myself, "God, how terrible it is that these kids are not getting benefit of the music that we had when I was younger," because I can take one phrase and write a modern song. I could do the lyrics. And I'm not musical. Say, "Let's Go Mud Wrestling Tonight, Let's Go Mud Wrestling Tonight, You and I, Let's Go Mud Wrestling Tonight. We will be in the mud, we will be in the mud. After the day is over, it's night so Let's Go Mud Wrestling Tonight!"

I really felt very sorry because I realize that the music that I'm telling you about now . . . music of my era . . . not only gave me relaxation, not only gave me a certain amount of stimulation . . . the lyrics of the songs actually educated me. I would say thirty percent of what I know about life today was gleaned from songs. You remember what you learned from a song. Today I heard Paul Robeson singing "Ol' Man River," and I remember seeing the movie with Paul Robeson—the best singer of all time, and the story where it had a mixed marriage, things going on now . . . the problems of the black people. He sang, "take me away from the White Man Boss." That phrase stuck in my mind because as I heard the song today . . . and this song was sung thirty or forty years ago . . . I had also read in the editorial page why Reagan isn't the best candidate for the blacks because they are losing a lot of what they have gained, and I began to realize what a long struggle these people are having.

Q: So, in other words, some of the music you listen to taught you about the people singing it and gave you knowledge . . . ?

A: Well, not only taught me about the people singing, but about life in general, conditions. For example, during the depression there was a big hit, "Brother Can You Spare A Dime?" and the words went, ". . . once I built a railroad . . . now I'm asking for a hand-out."

It wasn't just the person singing the song but the times. For example, during the war era we sang songs that were not only patriotic, but they taught us a lot about what we were fighting for, what was so important about saving America. In a lot of cases, the songs weren't written by the religious but they had some religious overtones and brought in some sense of faith.

Q: When you mention faith, does music help to increase your faith and help you understand more?

A: Yes, I always enjoyed singing. We sang in school, Boy Scouts, in the service. I was very happy to see that the Catholic Church, realizing that music was important in your spiritual feeling . . . music became a very important part. Not only are the prayers considered important, but also the singing because each song teaches you certain aspects of Christ's life, or to become part of the community.

Q: When I asked you about today's music, you talked mostly of rock. Is there any kind of music you respect today, that you can parallel with when you were younger?

A: (pause) Well, I would say some of the Beatles. For example, some of the top orchestras would play their songs and, as the songs mellowed, I really enjoy them. There are others like Joe Cocker singing the theme from . . . (thinking) "Soldier and a Gentleman" . . . "Officer and a Gentleman" . . . something about belonging up there.

Q: On songs you do like, do the lyrics or the melody stand out?

A: Very good question. This question has been asked on many talk shows, and I thought about it. In my case, and in a lot of others, it comes down to about fifty-fifty. The kids now would say, "I like the beat." Well, from my era, it was a time where everyone knew the songwriter and the guy who wrote the lyrics. Who in the world would tell you they enjoy the song "White Christmas" because of the tune, and the words didn't mean anything? I couldn't separate the two. The lyrics are a part of my life. The songs that educated me and gave me confidence when I was sad . . . they had to have words!

Q: What are some of your favorite songs?

A: "The Impossible Dream" from *Man from La Mancha* because it is a very inspiring song. "Theme from a Summer Place." It's a sad song that reminds me of our vacations . . . at the end of summer and we would see people packing up. The theme just fit the mood.

Q: So basically it was words that made you think of that?

A: No, it was the music. It has a very haunting melody. It was a tune that goes through your mind, a lilting melody. Sometimes it's good to hear the words, but in this particular song I prefer the instrumental.

Q: Do you feel you're an open-minded person to different types of music or do you stick to your own style?

A: No, I find that at my age I'm more open-minded. I discovered this while switching stations while driving. Since I'm a salesman, and do a lot of driving, I listen to the radio constantly, fifty percent talk shows and fifty percent music. I find I'm acquiring a taste for classical music. On some stations from Canada, they specialize in music from around the world. I enjoy hearing music from Greece, Italy, Spain, South America.

I will be very emphatic when I say there is so much music in the world that if I tell someone that I do not like the modern rock and roll music, I get angry when people say I'm not open-minded, because rock and roll is such a small percentage of the music in the world.

Q: Any conclusions?

A: When you asked me to do this interview about music, I feel that it's something that is really my bag because I couldn't go through a day without hearing any music. If Big Brother should try to brainwash me and find something that would make me crack, he should put me in a room with no music.

I'll put it in the form of a song (singing), "Without a song, the day would never end, without a song a man ain't got no friend, when things go wrong. . . ."

ELDERS

KEN

"... when I was in the service, when we had the band playing, it instilled a lot of things in you."

Ken is a disabled sixty-five-year-old. He is a retired Army
major and a retired factory worker. He was interviewed by a student
working part time at the group residence where Ken lives.

Q: Who are you?

A: I'm just an ordinary citizen now. I'm just one of the boys, I guess. I'm a father, a husband, and I was a family provider up until the time I got the way I am. I'm not able to go out and earn a living anymore, you know, and do the things I want to do, so I put everything on the back burner.

Q: So you had a full life?

A: Well, I think I had a pretty full life. I did more or less what I wanted to do. We bought a home, we had two kids, and I have a very good wife, an understanding wife, and she still is. We were able to raise two boys, give them an education, which we felt was pretty good. The youngest one is home yet, the other one is married. He is raising his own family now. One is twenty-six and the other is twenty-three.

Q: Did music influence your children while they were growing up?

A: I was always interested in playing an instrument, although I never did. I did have an accordion when I was small but I never learned how to play. I was fascinated by it. The notes and the music were fascinating so I joined the drum corps. Played the snare drum for about ten years. We used to go to all the parades and the county fairgrounds and all the state fairs.

Q: Was this while you were married?

A: Before I was married, I was about twenty-six years old when I met my wife. Then I put everything on the back burner. It was all singles, you know. They'd drink and play for somebody, somebody would throw ten bucks on the bar, then we'd all march around the bar buying drinks for everyone. Now I look back and I say what the hell did I do that stuff for? On hot days in the summertime your tongue would be sticking out while you're marching. You could be under a tree somewhere having a beer instead of in the street marching.

Q: This must have been very important to you.

A: Well, it was fun, it was something to do. The guys I hung around with, all they wanted to do was drink beer and they would go from gin mill to gin mill and that was their big thing. The beer in here wasn't good enough, they would have one or two here and then go somewhere else and have one or two more and before you knew it they were loaded and everything else and I didn't have any fun. What the hell, I had to take care of five drunken guys and that's no fun. Little by little I sort of went into the fire company there, to play with the drum corps. It was something, you know. There were a lot of guys and everybody wanted to do something with you. You didn't have to drink but everybody liked to drink. You know those firemen guys, that was the big thing, when they tapped a barrel of beer, everyone, everyone would stay till the barrel was finished . . . but that's where you would learn to play the snare drum.

Q: Who taught you to play the drum?

A: We had a drum instructor there, and we had a corps instructor, but I don't remember his name. He was the guy who led us up there. Did you ever see the guy with the big baton? He was our leader, and the other guy was the drum major, he told us how to play the drum. Each instrument had its own major. There was a fife major, a bugle major, and so on. He was the guy on the right flank you took all your cues from. The guy up there would blow the whistle and tell you what you were going to play next, either two or three or something, and the drum major would make sure you knew what one or two or three was. It was either "The Washington Post" or "Hail, Hail," or something. They would go into one of their favorites, especially past the reviewing stand.

Q: Tell me about your family.

A: The first one was Tim. I didn't think I had an influence on him about taking up music but we used to go to church and he would sit on the bench with the organist. He would touch the organ to feel the vibrations, he just loved to feel the vibrations of that organ. He would help the organist pass out song books and after that the organist took him aside and showed him a few things on the organ. My son thought that was wonderful. The organ player began teaching piano and organ, so Tim went to him for lessons and we bought a small organ. He continued to play on that thing and he formed a band. He used to go to band practice up on Broadway to a music studio where bands could get together and learn to play. Tim put together a four-piece band and would play for first communions and things like that, until they expanded a little bit.

Q: What type of music did they play?

A: Rock and roll and Polish music.

Q: What do you mean Polish music?

A: Polkas and Italian music. He used to sing about a guy in the airplane, the Italian airlines where he told everyone who could swim to sit on the left side and the ones who couldn't on the right side . . . this was a funny song but the kid was a natural, he was a ham.

Q: How long did they stay together?

A: They played for a few years. They used to call themselves the "Rhythm Makers." Then they put together a new band and they added a little more professional touch to it. He got involved with a couple of guys who were older than he was, so he specialized in singing Elvis Presley music, imitating Elvis Presley, and he was pretty good. Then they went from that to a band of his own . . . a big band . . . he had four trumpets, two slide trombones, and five or six saxophones. They called themselves the "After Hours." He used to play for a lot of school dances. He had the big band sound. They played rock and roll, he was crazy about rock and roll, and then they went into a show and put on the Blues Brothers. He was out of shape so he couldn't jump up and down off the stage . . . everyone would laugh because he had to run up the stairs to get back on stage, but he was actually going along with it so it appeared as if this is the way it was supposed to be. Shortly after this it seemed like each of the people in the band started going their separate ways and the band soon broke up. He is trying to put a band together right now.

What killed me was all the time and practice he would do. Then there was the organ, I don't know why an organ, but I even bought a station wagon just to haul that instrument around . . . not including the microphone stands, and then a piano, so finally I bought a van to haul the stuff around and I got sick of the van so I taught him to drive and let him drive the van and I didn't have to go with him anymore.

Q: So music has been a big influence on his life?

A: Yes, he was preoccupied with music; I didn't worry about him because he was always somewhere playing something.

Q: What about you, how has music influenced you and your life?

A: I never really took music, but it always affected me because when I was in the service, when we had the band playing, it instilled a lot of things in you. When you had to dismount a drill and things like that, it was so much nicer to dismount the drill with a band playing, you could keep time with the drums. I think the guys enjoyed it a lot more, with the playing. The thing is, the band did not have to be good as long as they could keep time. So, as I was growing up, I had an interest for music and it affected me and I'm sure it had an effect on some of the other guys. I always tried to make sure I had somebody in the company. I always had a bugler. The guys would always sing around a fire at night, sing some songs and get everybody singing these old songs.

Q: Let me ask you about our singing/music group we have in the clinic?

A: I think it was nice, but the only thing I couldn't see with some of the songs like "Happy Days are Here Again" . . . this song just goes against the grain, singing "Happy days are here again . . . ." But some of the other songs like "Shuffle off to Buffalo" and Christmas songs are all right . . . but some of the songs that didn't ring true to what we were actually feeling . . . .

Q: How do you feel the guys felt as a group?

A: In the beginning, I don't think anyone wanted to sing. Everybody sang not very good but everyone was singing. I think it does a lot of therapeutic good with guys singing. To do something instead of just sitting there and just moping. To me, when we went downstairs to the lobby to sing and we were joined by all those other people . . . here we are not that equipped . . . with all these people singing, made us sound a hell of a lot better, and everyone sang along, together with the piano player. I'll tell you it seemed to make the day.

Q: Do you think the quality of the music or just the fact of being together is important?

A: Being together, and everyone doing the same thing, it doesn't matter how loud you sing or how you sing, as long as you sing, as long as you take part.

Q: What is it that makes this group therapeutic?

A: I think it makes you forget your problems. What I'm saying is some of the songs we have here are songs you could remember from way back when it would lift your spirits up, especially around the holidays. They say the holidays are sad for a lot of people because a lot of things happen around that time. There are also a lot of good things that happen during the holidays that make you feel gay . . . happy and glad.

Q: What about the Christmas caroling we did?

A: That was nice. Right now I hear different people say, "You came around with that choir around Christmastime singing Christmas songs. Yeah, I remember you." It sort of makes you feel good that someone did remember you came around and sang or did try to make someone else happy besides yourself. I think it actually does help yourself to see you are making somebody happy or feel good. It makes you feel good too. I found out I could sing with other people. As long as everyone was singing and I got drowned out a little bit, I didn't feel so bad.

Q: What was your overall picture of this group?

A: I think it did great things for everybody. They were all singing together, they were all doing something together . . . it added to the comradeship of the group, that they are all in the same boat and we could sing about it. Some fellows I could see were sad . . . it touched some part of life. This could be positive because its good to think about things that happened years ago.

Q: Do you think that music is a good way to help reminisce?

A: Yes, for example when that psychologist has his group . . . sometimes he brings it out too harsh and nobody wants to hear about it that blunt . . . like a sock in the face. You know it's there but sometimes you don't want to talk about it. But I don't talk about it, it will be here soon enough. Music makes you mellow. It brings out feelings you didn't even know you had. They generate from one to another. If you see another fellow that you feel is worse off than you and you see him singing, you say, "He's trying, why not me?"

ANTHONY

"When you sing, you pray twice."

Anthony is sixty-seven years old, a retired mailman, and a
devout Catholic. Originally from a large Italian American family,
he is married and has three sons. Anthony was interviewed by
his grandson in a bright and cheerful kitchen.

Q: Okay, you're on the air.

A: I started when I was about eight years old. We had a Presbyterian
church across the alley from us, you know, but we were Catholics. I used
to go in there and they would have shows and singing things. I used to
enjoy singing all kinds of songs. That's how I started singing.

Then I went to junior high. I started singing in the glee club, then
we had a couple of plays. I had a part in the play singing. It was like
an operetta. The vice-principal down there said, "You know, some day
you're going to be a Caruso." She liked the way I used to sing.

Then I had to be in a recital at the school. I was playing the guitar.
I had to sing "Mexacali Rose." I practiced it for a while and then my
mother got scarlet fever and we were quarantined and that was that. I
couldn't go to school.

Then I got interested in singing in choirs—church music. I started
out at St. Anne . . . no, I started at St. Bartholomew. I was single then.
I started singing every Sunday at St. Bartholomew, we practiced every
week. Then I got married. My wife belonged to St. Anne so I started to
sing there. I sang there for two years. Then I said, "Well, I'll do them
both." So I sang at St. Bartholomew one Mass, and then over to St.
Anne for one mass. I kept that up for a while but I found that was kind
of hard to do so I quit St. Anne. I couldn't go back and forth so I stayed
at St. Bartholomew, and I'm still there. I sing the tenor part. I enjoy
singing for the good Lord. It's just something I like to do. Some people
like to gamble, smoke . . . . I don't smoke; I just enjoy music.

I sang down at the shrine. They had a few concerts. So I joined their

chorus and sang with them for a while. Then I sang in a couple of operas
. . . . I wasn't the lead, I was just in the chorus. We did "La Traviata" and
"Rigoletto." Then a friend and I went to the city and we sang in "La
Traviata."

I'm still trying to sing. I still carry a good tune. I was a mailman and
I always used to sing on my route. People used to enjoy it and I used
to enjoy singing . . . in warm weather, of course . . . not in the cold
weather. I would just sing a tune or two. I'm still singing today and I
enjoy it. That's about it.

Q: When did you start singing with St. Bartholomew?

A: In 1940 and I'm still singing there; 1950 I started at St. Anne.

Q: Tell me about the guitar.

A: I haven't played the guitar recently. I still have it but, ah . . . . (wiggling his fingers) I used to take lessons. My father sent me for about five
or six lessons. My father used to play the guitar. He used to take lessons,
and I started lessons on notes, you know . . . learning the six strings and
the corresponding notes. But my father said it was taking too long to
learn it, and it cost too much money . . . so he wanted me to learn to
play like he did, learn all the chords and sing like he did. But I still like
to play the guitar. If my arthritis doesn't bother me . . . I like to play but
my fingers get a little stiff.

Q: So your father played by ear?

A: Yeah. He was a singer . . . his father taught him songs. They used
to sing together. They learned their music just by ear. You could strike a
chord, and they knew what chord it was . . . they knew what range they
wanted to hit.

Q: So you sing over at the garage? [Anthony's son has an auto
repair shop.]

A: Oh, yeah. I sing over there. . . . When they've got the grinder
going, it's like music to my ears . . . it makes a certain kind of buzzing
that you can pick up and sing a tune to.

But I enjoy operas. We just went to see "La Traviata" again in Buffalo.
Larry bought us tickets. We enjoyed it. The tenor was mellow, but he
was too weak, you couldn't hear him in a crowd. But the girl, all she
had was one high note that you didn't hear too much. But Girmandi . . .
he's supposed to be the father . . . he had a good voice. We catch all the
operas, on television. My wife likes opera.

Q: Tell me a little more about singing in church.

A: Church. Well that's good because you learn a lot of Latin, use a lot
of Italian, you get your vowels, you get your nice tone quality, and your
voices always have to blend . . . the sopranos, the altos, the bass, and the

tenors . . . we always try to blend. We try to be mellow. You don't want to stand up there and yell.

The other day we were singing at a funeral. And someone came up and said, "Boy, I heard you sing and I thought there were twenty people upstairs! I turned around and there were only four!" We do all kinds of music for all occasions.

Q: What kind of feeling do you get when you're singing?

A: Well, you figure when you sing you pray twice, so it's gotta be a good feeling. You figure the good Lord gave you a good voice . . . why not use it? He gave me a voice . . . why stay home and be quiet? I go out and use it. It's something I enjoy.

Some people like to smoke, some people like to drink. . . . Give me the sheet music and an organ. I go walkin' down the mall, and they have little shows with the organs . . . I'll stop in and sing with the guy. My wife gets mad . . . "Come on, come on . . . Let's go!"

Q: What about modern music?

A: No. I don't care too much for pop. Years ago some of the stuff coming up had nice singers, like Mario Lanza. He used to be good. I used to enjoy his songs. Love songs, you know. Now I enjoy Luciano Pavarotti . . . he's good; a strong voice. I make it a point to hear him whenever he is in town or on TV. He comes out nice and smooth.

Q: So he's one of your favorite singers?

A: It's a toss-up between him and Mario Lanza. I like Mario a little better. He seems to have more gusto. Pavarotti is more . . . sweeter. Placido Domingo is good too, but . . .

Q: Do you watch the Grammy Awards?

A: Yeah, but you have to be in tune to that stuff . . . listen to the radio . . . and I don't have time for that. But give me Luciano and I'm happy.

Q: I hate to keep coming around to contemporary music . . .

A: Willie Nelson. I like a couple of his songs that he sings, like . . . (he sings a few lines from a Willie Nelson song) love songs and ". . . you are always on my mind. . . ." I like that one. Kenny Rogers. I don't like him too much. I listen and he just kind of talks . . . he doesn't strain himself, nothing. I don't care for him too much.

Q: What is it that you don't like about modern music?

A: I don't know. Maybe it's because I'm not a southerner. You know . . . they wear those long beards. Dolly Parton . . . I don't care for her too much either.

Q: What about dancing?

A: Oh, yeah. I like music for dance numbers. I like music with a slow beat. Sometimes a little faster like the jitterbug. I don't like tarantella . . . it's too fast; it takes too much out of you. I like a polka, but a jitterbug is usually what I dance to. Or you get a nice Willie Nelson song that has a good beat.

Q: Is there anything you would like to add?

A: Just that I enjoy singing and I do it every day . . . unless I have a cold or a sore throat or something.

Q: How old are you again?

A: Me? I'm sixty-seven. I've been singing since I was eight.

Q: So you've been at this a long time?

A: Oh yeah. I used to walk in that church across the alley. They would have Scout meetings and sing-alongs . . . and sing songs like "It's a Long Way to Tipperary." I would sing real loud and all the kids would turn around and look at me like, "Who's that nut?" But I didn't care.

ELAINE

". . . if anybody wanted to dance at a party
I was at the piano."

Elaine is seventy-five years old and was interviewed by her son.

Q: I want to know who you are and then what music is about in your life.

A: Oh. Well I'm a woman of seventy-five who has taught school, raised one son, and now I'm a retired old housewife. (chuckles) But I'm content with myself.

Q: And what's music about for you in your life? What's it been about?

A: Music is a very important part of my life. I started when I was seven playing the piano and I studied for ten years. I played, studied for five years, then I went away to boarding school and played five years there. I played when I was in boarding school for dancing in the recreation room, and I used to go into the Boston Symphony every Thursday on the bus. We always had musical appreciation before we went, as to what we were going to hear, and musical appreciation class when we got back to go over what we'd heard. And the first two years I went, you know, I enjoyed the music but I didn't think too much about it deeply and I was more interested in noticing the old Boston matrons coming in and what kinds of hats they had on, and so forth, because they were always there on a Thursday afternoon. And then I began to really like it. I looked forward to all the nuances and differences in the music and what not.

Then when I was teaching school I loved to play the piano and I played for the classes and then when they had school plays and musical things I played. I had a lot of Polish and Italian children who were quite musical, especially the Polish children. After school they would like to clean the erasers and the board because I would play some polkas for them and then these little Polish boys and girls would dance around the room clapping their erasers together, the little girls kicking. And they showed me Polish steps that they did when Polish families were together having a party. These Polish people were mostly workers on the large estates.

Q: What about the Italian kids? Did they show you anything?

A: Yeah, they like to sing. (laughs) They would stay behind and sing at the piano. If they were good and had done their lessons I'd stay an extra hour and play for them to dance or sing.

I've always enjoyed all kinds of music: band music, march music, dance music, classical music, and I'm particularly fond of piano music, of course. I like Chopin and Tchaikovsky, and I like Bach, now. I didn't like Bach when I was studying it; I thought it was too mechanical, but now I see it's very relaxing to play Bach.

Then, when I was married, I taught school and played whenever I was needed for anything, and I did play in a two-piano group for a while, but most of the piano players, pianists, were far advanced beyond me. They'd studied fifteen or twenty years, and they had appeared professionally, and they had been accompanists to well-known singers and that kind of thing. None of them wanted to play "Tea for Two," which I wanted to play. I played in the school with different music students in the music department when there was a concert. I always knew in the twenties and thirties all the popular songs. I started . . . my first jazz piece was "When the Red Red Robin Comes Bob-Bob-Bobbin' Along." I must have been about eleven or twelve. And "The Parade of the Wooden Soldiers" was another beauty. At the time of "Red Red Robin" there was "Bye Bye Blackbird"; it was a bird year I guess. (laughs) Then, too, I played for dancing; if anybody wanted to dance at a party I was at the piano.

Q: So even as a teenager, and at school . . .

A: Oh yes, and in teaching school. It came in real handy teaching school because a good many teachers can play simple little things, but if it's a musical review or something they get kind of lost, some of them. And I used to love to dance in my teen years. Between sixteen and twenty-two, when I really buckled down to teach, I was popular and liked to go to dances and have a wonderful whirl. I danced till my feet dropped off.

Q: What kind of music did you like to dance to?

A: Oh, I liked Jelly Roll Morton, and Red Nichols and his Five Pennies, and I went down to hear Duke Ellington at the Cotton Club once. Of course you could go into Harlem then, spend the night with a few college friends; wouldn't cost too much and you'd come out without being shot. I mean you might be all shot the next day, but you wouldn't be. . . . (laughing) And I saw the opening night of *Porgy and Bess*. The gal I roomed with was head of the dance department at the high school and she had tickets for opening night. I didn't have much money; I only got paid enough to just exist. Anyhow we went in to see *Porgy and Bess*. Must have been somewhere between 1935 and 1938.

And another thing I saw, not an opening night, but in its first few months, the one where the ballet first came in—"Oklahoma," where they first had ballet combined with jazz and the musical theatre.

Q: You took me to see that.

A: Yeah, and we took Grammy to see that. And let's see, I played in the two-piano group for a while, then I did play for the Gilbert and Sullivan, a few of their rehearsals when they couldn't get anybody better. (pause) Now, since I've been retired and up here I listen to the Gilbert and Sullivan hour which is on the radio, on Saturday; its a half an hour but I wish it was an hour. And I play along; I have the music for all the Gilbert and Sullivan so I play along with whatever they're playing. And I have tapes and records of Duke Ellington, Benny Goodman, a lot of Benny Goodman, and when my piano goes in with a tape I join in and I have a wonderful time playing along with the tapes and the records. And that "Stride Right"—who's that?

Q: Johnny Hodges and Earl Hines.

A: I'm particularly fond of "Tea for Two" and "Ain't Misbehavin'," and of Red Nichols' "You're My Everything," and Benny Goodman with "Tea for Two" and "There are Smiles That Make You Happy," that's another one I like to swing along to.

Then every Saturday night on radio they have early jazz records of the twenties and thirties and I have my music on the piano; usually by the time I find the music . . . because I can't tell ahead of time what they're gonna play . . . but if I do know where the music is I play along with that. And sometimes I tape it so then I can go back and find the music and play along. That's fun.

Q: So you use the sheet music at the same time the record player is on?

A: Yeah, yeah.

Q: You've got some things you can play by ear, right?

A: Oh yeah, but . . . I like the colored guy who did . . . Joplin. I have all of Joplin's music and Joplin's records, so sometimes when there is nothing on the tape or records I'll play the Joplin records along with my piano, if I'm in a Joplin mood. That's where the music comes in handy, is . . . when you're sad about something . . . you can play "Andante Cantabile" or something and just feel so sad. And then if you're happy you can play "Forget your troubles, come on get happy, get ready for the judgment day," you know.

Q: So you do it to match your mood?

A: Yeah. And then if I just want a change of scenery I'll just sit down and play whatever is convenient. It's a marvelous outlet.

Q: What are you letting out?

A: Well, I mean if you're sad you play sad music and then you don't feel quite so sad. Or if you're happy you can play happy music and . . . it's the same reason I like to play golf. If I'm mad and I go out on the golf course I forget what I'm mad about if I just sock the ball. After I've socked the ball a few times I'm not mad any more.

Q: So it changes your state of mind.

A: (chuckling softly)

Q: What about playing drums? There was a picture of you I remember . . .

A: Oh I just played drums in the school orchestra because they needed somebody for rhythm; I was pretty good at rhythm. So my brother who was in college sent me a set of drums that he wasn't using. And I didn't have any lessons so I just faked it. I really faked it, because I had a music stand with music you know? I guess everybody knew I was faking, but I accompanied and came along and it went along all right. I flipped over my drum music whenever everybody was flipping over their music. But I could read music well because of my ten years of piano.

Oh, that's another thing I did, I did a lot of page turning for artists who came to the school to play, give concerts, or for people in the music department. If I wasn't playing myself, I would sit and turn the music, even though the music sometimes I couldn't read completely, I'd just have a general idea of where they were and it was about time to turn the page. For some reason or other I wasn't embarrassed about it. I enjoyed it and I wasn't aware that I might make a boo-boo. I never did make a boo-boo.

Q: Were you worried about that when you were playing piano by yourself?

A: No, but I mean as you get older you get more self-conscious. And I was in a four-piano . . . there were four pianos playing once at Abbot, and I had the bass in the ballet "Rosamunda" and I was a bass part on one piano . . . dumpdittydumpditty dump dump dum, dump dump dum, dum dittyum . . . that one. We were going along fine and the teacher, Miss Hessell, who was my piano teacher, she said, "Stop everybody! Somebody is playing the bass too loud. I want to hear that again." So I was oom pah, oom pah, oom pah, you know in the bass. . . . "It's Elaine. Elaine, this is a ballet of people, not elephants!" (laughing)

Q: What music do you like best of all the music there is?

A: I like dixieland. The old dixieland. And good dixieland. I don't like . . . well, now there's a local jazz group, I hope they won't be insulted, they've been giving concerts around here once in a while, and they had them on radio the other night. They were imitating the early dixieland jazz but they didn't make it. They were too loud, too blatty, the drums were too heavy, the horns were too loud, they didn't play well together. You know, when the solo parts came on they were too loud. And, right after they played this thing, they played a Jelly Roll Morton record where everybody just swung together. They accompanied, they quieted down when the soloist came on and accompanied him, and when they got together they just swung together. And the difference between the real thing and the imitation was quite obvious.

Q: You like the real thing.

A: And I like Strauss waltzes; in the spring particularly I love to play Strauss waltzes.

Q: You like playing them more than listening to them? . . . because everything you've been saying is about playing, from the time you were a little girl until . . .

A: I like both. I like both. I like listening. I like to go up to the concerts at Tanglewood in the summer but I don't like to drive late at night. I like to go to the morning rehearsals on Saturday, and the Sunday afternoon concerts. And then the Friday and Saturday concerts on radio I like to listen to . . . listen to it on the hi-fi, put your feet up on a chair and relax and see if they go over the mistakes and see if they don't make the same mistakes they were trying to rub out in rehearsals.

Q: But almost everything you've said to the question "What's music about for you?" has been playing the piano, for people or with the tapes and the records . . . .

A: Well, that was my thing. I didn't do anything else really.

Q: And you were just playing carols for the family.

A: Yeah, I just finished playing the carols for everyone and I enjoyed it very much. I hadn't practiced it or even gone over it and I blundered in a few places, but it was fun. It's something that you can use all your life! Either for yourself or for other people. For instance, if I was in a home and ninety years old or something and still able to play the piano and they needed somebody to play I wouldn't hesitate to sit down and play for some old folks. I wouldn't mind that at all. But I'm not about to do it now, I've got too many home chores to do right now.

Is the tape still going? I can tell you about musical evenings when I was little. Our families, there were three or four families in town who enjoyed music. And we would meet. My father was a fairly good tenor and we used to meet at the Alston's house—other people who were musical—we'd go to the house for dinner, or they would come to us for dinner, and then we'd have a musical evening.

Now I remember my brother Bob who died very early, he played the fife and the piccolo and an ocarina. When he was sick he used to listen to the birds and then repeat it on the flute or the piccolo, and then they'd talk back and forth to each other. It was really quite beautiful. And he carved out of wood, little birds and little animals, terribly talented. . . .

Then my mother played the piano, the violin and the guitar. And she sang well. Your uncle played the drums, and I played the piano and sang, not very well. In choral groups they could never figure out if I was an alto or a second soprano. Anyway, people would sing and play and dance and then we'd have charades. You didn't have the radio, you didn't have the TV, or you'd play cards and then stop to sing a song or two. And the Alston family, one boy played the guitar and sang very well. I don't know, it just seemed . . . we entertained each other. Your grandfather sang things like "In the morn I bring you violets, which . . . at evening I have culled, and . . . I bring you roses" or something, "promise me that one day you and I shall go together to the sky beyond" or something. (laughing) That kind of stuff. Sentimental ballads.

Q: And he loved marches too.

A: Oh, he loved marches. When they played "The Second Connecticut" on Fourth of July tears would roll down his cheeks. Not only did he like marches, but he was patriotic.

Q: What kind of music did your mother like most?

A: Oh, light music. I wish I knew those waltzes that she played on the piano that I was just crazy about, but I never did think to ask her what they were. And polkas. You know, in her day . . . she graduated from Smith in 1896, and she was forty when I was born—I was the last gasp . . . she taught in high schools and girls schools, before she was married at twenty-nine, and those polkas . . . she would polka all by herself. If she was feeling particularly flip or in the mood she'd go hopping around, skipping and hopping and dancing the polka. (laughing)

Q: So there was a lot more live music in those days.

A: Oh yes. Much more dancing too. Everybody . . . your aunt played a little piano, had a true voice and was a whiz of a dancer. This was the way you spent your evenings, or when people got together they did things like that.

"Well, I was beautiful then and, boy, could I dance."

Helene is eighty-three years old and was interviewed by her grandson.

Q: What is music about for you?

A: Oh, I love music! . . .

Q: Well, tell me some things about music for you. Tell me why you love music.

A: Music brings back memories . . . memories of when I was younger. Everyone was alive then and things were so good. I was the youngest of six kids. I was the last one left at home. Me and my brother. My mother, she said to me . . . before I die, I want you to get married.

You want to know about music? I remember when she told us that. . . . We were sitting in the kitchen listening to the radio. That's what we did for entertainment then. The whole family sat around and listened to the radio. Since me and my brother were the only two left at home, just the three of us were listening. My father had died a few years earlier. Anyway, this song came on the radio. I can distinctly remember it. It was a Polish song. I don't remember the name of it now but when my mother heard it she said, "Remember that song at your sister's wedding? I want you two to get married before I go. And I want them to play that song at your weddings. It is such a beautiful song."

I had so many men after me then, but I didn't like any of them enough to marry one of them. Shortly after that I met your grandfather. I met him on a streetcar. Oh how I hated him then. He was always standing behind me and, like, pushing me when the streetcar jolted. I hated that. Then we got in an accident . . . the streetcar fell off the tracks. We had to give our names. When I wrote mine down he must have seen it and one day he came to my house and was honking for me outside. I said to my mother, should I go? She said go ahead . . . so I did. We went for a car ride. Then he asked me to a dance. There was a dance at one of the clubs in our neighborhood. We danced a lot! I love to dance! We used to go to dance halls—not like the ones you kids have today. They weren't like bars. We had fancy ones like the Ritz.

This was the big band era. We did the foxtrot, and oh, how I loved to waltz! Your grandfather was a good dancer, too. When we were younger, my girlfriends and I, we used to go to dances all the time. I was such a good dancer. All the boys wanted to dance with me. My girlfriends were so jealous. Well, I was beautiful then and, boy, could I dance. I loved to waltz and the music was so beautiful then. Not like today. Today I don't know how you kids listen to that junk. It doesn't make any sense. You can't understand any of the words. It has no meaning.

Yes, I can remember beautiful waltzes. They have words too, you know. I remember how we used to go to dances then. It had such meaning. Those memories are so special to me. It's what I have now. Memories of my old friends and family. I remember how my mother and I used to dance in the kitchen. We danced to our ethnic music. Polkas. I love to polka. I guess polkas always remind me of my mother. Everything was so good then. We never cursed, never fought.

That's why I love my polkas so much. They remind me of my family, of when I was young. I led a very fulfilled life. It was very happy. Polish music is my heritage music. It is my favorite. It is so sentimental and also sometimes silly. Did you ever listen to some of the words? I also listen to polkas just for the pure joy of listening to good entertaining music. Sometimes it makes me laugh. It puts me in a good mood. Polish music is my heritage music and I love to listen to it.

Q: Do you enjoy any other music?

A: I love Lawrence Welk and Perry Como. They play waltzes and have sentimental lyrics. I love the Christmas music Perry Como plays. He plays it even when it's not close to Christmas. This music is so beautiful. Church music is also beautiful. Without this music church wouldn't be the same. Church music really makes you feel good. I like to sing church music. It makes me feel peaceful and close to God. I love "The Peace Prayer of St. Francis." That song reminds me of my sister. You see, that's the song we played at her funeral. It was her funeral prayer. Certain songs remind me of certain people. They make me remember the loved ones in my life. My memories are important to me.

Q: So songs bring back memories. Does any other kind of music? Like instruments, certain melodies, things like that?

A: When I hear an accordion, I can picture your father learning to play the accordion. This was back in the fifties when rock and roll was around. But your father wanted to play the accordion. He took lessons and made us so proud. It's good to have a talent. A musical talent is really special to have.

But, as your father got older, he became interested in rock and roll and stopped playing the accordion. He wanted to play the guitar instead. I don't like rock and roll. It has no meaning. It's gibberish. Music when I was a girl was beautiful. Then it changed. The sentiment went out of it. The words were stupid and didn't say anything. I liked the music in my day. It was slow, and easy to dance to. The music in my day prompted beautiful dances like the waltz. Rock and roll didn't prompt any beautiful dances. People jump around to rock and roll. That's not dancing.

Music, good music, makes me feel like dancing. I guess that's another reason why I love music so much. It makes me feel good and it makes me want to dance. Dancing is fun. It's a form of entertainment prompted by the right music.

Q: Why does music make you feel good?

A: Music makes me feel good in a lot of ways. Some music relaxes me. Some music lifts my spirits, and some music brings back memories. All the memories that music brings back are happy memories. I think this is because I had such a happy life filled with a lot of music. That's why songs bring back so many memories.

SAMUEL

"It takes the fear away from you."

Samuel is eighty-three years old, black, and a retired steel worker. He was interviewed by a student at the same group residence where Ken lives.

Q: Who are you and how do you perceive yourself? Tell me a little about you and who you are?

A: My age and my feelings . . . I feel just about as good now as I did twenty years ago. I can eat just as good, I can sleep just as good. If I had a job to do, I could do the same type of work, because I broke in working hard. Worked for myself, started when I was thirteen years old. Around then my father was courting again, my mother had done died. When he started courting and we lived in the country . . . he couldn't be home at times, he'd go to town and stay the whole week, come home maybe on Sunday . . . see how we done, bring a little food, and go back. One thing that people say, hard work is going to kill ya, but hard work is going to make you strong, make you know how to do things for yourself. You don't need to depend on nobody else. I know now the job I did was a hard job but I was young . . . get home from work around two o'clock, eat, go right on to the baseball field and start practicing the black diamond. . . . (laughing) Hit them out there . . . knock them home . . . flies . . . pitching . . . get in the infield . . . play shortstop . . . well, I just do it all.

Q: When you were young . . . how did music influence you as a boy?

A: Well . . . we had a what-ja-ma-call-it, a gramophone . . . we didn't have no TV there . . . one of those boxes you wind up, you put a record on it and play it. Then we wasn't allowed to play no blues or nothing.

Q: Was there something wrong or taboo about singing the blues?

A: Well, my parents did not allow it, and whenever we'd sing the blues or something, we'd be off down the hill in the woods or the field or something. But the church songs . . . every Wednesday night were prayer meetings, Friday night was choir rehearsal. Friday night we would sing different songs and one song I used to really love was, "Come, we're going to walk to the white robe . . . a one of these days, I'm going walk up and one day I'm joining on repaying, going to walk up with the white robe one of these days." Yeah, we had a gang of these songs we used to sing.

Q: How old were you when you did this?

A: Around about fifteen, because I joined the church around the time when I was thirteen years old, and I been to church ever since. Yeah, I think that helped me more than the doctor or anything because I ain't never been sick but once, and that's when I had appendicitis, operated on for appendix, and I ain't been to no doctor since then and ain't been sick since and ain't felt bad or nothing.

Q: Why do you think you have been so healthy?

A: Well, I think the Lord just keeps me strong enough to keep me going because years ago you couldn't buy shoes or a pair of pants or something like that but now, anything I want, I'm able to get. I had a few old clothes that I gave away, even got old shoes and gave them away. The Lord just blessed me like that, and I think that came from being obedient to Him. I never gets in bed until I thank the Lord for keeping me safe throughout the day. As I sleep He watches over me, you know. I wake up feeling good.

Q: Do you think your singing or music has anything to do with this?

A: Yeah, yeah. If you ask the Lord for something in earnest and mean it, He'll pick a way for you. You might not get what you want right now, but the very time you're not thinking about it, that's the time you get it. I know a lot of times my little old check . . . I get a little old check from where I used to work . . . say, now the house insurance is due, the car insurance is due, and you have to have something to eat, and the old house needs a painting. What you going to do?

Q: Do you still sing in a choir?

A: Why sure! Every first Sunday of the month. We practice Friday night and Sunday we sing. We all have our book, we all read, we all look at it, try to keep your tune and your parts, and with the piano playing it sounds real good.

My daughter plays in the choir, the youth choir. Now we have two . . . no, three choirs. The youth choir, the women's choir, and the men's choir. There's six of us men. We sing, and I sing tenor. You get them voices together, you sound good!

Q: Do you practice at home?

A: Sometimes I be fumbling around and I'll go down in the basement, I sit down there tap my foot and sing it a little bit, I try to keep my voice together.

Q: Does this remind you of when you were young and used to sing the blues?

A: Yes, if you're a good gospel singer you were a good blues singer. If you could sing the blues you could sing gospel music.

Q: How do you think gospel music and the blues came about?

A: From old songs. My grandmother was a slave. She used to tell us about the white people up north, they used to come through there taking horses and she said she would take the horses down to the woods and hide them. After they would come through, a couple of days, she would come back out with the horses. She lived on one plantation and my grandfather lived on another plantation. Now, my grandfather's name . . . my grandfather had that white man's name because he was that man's slave. My grandmother and grandfather, they courted and raised a family. You had to get permission from your master for to get married, or to court or anything like that. Now this woman had to do the washing, ironing, and work in the field too, for the white people. They give them twice a week to see each other. My grandfather had to travel five miles and he had to be back at his place in time to go to the fields.

Q: Did they sing in the fields?

A: Oh, yes. Sing those songs like, "If I Had My Way I'd Tear These Buildings Down," "Time Has Been, Shall Be No More," and one time you would hear them singing this one, "Been Working All Day." Now you better not do anything wrong that day because if you do grandmother would tear you up, she would whoop ya. After she would whip you, she would sit down and talk to you. "Grandmother isn't whipping you because she hates you, she's whipping you because she loves you. If I don't whip you now, when you get older you going to be in somebody's jail." And then . . . about then they had what they call country roads . . . they take the prisoners and cut a brand new road, chain gangs, they would sing on these chain gangs, they would sing on these chain gangs. After she told me that . . . I wasn't to do any of these things you see, they keep you honest. Now I'm eighty years old and never been arrested, never been on a witness stand, honest.

Q: Do you know where your African roots are?

A: But it may have been South Africa. The real Africans are real black. They just as black as that—they shine like a new pair of patent leather shoes.

Q: Samuel, tell me a little about the music and sing-along group we have here in the clinic twice a month.

A: Well, it brings us closer and gives us the chance to understand each other more better and, maybe some of them don't know the song, it gives them a chance to learn the song. You know, if they sing it's going to help out the lungs.

Q: Do you think it helps you remember things?

A: Why sure it does. Well, if you just sit down and talk about something you soon forget about it. If you sing today, well tomorrow you think about it and sing it again, just keep on, keep on till it stays on your mind. Sometimes you try to think of something but this song stays on your mind.

Q: How about your own experience with singing in the group?

A: Well, I'll tell you what, now I used to stutter bad. I don't stutter bad now. I used to have to sing to talk. If I would say good morning I would sing it "good morning" . . . but now that singing done helped me and it still helps me. Lots of time now, I go down in the basement, get my smokes, and start to singing. It seems like my throat clears up, my head clears up. My blood seems like it be moving around. Now exercise is all right for your limbs, but your blood needs to exercise too. Singing helps me think, and puts me in a mood for talking. Yeah, when I used to talk, I used to sing and sing the words out, but now I cut them short.

Q: Do you think this helps you socialize with other people?

A: Sure it do. It takes the fear away from you. Sometimes you know you might get up and feel embarrassed but after you get up there, you get started . . . you're all at leisure, you see. Next time it'll get better . . . next time get much better. That's a good way, as in our church we have the united choir, where we all stand up united and the lady plays the piano there. If you can't sing, if you haven't got the tune to sing a song, she play and she sing it and you follow her.

Q: How does this make you feel?

A: It makes you feel good. Yeah, it makes you feel like you're doing something for the Lord, and for yourself too. Well, you just feel satisfied. Yeah.

Q: So you get a lot of satisfaction from singing with the other patients and in the choir. Do you think this singing group in the clinic should continue?

A: Yes . . . well, what I mean . . . we all come here, we all sing together, talk together, eat together . . . be together while we're here. So when we depart, upon having to die or something . . . well, we could look on and say that was my friend . . . we could say we done such and such together.

CHARLES KEIL

Appendix
Music in Daily Life Guidelines

The following general instructions to interviewers were used in the spring semester of 1988, about halfway through the process of collecting the interviews. These instructions may not have been read very carefully by interviewers, but they capture the exploratory spirit of our research.

Introductory Notes for the Music in Daily Life Project

I have stopped looking at what we will be doing as a variety of social science. There is nothing very precise, repeatable, predictable, verifiable, law-seeking, etc. about finding another person and talking with them about music. I'm not even sure that "science of the spirit" or what the Germans call *Geisteswissenschaften* is loose enough a term, but I like the way Bruno Bettelheim describes Wilhelm Windelband's definition:

"The *Geisteswissenschaften* he called idiographic, because they seek to understand the objects of their study not as instances of universal laws but as singular events; their method is that of history, since they are concerned with human history and with individual ideas and values. . . . Idiographic sciences deal with events that never recur in the same form—that can be neither replicated nor predicted [but that can be understood]."[1]

I like the references to spirit and to "idiographic," and one possible title for the book that I hope will result from this spring's work could be "My Music: Studies in Idioculture" because that is one way to look at what people are doing with music in this society: building an idioculture, an idiosyncratic, idiolectical, even idiotic musical world that each person can call his or her own. My first impulse and primary purpose is to celebrate the unique selection of musics to be "into" and the unique configuration of ways to be "into" those musics that emerges from each interview. Our musical life has never been more mass mediated and commodified than it is today and yet individual musical lives, as evidenced in the interviews done so far, are highly variable, very idio- and not slightly so.

A second purpose, in contradictory or paradoxical relation to the first purpose, is to understand how all these musical lives are the same and in most of that sameness, probably "part of the problem." A hundred walkman users may be listening to a hundred different musics, but they are all encased in headphones and letting mediated music substitute for full environmental and social awareness in present time. People use a wide variety of musics as drugs to "pump up" their selves to face the day and another whole range of musics to "catharse" or "let go" of their bad moods at the end of the day. Is this really like a drug? If so, isn't music a "good" drug? These two examples and the questions that flow from them can be multiplied many times and I don't want to evade ANY issues in the book or collection we're assembling this spring.[2]

I would like to urge you to keep both purposes in mind but separated and prioritized as much as possible. In other words let's focus on elaborating and celebrating each person's musical world first and foremost. Later on we can look for patterns of musical life in the U.S.A. that suggest problems and begin to explore those problems. This is a little too simple—first celebrate American individualism in the interviews, then debunk it later in an analysis—because as you are doing an actual interview and then later as you are editing and/or interpreting an interview done by yourself or someone else you will be constantly presented with choices and more choices of what to ask about next, what to leave out of a text, what to draw attention to with an interpretation. I'm suggesting that we keep the contradiction or paradox in mind, meditate on it, reformulate it various ways, read about it (D. Riesman's *The Lonely Crowd*, P. Slater's *In Pursuit of Loneliness*), but when interviewing lean toward the optimistic idio-participatory side of the contradiction, knowing that later on we'll be looking at the negative side of the puzzle. Somebody says, "I really love Bruce Springsteen and his music, can't help it, I get weepy over 'Born in the USA,' you know? But sometimes I wonder if I haven't just swallowed the hype about his being a working-class hero from New Jersey with the symbolic black guy by his side, you know what I mean?" and then pauses, looking at you for some direction or an answer. A choice to make. You can wait a bit, nod sympathetically and hope that the person will go on and explain some more. Then you can say "Could you explain that a little bit more?" and wait a bit for the person to think it through. But if push comes to shove and neutral encouragement is not helping the person clarify their thoughts, I'd try "Why do you love Bruce Springsteen's music so much?" or "What makes you weepy when you hear 'Born in the USA'?" rather than "What makes you think you're a victim of hype and promo?" At the risk of losing this person's incisive analysis of the consciousness industry I'd rather get deeper into how he or she participates in the Springsteen persona. If the fear or embarassment about being manipulated by the media comes up a second or a third time, maybe go with the critical side of the flow, or try to remember to come back to the problem later in the interview. But in general, or when in doubt, keep the vibes positive and orient yourself toward the person's involvement in the music.

How to Interview

Basically the whole course is about the quality of our interviews, so quickly getting better at doing them is the trick. Experience is the best teacher. Honesty is the best policy. Listen and learn.

An "open-ended, nondirected, ethnographic interview" is what social scientists would probably call our method or approach to unpacking what is in someone's mind about music in his/her daily life. I put the phrase within quotation marks because "open-ended" doesn't really mean that the interview goes on forever and ever; we just hope that people will stretch out and take as much time as they need to explain their relation to music. "Nondirected" is inevitably an even bigger fib or euphemism since you have come to a person asking for an interview and that person will take any words that come from your mouth as some sort of direction; as in the Springsteen example above, people are often looking for guidance, direction, minor or major indications of what will keep the conversation going, the interviewer happy. "Ethnographic" suggests that you are trying to "graph" the values of the other's "ethnos" or tribe, and not your own values, but in this instance both interviewer and interviewee are members of the same American tribe or of "clans" within it, and of course your own idiosyncratic values and attitudes will shape what you say, ask for, choose to follow up on or to ignore, and how you say it. "Interview" is the most truthful word in the phrase, suggesting that the "view" that emerges will be constructed "inter" or "between" the two of you.

So think of these terms as vague ideals, fuzzy reference points borrowed from the world of social science. Ideally, you the interviewer should say very little and the person interviewed should say a lot. Ideally, the subject should take charge and take the topic anywhere they want to go with it. Ideally, the subject's values, attitudes, beliefs, memories, hopes, etc. will come tumbling out in just the order that expresses him or her perfectly. Ideally.

More realistically, you will be having a conversation, a dialogue, an "interview" (as defined above) with someone about music in front of a tape recorder. The "ideals" above can make you feel awkward, constrained, under pressure to say less, not skew or distort what someone is telling you, not argue with them, etc. but for the other person to be real, be themselves, you have to be real too, no b.s., no holding back, honestly concerned to develop a good understanding of what music is about for this other person. You are not just the human attached to the tape recorder in order to elicit answers for the tape. For some people a smile and an attentive ear is all they need to talk for hours, but others develop their thinking best in a more give and take or argumentative style: "Whaddya mean, 'Who are you?' I'm me, can't you see! And who the hell are you anyway?" Better be ready to say a few good words about yourself and what you are doing. Hopefully, the other side of this "inter-view" doesn't want to argue from the start, but if that's the "style" or "way" of the person you are conversing with, "go with the flow" and have a good time. And certainly, later in the interview, if something keeps coming up that you don't quite understand or that you disagree with, jump in and seem foolish or say you disagree.

You came with the tape recorder. You have your questions. These factors tip the conversational balance in your direction from the start. Try to listen real well. Try not to dominate the conversation. But give whatever you need to in order to help the other person express their ideas about music.

Notes

1. Bruno Bettelheim, "Reflections (Freud)," *The New Yorker*, 1 March 1982, 70. Quoted in " 'The Thick and the Thin': On the Interpretive Theoretical Program of Clifford Geertz" by Paul Shankman, *Current Anthropology*, 25, no. 3 (June 1984): 264.

2. The plan in 1988 was to put the interviews in the first half of this book and essays about those interviews in the second half.

Index

Index / 216

Motown, 88, 116
movies, music in, 20, 39, 181–82, 185
Mozart, Wolfgang Amadeus, 41, 59, 136, 139, 167
music business. *See* commercialism; media manipulation
musical evenings, 203
musician. *See* listening; playing an instrument; performing

Near, Holly, 86–87
need for music, 41, 51, 91, 186
Nelson, Willie, 47, 120, 160, 180, 196–97
new wave music, 57, 80, 111

oboe, 28–29, 94
oldies, 50, 53, 111, 119–20, 155, 176–77
opera, 54, 113, 170, 195
organ, 139, 176, 190, 191

Parton, Dolly, 161, 168, 196
Pavarotti, Luciano, 173, 196
performing, 57–58, 76, 132, 136, 149–50, 191. *See also* playing an instrument
piano, 7, 28, 47, 148–49, 171, 198–203
Pink Floyd. *See under* Waters, Roger.
playing an instrument: advantages of, 33; expression, 54; lessons, 151, 195, 201–202; and parents, 126, 149, 150–51; practicing, 45, 55, 58, 126, 130–31; psychology of, 129; professionally, 128–33; with recordings, 130, 200; for self, 94; starting out, 56, 125. *See also* accordion; drums; guitar; oboe; organ; performing; piano; trumpet; violin
Pointer Sisters, 73, 88
Police, 89
politics, music and, 81–82, 86–87, 103–105
polka, 114, 151, 197, 198–99, 203, 205
Presley, Elvis, 50, 156, 191
Psychedelic Furs, 80, 84
punk, 117, 121, 137

race, 88–89, 114, 116, 132, 184, 209
radio, 20–21, 37–38, 109, 114–15, 134, 159–62, 174, 182, 185, 200, 204. *See also* commercialism; control; media manipulation
ragtime, 30, 31, 104, 200
rap, 24–25, 43, 45, 49–50, 52–53, 61. *See also* creating

reggae, 38, 141
relaxation, 137, 140, 174–75, 176, 183. *See also* easy listening; escape; sleeping
Roches, 71, 86
rock and roll, 17, 23, 49, 73, 78, 99–101, 140, 146, 156–57, 168, 172, 184, 186, 191, 206
Rogers, Kenny, 48, 196
Rolling Stones, 57, 115

school: band, 26, 29, 44, 127; dancing in, 9–10, 25; music in, 12–15, 18–19, 44, 128, 198; singing in, 8–9, 11, 46, 170. *See also* teaching with music
sexuality, 122, 146, 147, 157–58; homosexuality, 83. *See also* dancing
Sinatra, Frank, 160, 172, 182; imitation of, 46
singing, 48, 110–11, 139, 183, 192, 194–97; for an audience, 76; in a choir, 149, 208; and emotion, 32; and health, 210; with machinery, 195; with others, 32, 192–93, 210; at weddings, 77; and work, 195. *See also* creating; family; friends; school; songs; spirituality
sisters, 71, 163, 121–22
sleeping to music, 90, 101; lullabies, 10–11, 166. *See also* relaxation
Smith, Jimmy, 128, 177, 178
society, importance of music in, 39, 41
solitude. *See* escape; listening
songs: dismissal of, 135; expressing feelings, 74, 77–78; in one's head, 38, 46, 58, 90, 173; old, 192; patriotic, 182; slavery, 209. *See also* love
spirituality, music and, 41, 74–79, 135, 164, 184–85, 196, 208; music in church, 77, 149, 185, 194, 205. *See also* gospel
stars, music, 40, 63, 70, 81, 84, 90–93, 157–58, 160, 166, 179, 182. *See also* concerts; fandom

taste, changing over time, 72, 82, 119, 139, 141, 171, 181
Taylor, James, 73, 119, 123
teaching with music, 145–46, 198–99. *See also* school
technology, 91, 102, 148–49, 170, 176, 207
television, music on, 19–20, 21, 48, 58, 72, 77, 113, 125, 196. *See also* MTV
Tiffany, 21, 38
Top Forty, 82, 110, 115

UNIVERSITY PRESS OF NEW ENGLAND publishes books under its own imprint and is the publisher for Brandeis University Press, Brown University Press, University of Connecticut, Dartmouth College, Middlebury College Press, University of New Hampshire, University of Rhode Island, Tufts University, University of Vermont, and Wesleyan University Press.

ABOUT THE EDITORS The Music in Daily Life Project represents an unusual collaborative effort among some forty undergraduate interviewers and graduate student editors. Crafts, Cavicchi, and Keil brought this text to completion and are standing in for the larger team at the State University of New York at Buffalo that developed the Music in Daily Life Project over a four year period.

SUSAN D. CRAFTS holds degrees in anthropology and environment and is completing her Ph.D. in sociology at SUNY-Buffalo. She is currently working on an ethnohistorical study of Canadian folk music.

DANIEL CAVICCHI is a graduate of Cornell University and SUNY-Buffalo and is pursuing a Ph.D. at Brown University where he is conducting an ethnography of popular music fans.

CHARLES KEIL is Professor of American Studies at SUNY-Buffalo. He is author of *Tiv Song* (1979) and *Urban Blues* (1966) and co-author of *Polka Happiness* (1992).

Library of Congress Cataloging-in-Publication Data

My music / [compiled by] Susan D. Crafts, Daniel Cavicchi, Charles Keil and the Music in Daily Life Project.
    p.   cm. — (Music culture)
Collection of interviews.
"Wesleyan University Press."
ISBN 0–8195–5257–7. — ISBN 0–8195–6264–5 (pbk.)
    1. Music, Influence of.   2. Popular culture.   3. Music and society.   4. Popular music —History and criticism.   I. Crafts, Susan D.   II. Cavicchi, Daniel.   III. Keil, Charles. IV. Music in Daily Life Project.   V. Series.
ML3920.M98   1993
781′.1—dc20   92–56907

∞   MN